T0360117

Wakefield Press

Flinders Essays in Economics and Economic History

A Tribute to Keith Jackson Hancock,
Metodey Polasek and Robert Henry Wallace

FLINDERS ESSAYS IN ECONOMICS AND ECONOMIC HISTORY

A Tribute to Keith Jackson Hancock, Metodey Polasek and Robert Henry Wallace

Edited by Ralph Shlomowitz

Wakefield Press

Wakefield Press
1 The Parade West
Kent Town
South Australia 5067
www.wakefieldpress.com.au

First published 2009

Cover and text designed by Liz Nicholson, DesignBITE
Typeset by Michael Deves, Wakefield Press
Printed in Australia by Ligare Pty Ltd

National Library of Australia Cataloguing-in-Publication entry

Title:	Flinders essays in economics and economic history: a tribute to Keith Hancock, Metodey Polasek and Robert Wallace / editor, Ralph Shlomowitz
Publisher:	Kent Town, S. Aust.: Wakefield Press, 2008
ISBN:	978 1 86254 787 2 (pbk.)
Subjects:	Hancock, Keith, 1935–
	Polasek, M. (Metodey)
	Wallace, Robert
	Economics
	Economic history
	Economic development
	Economic policy
	Economic zoning
Other Authors:	Shlomowitz, Ralph
Dewey Number:	330

Keith Hancock, Robert Wallace, Metodey Polasek

Contents

Preface

This book consists of papers prepared for a mini-conference on 30 September 2005 to honour the careers of the three founders of the discipline of Economics at Flinders University: Keith Hancock, Metodey Polasek and Bob Wallace. The contributors include their ex-colleagues and friends, and the papers cover diverse topics in the disciplines of Economics and Economic History which have been closely linked at Flinders University. I am indebted to Mrs Iolanthe Whitaker for assistance in organising the mini-conference and in arranging these papers for publication.

Ralph Shlomowitz

Foreword

I am delighted to write the Foreword to the volume in honour of my three old, dear friends, Bob Wallace, Keith Hancock and Mat Polasek. I met Bob in the early 1950s when he was a couple of years ahead of me at the University of Melbourne, Keith, two years later when he started as an undergraduate at Melbourne and Mat, when I came to Adelaide in 1958 after he had recently graduated. We have remained friends and colleagues ever since.

Bob was one of my teachers at Melbourne. I attended his first ever set of lectures, on international trade theory to the honours class of 1952–53—Cliff Woods, Alan Barton, Geoff Bills and myself. I taught Keith when he was an "out patient" at Queens and I was the economics tutor—more of that later. I came to know Mat when he worked in Adelaide and then, after doing his Ph.D at Duke, when he taught at Flinders with Keith and Bob.

The Wallaces and the Harcourts became the very closest of friends with many family meetings on both sides of the world. We both had four children, Joan and I married about a year after Pat and Bob and when Bob took up his lectureship at Adelaide after his B.Phil at Oxford, Adelaide was even more so the place Joan and I most wanted to go to after doing my Ph.D at Cambridge. I was appointed to a research assistant post in 1957 but then the Murray Commission reported and with Bob's encouragement and support I was lucky enough to get the economics lectureship that was created as a result of the Commission's recommendations. I had been interviewed in early 1958 by Peter Karmel who was on leave in Belfast and the news of my appointment was received one day out of Colombo on our way home in March 1958. I thought that the doors of Heaven had opened and I was right, those first six years in Adelaide were indeed Heaven on earth. There I worked with Peter and Bob, met Eric Russell, Frank Jarrett, John Grant, Russell Mathews, Ron Hirst and with Bob helped recruit Keith and others—Donald Whitehead, Alan Barton, Maureen Brunt, Hugh Hudson—to the expanding, exciting Adelaide department.

Bob's lectures at Melbourne were a revelation: painstakingly prepared, incredibly deep and honest, enthusiastically presented, he developed a wonderful rapport with his class, whetting our intellectual appetites, stimulating our curiosity by making us keen to see where his probing, sceptical and highly intelligent narratives would take him—and us. Bob believed in challenging his audience by never dodging difficult issues, at the same time thinking up ingenious ways to illuminate the arguments by both words and pictures, using homely analogies, and, by getting behind the purely formal presentations of arguments, trying always to relate theory to the real world it was intended to illuminate. Generations of Adelaide and Flinders students have benefited from his selfless devotion first and foremost to teaching. His first year lectures and tutorials are role models of high standards coupled with enthusiasm and challenges which, in my experience, few could match. His honours lectures equally were at the right level and posed the proper tests of ability, understanding and judgment.

Not that Bob has been a slouch in research and as a sympathetic and critical reader of his colleagues' work. He has been associated with a number of excellent books aimed at both improving our knowledge of, for example, our financial institutions and providing first class teaching material in, for example, *Economic Activity*. His monetary chapters in that volume are masterpieces of acute analysis of difficult concepts and issues presented at exactly the right level for serious students starting on their economics education. His volumes with Ron Hirst and Merv Lewis and, of course, the Australian Samuelson in which the Master's text was put through the same demanding examination as Bob's pupils, are important landmarks in the Australian economics literature, as is, too, his pioneering work with Mike Artis on Australian fiscal policy. Moreover, one of Bob's early papers, written jointly with Peter Karmel and published in the first issue of *Australian Economics Papers* in 1962, was over 40 years ahead of its time; it provided a resounding critique of the limitations of representative agent models when applied to the workings of the economy as a whole. Peter and Bob combined their respective comparative advantages to analyse the systemic outcomes of individual banks' behaviour. Recently the *Cambridge Journal of Economics* received a paper on the same subject; its youthful author was, surprise, surprise, unaware of Peter and Bob's seminal paper, possibly because the author belongs to the modern trained generation of economists who think that economic theory began about 10 years ago with a moving peg.

My friendship with Bob was not confined to the lecture room and joint work. When I was an undergraduate, he "coached" Bert Prowse and me in order that we could break the five minute mile barrier, which we duly did (I think) one evening at the Melbourne University cricket/football oval surrounded by the University's colleges. It nearly broke me, I can tell you, but Bob could not have blown a candle out involuntarily at the end. He was a very fine long distance runner and, of course, played an excellent game of hockey well into his middle age, with his two sons in the same team. I envy him; I played Aussie Rules until I was 47 but never with either Robert or Tim in the same team. (Tim and I did play in the same cricket teams on occasions.) Bob was also a great influence on my political views—alas, I am now far to the left of him as his quizzical sceptical traits have made him almost anarchistic in his take on what political parties and their policies can achieve. But Bob was a great support and help when I took a leading role in the anti-Vietnam war protests of the 1960s and 1970s in Adelaide (the CPV and all that).

I must also mention our mutual admiration for the first TV series of the Forsyte Saga. We would watch each Sunday night for the six months it was on, ring one another for an in-depth analysis immediately afterwards and then the first 15 minutes of my combined honours class on capital theory at Flinders on the following Mondays would consist of a seminar with Bob and the students on it. Bob and I had a series of closely fought and highly enjoyable squash games for many years, to which we both looked forward immensely and neither of us cared who won. Frank Jarrett and I had some fiercely fought battington contests against Bob and Jim Bennett at Adelaide.

Most of all, Joan and I greatly admired the fortitude with which Bob and the children faced life after Pat's tragically early death, a fitting tribute to the ideals of united love that Pat bequeathed to them.

When Keith started at Melbourne, Jean Polglaze asked me to look out for this exceptional student from Melbourne High who she feared was attempting too much by trying to combine law, history and economics in an undergraduate degree. (Jean was always very "paternalistic" in attitude to students.) I came to know Keith in the tutorials I gave at Queen's—I very pompously insisted on gowns and surnames!—and I was immediately struck by his great intelligence and how articulate he was. It is no accident that he was one of the great debaters (and bridge players) of his generation. I spent a lot of time during my

Master's years at Melbourne drinking coffee with Keith and Joan (Taggart) in the Shop refectory; they were finishing off their undergraduate degrees before they married and went to LSE where Keith worked with Henry Phelps Brown for his Ph.D.

As I mentioned above, Bob and I recommended Keith to Peter Karmel when Keith was looking for a post back in Australia. When Keith was at Adelaide in the late 1950s, early 1960s we not only met daily in the wonderful Adelaide tea room for endless discussions on economics, politics and sport, we also played together in the Graduates cricket team which John Dillon and I started in 1962. It included as well as we three, Eric Russell, Deane Terrell, Dick Blandy and Keith Jones from the department. We went top in our first year. Keith was our ever reliable wicket keeper, Dick and I were the openers, and Eric, John and Deane, our outstanding all rounders.

When I returned to Adelaide in 1967 after nearly four years at Cambridge, I joined Keith as a co-editor of *Australian Economic Papers* (I had been Hugh Hudson's assistant editor when it was started in 1962.) Though Keith and my views on politics and economics sometimes were far apart, not least on the Vietnam War and incomes policies, we only ever had one disagreement in all those years. I found him the easiest of persons to work with and though our editorial styles were very different, I admired the seriousness and thoroughness with which he performed his editorial tasks. There are many articles in the journal from those years that benefited greatly from his close readings, suggestions and rewritings.

As we know, Keith went on to other successes following his years as a youthful professor at Flinders, first as Vice-Chancellor and then as Joe Isaac's successor at the Arbitration Commission (his first associate was one Tim Harcourt), and now as senior states person at Adelaide and Flinders, able now to write those well thought out and thoroughly researched papers that his administrative years, to some extent anyway, threatened to rob our profession of.

The public image of Keith is often of someone rather forbidding and formal. Indeed, when I was rung by Keith on editorial matters, he would always say when his secretary put him on the line, "Hello, Geoff, how are you?" before we got down to business. But all this was his frontal façade. I also know him as the most delightfully irreverent down-to-earth character, loving sport, especially the races, and a few beers or latterly wine, and sometimes more than a few, with a most engaging Rabelaisian wit. Joan (Hancock) and Keith once gave me a lift from Adelaide to Victoria and we had not exhausted our stock of often unrepeatable stories by the time we reached Ballarat where they left me. I have had the good fortune to know all four Hancock children, to teach Jim at Adelaide, talk to Kate about her master's thesis and Bill about his work in Italy and the UK. I count them amongst my favourite young people and I remember with much pleasure having conversation and bangers and mash with Ben and Keith when they came to visit us in Cambridge. Joan and I value enormously our sustained friendship with the Hancock families, one and two, for whom our affection is great. We especially value Joan's frequent visits to us in Cambridge and ours to Joan in Adelaide.

I always admired Mat's seriousness of purpose and transparent honesty and sensitive intelligence. I viewed with awe the harrowing story of his adventures before and after he reached Australia after the Second World War, and was always delighted by his academic achievements, his Ph.D from Duke and his closely researched work on international trade and international financial issues. He has many of the characteristics of his mentor and mine, the late Eric Russell—integrity, a deep respect for facts, the importance of understanding data sources and never pushing theory beyond its legitimate boundaries. He is a deeply devoted teacher and scholar, taking no short cuts and always believing in what he is presenting to students and readers. Peter Karmel's masterly introduction to statistical methods lives on in Karmel and Polasek.

I admire his love for his family, his pride in Pam's music making (at which he is no mean dab hand himself), and in his children's achievements. He was an exemplary colleague—selfless, supportive, excellent company, a fount of authoritative information and understanding.

I count myself most fortunate to have had my life entwined with three such fine people. I am so glad their splendid teaching and other contributions at Flinders are to be acknowledged in this volume and most honoured now to ask its readers please to read on.

G.C. Harcourt
Jesus College, Cambridge
April 2005

Europeanization or Globalization? What do Business Cycle Affiliations Say?

Michael Artis

University of Manchester and CEPR

Abstract

The paper derives deviation cycles for OECD countries and examines their synchronization through cross-correlations and the application of clustering techniques. Dividing the whole period (1970–2003) into three sub-samples allows an assessment of changes in business cycle affiliation over time. The UK, for example, appears to move from a US association to a European one. The paper also reports the results of applying a non-parametric procedure to test for business cycle association. This test suggests that the European grouping is not a very distinctive one. "Globalization" may be overwhelming "Europeanization".

Introduction

This paper focusses on cyclical affiliations. This term is meant to refer to the alleged tendency for some countries' business cycles to cluster together with others. One affiliation of arresting interest is that of "the European business cycle". There are several papers which claim to discern the existence of such a cycle (e.g., Artis et al. 2004; Kaufmann 2003) and there is an obvious reason to be interested in such a notion in the context of European Monetary Union. The European Business Cycle forms the subject of analysis for the CEPR's EuroArea Business Cycle Dating Committee and its coherence is a positive indicator for monetary union. But we are increasingly aware of "globalization" as a feature that may be overwhelming sub-global convergence. The paper starts with a homily.

Some years ago, with my colleague Wenda Zhang, I wrote a paper (Artis and Zhang, 1997) in which we employed the OECD's trade cycle data base and a presentational device first deployed by Baxter and Stockman (1986) to indicate the possible arrival of an European cycle, associated with the Exchange Rate Mechanism (ERM) of the European Monetary System.

In that paper we took industrial production deviation cycles estimated by the OECD on the basis of a modified NBER algorithm and showed the cross plots of the cross correlations of those cyclical deviates vis-a-vis the US and vis-a-vis Germany for a sequence of two periods. The first of these was typified as a "pre-ERM period" (1961:1 to 1979:3), the second as the ERM period (1979:4 to 1993:12). The interest in the picture was that where the observations for the first period suggested a broad "world cycle", in the second a number of countries could be seen as having moved strongly towards a stronger affiliation with Germany, with Germany and the US themselves much less closely related to each other. The UK was a prominent exception, with the European countries that had moved towards a stronger identification with Germany being those that were associated with the ERM either as full or as "apprentice" (shadowing) members. It might have been thought that this movement would be strengthened in subsequent years. Figures 1–3 show that this has not been so.

These figures plot the cross correlations of the cyclical deviates of industrial production, again as identified by the (now revised) OECD trade cycle data base, now for three periods. The first of these is labelled the pre-ERM period (Figure 1), and the world cycle phenomenon seems again a loosely reasonable characterization. In the second period (Figure 2), as in the original paper, a number of European countries have moved above the line—leaving the UK and the Northern "periphery" below the line. In the third period however (Figure 3) matters look very different. The US and Germany are now themselves highly correlated and it makes no sense to speak of a distinctive German affiliation.

It seems that we have to revisit the notion of a European business cycle, or at least refine what we mean by it. The first part of this paper is devoted to looking for evidence of business cycle affiliations employing a multi-country quarterly GDP data set and focussing on the notion of the deviation cycle. To

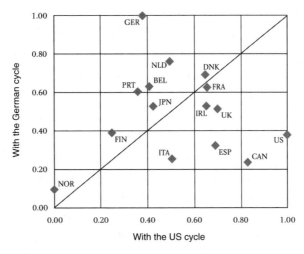

Figure 1. *Business Cycle Cross Correlation (OECD trade cycle database),*
pre-ERM period 1961:1–1979:3.

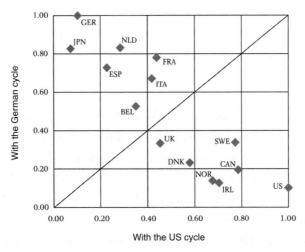

Figure 2. *Business Cycle Cross Correlation (OECD trade cycle database),*
ERM period 1979:4-93:12.

begin with, clustering techniques—both hierarchical and fuzzy clustering
methods—are used in an attempt to "let the data speak" as to whether there are,
or not, well-defined business cycle affiliations. Then a non-parametric technique recently employed by Bovi (2003) is used to assist in the same endeavour.

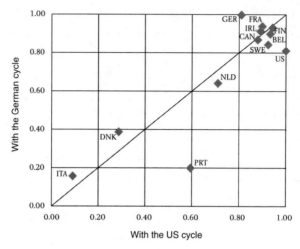

Figure 3. *Business Cycle Cross Correlation (OECD trade cycle database), post-ERM period 1994:1–2000:12.*

The measurement of cycles

In order to comment on business cycle affiliation it is necessary in the first instance to have a good idea of how to measure the cycle. Economists have made considerable progress in this respect in recent decades.

Business "cycles", as such, are not entirely well-termed, since the term "cycle" suggests a degree of regularity which is not found in practice. Nevertheless the idea is that it is possible to observe broad-based movements in the economy which have an oscillatory character, even if those oscillations do not occur with a strictly uniform periodicity and vary in the total length of time taken to work themselves out. Very important ground-clearing work was undertaken by Pagan and others (see Harding and Pagan, 2001, 2002) in resurrecting and clarifying the notions of the classical and the growth (or deviation) business cycles. The non-parametric algorithms which have resulted have permitted further refinements: for example, Artis, Marcellino and Proietti (2002) base their algorithms on a Markov-Chain approach which provides a flexible, yet rigorous framework for the identification of cycles. In these excursions, a dating algorithm identifies (strictly alternating), peaks and troughs and imposes minimum phase (expansion and recession) lengths and a minimum length for the cycle as a whole. They provide the opportunity to add amplitude restrictions in addition.

A cycle-dating algorithm may be applied to an original or to a transformed series describing the economy. The most common transformation (in addition to seasonal adjustment) is that of de-trending; here too, economists have made significant progress in recent decades. The suggestion by Baxter and King (1995) to make use of frequency domain analysis has proved highly important in this regard. Their argument is that since we "know" what the typical periodicity of a business cycle is, we should use this information to clean the data of periodicities which are greater or lower than those that span the cycle. These other periodicities should be thought of as mere blips and bumps (or seasonal cycles) in the case of the higher frequency oscillations or, or in the case of the lower frequencies, as longer run movements perhaps of the type associated with the adoption of a new technology or process. At any rate, this approach has given the profession new confidence in detrending and without completely laying all doubts to rest (see for example, Harvey and Trimbur (2003)) has substantially qualified the reservations that an earlier generation had entertained in reaction to a series of critical papers (e.g., Harvey and Jaeger (1993)) which had shown that existing methods could lead to the spurious identification of cycles which were not present and to other damaging mistakes. For purposes of the current paper, the point is that recent work seems to have allowed the efficient identification of cycles, from which one may proceed at least to *measure* affiliations between countries with some confidence. Explaining affiliations is another, more difficult, task which has to be left to another paper.

Affiliation

Commonly, measures of affiliation between business cycles are in fact measures of synchronization and a standard means of assessing this is to measure the cross-correlation between the detrended series. A standard product would therefore be a cross-correlogram showing the cross-corrrelations of the countries analysed in the sample under consideration The cross-correlogram shows all the pair-wise cross-correlation coefficients that can be estimated and lends itself to an application of clustering. However there are still other characteristics of business cycles that could be taken into account, although as soon as more than one characteristic is involved a weighting problem arises. Clustering methods can be applied to multi-dimensional problems of this type (see Artis

(2003, 2004) for an example) although they cannot avoid the need for weighting (albeit this might be of a studiedly "neutral" type). Another drawback of the traditional cross-correlogram approach is that it is confined to pair-wise comparisons, when often enough a comparison of *groups* is what is required. Shortly below we take advantage of recent papers by Bovi (2003, 2004) to show how this weakness may be redressed. Table 1 indicates the data set we are using, the countries involved and the time periods for which the (quarterly) GDP series are available.

Table 1. Country sample in business cycle analysis.

	Country	ISO-Code	Sample size
1	Austria	AUT	1970–2003
2	Finland	FIN	1970–2003
3	France	FRA	1970–2003
4	Germany	DEU	1970–2003
5	Italy	ITA	1970–2003
6	Spain	ESP	1970–2003
7	Sweden	SWE	1970–2003
8	United Kingdom	GBR	1970–2003
9	EU15		1970–2003
10	US	USA	1970–2003
11	Canada	CAN	1970–2003
12	Japan	JPN	1970–2003
13	Switzerland	CHE	1970–2003
14	Australia	AUS	1970–2003
15	Korea	KOR	1970–2003
16	Netherlands	NLD	1977–2003
17	Portugal	PRT	1977–2003
18	Norway	NOR	1978–2003
19	Belgium	BEL	1980–2003
20	Mexico	MEX	1980–2003
21	New Zealand	NZL	1982–2003
22	Denmark	DNK	1988–2003
23	Ireland	IRL	1997–2003

Cyclical histories

Using these data we proceed to derive deviation cycles using the H-P band-pass method described in Artis, Marcellino and Proietti (2002). That is, the data are filtered twice through low-pass Hodrick-Prescott band pass filters to isolate those frequencies with periodicities that correspond to the business cycle (i.e. 1.25 to 8 years in this case). The cross-correlogram that results from computing the pair-wise cross-correlations between all the countries in the sample is shown as Table 2. Then, the dating algorithm described in Artis, Marcellino and Proietti (2002) is applied to identify cycles in the detrended output series. This yields up to ten complete deviation cycles, depending on the country and the data available. Table 3 then contains a summary of the business cycle "stylized facts"[1] as revealed by the algorithm. The number of cycles identified varies across countries partly because data availability varies across countries, as reported in Table 1. The dating algorithm of the deviation cycle, roughly described above, also insists that a peak (trough) can never be identified at a point which is below (above) trend, even if it should be associated with an inflexion in the rate of change of output relative to trend (this distinguishes the deviation from the growth rate cycle—see Artis *et al* (2002), Appendix B). By construction, the deviation cycle should be a more or less stationary series, so that it is not surprising that average expansion and recession probabilities (which are the fractions of time that the economy is in one or other phase) should be roughly equal at around 0.5. The average duration, in quarters, of the two phases is also roughly equal at 7–10 quarters, but with a number of outliers—Denmark for example has recession durations that average over 11 quarters and Portugal of 17 quarters whilst extra-long expansion durations are registered for Switzerland and the Netherlands. Average amplitudes, measured as the proportionate increase from trough to peak for expansions and from peak to trough for recessions are not at all symmetrical. Expansion amplitudes are generally much higher than recession amplitudes, though the latter are not often negative. "Steepness" is measured as the quotient of amplitude and duration: the relative symmetry of durations and the asymmetry of amplitudes thus reflects in very unequal measures of steepness in expansion as opposed to recessions—the former being very much higher than the latter in all countries.

The cross-correlogram already yields evidence of business cycle affiliations in that it is obvious that there are relatively high cross-correlations between particular pairs of countries but clearer pictures emerge from the application of cluster analysis to these data[2]. To begin with, hierarchical ("hard") clustering methods are applied, first to the cross-correlation data for the whole period,

Table 2. Cross-correlations, full sample 1970–2003.

	AUT	FIN	FRA	DEU	ITA	ESP	SWE	UK	EU15	USA	CAN	JPN	CHE	AUS	KOR	NLD	PRT	NOR	BEL	MEX	NZL	DNK
AUT																						
FIN	0.27																					
FRA	0.69	0.43																				
DEU	0.76	0.16	0.65																			
ITA	0.68	0.44	0.65	0.64																		
ESP	0.61	0.50	0.68	0.45	0.57																	
SWE	0.05	0.59	0.09	0.01	0.31	0.02																
UK	0.38	0.48	0.59	0.43	0.43	0.44	0.37															
EU15	0.79	0.49	0.82	0.84	0.81	0.68	0.21	0.68														
USA	0.33	0.22	0.41	0.56	0.36	0.27	0.06	0.65	0.62													
CAN	0.25	0.49	0.41	0.35	0.48	0.29	0.37	0.50	0.50	0.72												
JPN	0.28	0.18	0.33	0.50	0.21	0.20	-0.05	0.34	0.45	0.32	0.10											
CHE	0.69	0.45	0.56	0.67	0.67	0.48	0.11	0.28	0.68	0.44	0.49	0.32										
AUS	0.09	0.45	0.21	0.16	0.38	0.03	0.34	0.24	0.31	0.49	0.75	0.10	0.43									
KOR	0.21	-0.07	0.29	0.28	0.21	0.31	-0.02	0.43	0.32	0.24	0.08	0.19	-0.05	-0.21								
NLD	0.56	0.28	0.43	0.82	0.58	0.31	0.19	0.16	0.66	0.52	0.46	0.27	0.75	0.30	0.03							
PRT	0.54	0.32	0.56	0.33	0.49	0.59	-0.05	0.01	0.39	-0.27	0.02	0.17	0.31	-0.01	0.08	0.30						
NOR	-0.22	-0.25	-0.15	-0.25	-0.03	-0.27	-0.02	0.09	-0.19	0.06	0.10	-0.34	-0.28	0.01	0.07	-0.19	-0.01					
BEL	0.66	0.32	0.64	0.52	0.52	0.66	0.02	0.25	0.65	0.35	0.44	0.26	0.44	0.19	0.38	0.52	0.55	-0.11				
MEX	-0.02	-0.03	-0.01	0.16	-0.14	-0.01	-0.23	-0.31	-0.04	0.24	0.21	0.17	0.32	0.30	-0.24	0.20	-0.03	-0.20	0.21			
NZL	-0.26	0.23	-0.08	-0.34	0.03	0.02	0.46	0.59	-0.06	0.27	0.45	-0.23	-0.23	0.31	0.38	-0.23	-0.15	0.25	0.08	-0.21		
DNK	-0.47	0.03	-0.21	-0.61	-0.30	-0.39	-0.07	0.15	-0.33	0.55	0.29	-0.47	-0.28	0.42	-0.35	-0.37	-0.38	0.53	-0.21	-0.06	0.11	
IRE	0.73	0.31	0.71	0.81	0.76	0.65	0.12	0.64	0.61	0.19	0.84	0.09	0.81	-0.15	0.51	0.82	0.75	-0.03	0.67	0.51	0.16	-0.37

Table 3. Business cycles: stylized facts, 1970–2003*.

	AUT	FIN	FRA	DEU	ITA	ESP	SWE	GBR	EU15	USA	CAN	JPN
Number of cycles P-P	10	7	7	9	8	8	8	7	9	8	8	10
Number of cycles T-T	9	8	7	8	8	8	9	7	9	9	8	10
Average Expansion Probability	0.64	0.40	0.49	0.50	0.49	0.49	0.52	0.50	0.55	0.59	0.66	0.43
Average Recession Probability	0.36	0.60	0.51	0.50	0.51	0.51	0.48	0.50	0.45	0.41	0.34	0.57
Average Duration of Expansions	8.70	7.86	9.43	7.56	8.25	9.57	8.88	9.71	7.78	10.00	11.13	5.90
Average Duration of Recessions	5.44	10.13	10.00	8.50	8.75	9.85	7.22	9.57	6.44	6.22	5.75	7.70
Average Amplitude of Expansions	0.0912	0.1096	0.0967	0.0724	0.0881	0.0970	0.0909	0.0990	0.0695	0.1156	0.1263	0.1558
Average Amplitude of Recessions	0.0038	0.0199	0.0238	0.0081	0.0084	0.0467	-0.0177	0.0120	0.0171	0.0124	0.0030	-0.0450
Steepness of expansions	0.0104	0.0139	0.0103	0.0096	0.0107	0.0101	0.0102	0.0102	0.0089	0.0116	0.0114	0.0264
Steepness of recessions	0.0007	0.0020	0.0024	0.0009	0.0010	0.0047	-0.0002	0.0012	0.0027	0.0020	0.0005	-0.0058

	CHE	AUS	KOR	NLD	PRT	NOR	BEL	MEX	NZL	DNK	IRL
Number of cycles P-P	7	9	9	5	4	10	5	5	5	4	2
Number of cycles T-T	6	10	8	4	4	10	5	4	5	3	2
Average Expansion Probability	0.61	0.59	0.60	0.56	0.37	0.46	0.44	0.55	0.49	0.39	0.46
Average Recession Probability	0.39	0.41	0.40	0.44	0.63	0.54	0.56	0.45	0.51	0.61	0.54
Average Duration of Expansions	11.71	8.89	9.00	12.20	10.00	6.30	8.40	10.60	8.60	5.50	6.50
Average Duration of Recessions	8.83	5.60	6.88	11.75	17.00	7.30	10.80	10.75	8.80	11.33	7.50
Average Amplitude of Expansions	0.0934	0.1053	0.2172	0.1028	0.1282	0.1195	0.0806	0.1687	0.1471	0.0471	0.1884
Average Amplitude of Recessions	-0.0293	0.0121	0.0433	0.0175	0.0541	0.0129	0.0203	-0.0605	-0.0157	0.0264	0.0670
Steepness of expansions	0.0080	0.0119	0.0241	0.0084	0.0128	0.0190	0.0096	0.0159	0.0171	0.0086	0.0290
Steepness of recessions	-0.0033	0.0140	0.0063	0.0015	0.0032	0.0018	0.0019	-0.0056	-0.0153	0.0109	0.0089

* sample start dates vary; see Table 1.

9

then to a two-dimensional measure in which cross-correlation data are combined with pair-wise "distance" measures. The latter are measured as the RMS of the distances between any two countries' detrended data, the assumption being made that the average levels are the same. The declining amplitudes of the cycle in recent years should imply a decline in the distance between economies' cycles, even if synchronization remains the same. A clustering algorithm starts with a distance matrix showing some measure of dissimilarity between the countries located along the axes; this will be a square matrix with a diagonal of zeroes and symmetric above and below the diagonal. The algorithm then first forms a cluster from the two observations which are closest together; replacing these by another value, the algorithm then proceeds to find the next smallest difference between any two observations (counting the just completed first cluster as one of these) and so on. The initial values entering the distance matrix are in the form of dissimilarities between (in our case) countries in respect of some characteristic (possibly several characteristics)—so the algorithm will cluster together countries which are similar in respect of that characteristic (or set of characteristics). In the case illustrated in Figure 4, the characteristic, x_{ki}, is a measure of the cyclical synchronicity of the country in question *with all the other countries*. Clustering algorithms are long on alternative measures of distance (the measurement of the difference between observations) and on alternative ways to compute the "replacement" value of a cluster after one has been identified. They are short on measures of significance or adequacy (though some appear in the context of "fuzzy" clustering). In the construction of Figure 4, we selected the distance measure as the Euclidian distance, i.e. as

$$\sqrt{\sum_{k=1}^{22}(x_{ki}-x_{kj})^2}$$

and the cluster replacement measure as that of average linkage. Experimentation with alternative distance measures did not in general reveal any significant difference. The clustering algorithm reveals, it seems, a cycle cluster based on the US, Canada, Great Britain and Australia and a "European cycle" itself based on two clusters, one involving Germany, Austria, Switzerland and the Netherlands, and the other involving France, Spain, Belgium, Italy,

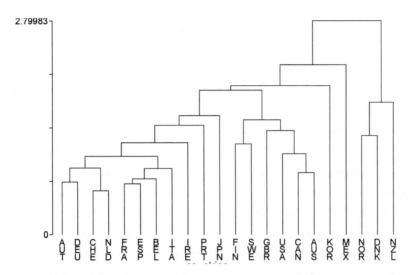

Figure 4. *Hierarchical average-linkage cluster tree (dendrogram) using Euclidean dissimilarity measure based on cross-correlations of cyclical deviates, full sample 1970–2003.*

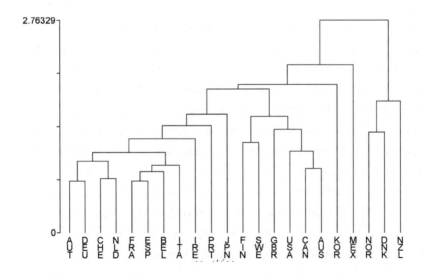

Figure 5. *Hierarchical average-linkage cluster tree (dendrogram) using Euclidean dissimilarity measure based on the combined cross-correlation and distance measures, full sample 1970–2003.*

Portugal and Ireland; but at the level at which these two are joined, there is also Japan. And then a number of other European countries—especially, the UK (denoted GBR), Sweden, Norway and Denmark are not so close. This is, if nothing else, a warning not to invest the notion of a "European" cycle as such with too much that is idiosyncratically European.

Contemporaneous cross correlation is not the only dimension in which we might want to measure similarity of business cycle experience. Some investigators (e.g., Massman and Mitchell (2002), Barrell and Weale (2003)) have suggested as an alternative the distance *between* cycles, as might be measured for example by the RMS of the squared differences over a period of time. The suggestion responds to the idea that whilst (for example) synchronization may not change over time, the amplitude of cycles may do so and thus the difference between cycles, for a given degree of synchronization, may increase or diminish. Figure 5 repeats the clustering exercise of Figure 4 for a combination of the cross correlation and distance measures, defined as

$$\sqrt{(1 - r_{ij})^2 + dist_{ij}^{\;2}}$$

where r_{ij} is the cross correlation and $dist_{ij}$ is the RMS distance between the cycles of countries i and j. As in the case of the simple cross-correlation this measure is computed over all j for each i. The picture provided by the clustering over this composite measure is however very little different from the picture provided when using the cross correlation measure alone. Figures 6, 7 and 8, however, use the composite measure, but in three sub-samples: 1970–79, 1980–92 and 1992–2003. These should give a picture of how cyclical affiliations may have varied over time. Figure 6 shows that in the first period there is no very well-defined European cluster though most European countries cluster away from the US and Canada; the UK (GBR) is shown as closer to some European countries than to the US in this period. In the second period a clearer European grouping emerges, albeit with some prominent exceptions and with the inclusion of Japan in the Euro group. In the third, most recent period, two European groupings can be seen to emerge—with Sweden, Finland and Norway being exceptional and Canada (this time departing from Australia) moving to the Euro-group. The groupings seem less clear and less constant through time than might have been expected.

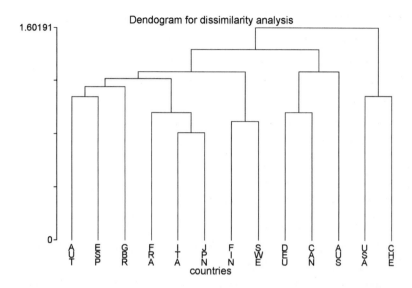

Figure 6. *Hierarchical average-linkage cluster tree (dendrogram) using Euclidean dissimilarity measure based on the combined cross-correlation and distance measures, 1970–1979.*

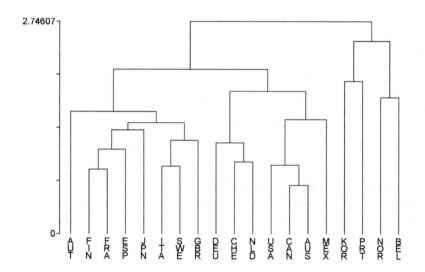

Figure 7. *Hierarchical average-linkage cluster tree (dendrogram) using Euclidean dissimilarity measure based on the combined cross-correlation and distance measures, 1980–1992.*

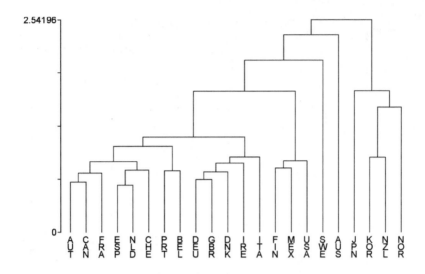

Figure 8. *Hierarchical average-linkage cluster tree (dendrogram) using Euclidean dissimilarity measure based on the combined cross-correlation and distance measures, 1993–2003.*

We may now turn to the fuzzy clustering analysis. In fuzzy clustering less information is wasted than in hard clustering: countries may be typified as having "membership coefficients", belonging (say) as to x % to one group or cluster and as to $(1 - x)$% to the other (in the case that only two clusters are distinguished). More generally the analysis furnishes the possibility of discerning whether there is a "distinct" set of groupings or not. To approach this question we use one of the "goodness of fit" measures associated with fuzzy clustering, which is the measure of average silhouhette width. Maximising the average value of the cluster silhouhette width seems a plausible way to determine the "optimal" number of clusters (Kaufman and Rousseow (1990)) provide a definition of this and of other measures associated with fuzzy clustering).

The average silhouette measure is bounded by ±1, with positive values indicating that the clusters are relatively well defined. In Table 4, which covers the whole period this criterion produces two clusters, of which one (cluster 1) is a good deal larger than the other. It involves most of the advanced industrial countries including both (most of) Europe and North America. Two clusters also are detected in the first subperiod (Table 5), more or less even in numbers of members. The UK is clustered with Canada and the USA; most other

Table 4. Fuzzy clustering, correlation of business cycles, full sample: 1970–2003.

	coefficients		silhouette width	belongs to cluster
Austria	0.64	0.36	0.79	1
Finland	0.52	0.48	0.49	1
France	0.70	0.30	0.81	1
Germany	0.67	0.33	0.78	1
Italy	0.72	0.28	0.79	1
Spain	0.69	0.31	0.76	1
Sweden	0.38	0.62	0.25	2
United Kingdom	0.55	0.45	0.50	1
EU15	0.74	0.26	0.81	1
United States	0.51	0.49	0.41	1
Canada	0.51	0.49	0.46	1
Japan	0.51	0.49	0.45	1
Switzerland	0.71	0.29	0.77	1
Australia	0.38	0.62	0.06	2
Korea	0.45	0.55	−0.11	2
Netherlands	0.72	0.28	0.75	1
Portugal	0.55	0.45	0.51	1
Norway	0.35	0.65	0.61	2
Belgium	0.76	0.24	0.76	1
Mexico	0.39	0.61	0.19	2
New-Zealand	0.32	0.68	0.54	2
Denmark	0.34	0.66	0.62	2
Ireland	0.70	0.30	0.72	1
Silhouette width	0.66	0.31		

Number of clusters	2
Average silhouette width	0.55
Dunn's coefficient	0.55
Normalised Dunn's coefficient	0.10

European countries are clustered separately. The second subperiod (Table 6) finds a larger number (5) of clusters to be optimal, suggesting a higher degree of idiosyncrasy in the period. Not even France and Germany are found to be in the same cluster in this period, although they are in the same clusters in the preceding and succeeding periods[3]. Table 7, finally, finds 3 clusters to be optimal for the most recent decade, one of these being a fairly prominent "European" grouping, including the UK.

Table 5. Fuzzy clustering, correlation of business cycles, sample: 1970–1980.

	coefficients		silhouette width	belongs to cluster
Austria	0.55	0.45	0.55	1
Finland	0.44	0.56	0.17	2
France	0.50	0.50	0.40	1
Germany	0.58	0.42	0.56	1
Italy	0.53	0.47	0.51	1
Spain	0.53	0.47	0.49	1
Sweden	0.45	0.55	0.09	2
United Kingdom	0.49	0.51	0.00	2
EU15	0.53	0.47	0.51	1
United States	0.47	0.53	0.24	2
Canada	0.45	0.55	0.23	2
Japan	0.58	0.42	0.50	1
Switzerland	0.55	0.45	0.50	1
Australia	0.41	0.59	0.50	2
Korea	0.54	0.46	0.29	1
Netherlands	0.60	0.40	0.56	1
Portugal	0.53	0.47	0.37	1
Norway	0.49	0.51	0.21	2
Belgium	0.57	0.43	0.53	1
Mexico	0.51	0.49	−0.03	1
New-Zealand	0.45	0.55	0.35	2
Denmark	0.41	0.59	0.43	2
Ireland	0.59	0.41	0.57	1
Silhouette width	0.45	0.27		

Number of clusters	2
Average silhouette width	0.37
Dunn's coefficient	0.51
Normalised Dunn's coefficient	0.01

The McNemar test

In this section of the paper we deploy a non-parametric technique to ask questions about the coherence of particular groupings. The procedure involves the "McNemar test" and has been given prominence recently by Bovi (2003, 2004). Many of the papers in the stream of literature associated with the identification of the European business cycle look outwards, over a period of time, from inside a European group, seeking to identify a closer union (or otherwise).

Table 6. Fuzzy clustering, correlation of business cycles, sample: 1980–1992..

	coefficients					silhouette width	belongs to cluster
Austria	0.09	0.13	0.16	0.33	0.29	0.25	4
Finland	0.23	0.06	0.15	0.46	0.10	0.47	4
France	0.11	0.06	0.10	0.61	0.12	0.66	4
Germany	0.12	0.14	0.42	0.17	0.15	0.80	3
Italy	0.13	0.05	0.24	0.49	0.10	0.34	4
Spain	0.07	0.05	0.08	0.64	0.16	0.62	4
Sweden	0.10	0.05	0.18	0.55	0.13	0.48	4
United Kingdom	0.17	0.07	0.13	0.41	0.21	0.51	4
EU15	0.09	0.04	0.18	0.59	0.10	0.43	4
United States	0.40	0.07	0.35	0.10	0.08	0.60	1
Canada	0.58	0.05	0.24	0.08	0.05	0.76	1
Japan	0.14	0.08	0.25	0.42	0.12	0.26	4
Switzerland	0.12	0.03	0.73	0.08	0.04	0.68	3
Australia	0.69	0.04	0.16	0.06	0.04	0.76	1
Korea	0.03	0.07	0.04	0.06	0.80	0.63	5
Netherlands	0.10	0.05	0.73	0.08	0.05	0.84	3
Portugal	0.13	0.24	0.11	0.19	0.33	0.67	5
Norway	0.13	0.47	0.15	0.09	0.16	0.73	2
Belgium	0.04	0.79	0.05	0.04	0.08	0.71	2
Mexico	0.62	0.06	0.13	0.12	0.07	0.68	1
Silhouette width	0.70	0.72	0.78	0.45	0.65		

Number of clusters	5
Average silhouette width	0.55
Dunn's coefficient	0.39
Normalised Dunn's coefficient	0.24

The important point made by Bovi is that this should be complemented by an analysis of whether any such development has proceeded faster or slower than similar processes elsewhere. Bovi himself uses long run data on classical cycles to look at this question, focussing in particular on the position of the UK. Our data sample in this section of the paper is much shorter and we shall not ask exactly the same questions of the data.

How does Bovi's procedure work? Bovi himself recognizes a contribution by McNemar, made as long ago as 1947 (McNemar 1947). The key here is a contingency table approach, as in Table 8. We can divide our observations into

Table 7. Fuzzy clustering, correlation of business cycles, sample: 1992–2003.

	coefficients			silhouette width	belongs to cluster
Austria	0.33	0.11	0.56	0.79	3
Finland	0.57	0.18	0.26	0.43	1
France	0.23	0.11	0.66	0.82	3
Germany	0.22	0.13	0.65	0.82	3
Italy	0.22	0.20	0.58	0.74	3
Spain	0.34	0.11	0.54	0.71	3
Sweden	0.32	0.42	0.26	0.12	2
United Kingdom	0.26	0.11	0.63	0.74	3
EU15	0.32	0.10	0.58	0.68	3
United States	0.63	0.17	0.20	0.61	1
Canada	0.25	0.09	0.67	0.78	3
Japan	0.26	0.56	0.18	0.54	2
Switzerland	0.24	0.08	0.68	0.76	3
Australia	0.42	0.37	0.21	0.52	1
Korea	0.15	0.71	0.14	0.58	2
Netherlands	0.37	0.08	0.54	0.65	3
Portugal	0.38	0.19	0.43	0.50	3
Norway	0.24	0.61	0.16	0.47	2
Belgium	0.35	0.10	0.54	0.67	3
Mexico	0.65	0.16	0.19	0.61	1
New-Zealand	0.13	0.76	0.10	0.67	2
Denmark	0.23	0.10	0.67	0.73	3
Ireland	0.19	0.07	0.74	0.81	3
Silhouette width	0.55	0.48	0.73		

Number of clusters	3.00
Average silhouette width	0.51
Dunn's coefficient	0.44
Normalised Dunn's coefficient	0.20

four cells (as in Table 8). When all the countries in Group 1 are in the same business cycle phase (that is, "in synch."), there will be some periods in which the countries making up Group 2 are also "in synch"—the intersection of these two sets gives the cell labelled N_{11}, the number of observations in which both groups are "in synch". Similarly, while the members of Group 1 are "out of synch" with each other, there will be some periods when the members of

Table 8

| | | Group 2 | |
		In-synch	Out-of-synch
Group 1	In-synch	N_{11}	N_{12}
	Out-of-synch	N_{21}	N_{22}

Group 2 are also out of synch: the intersection of these two sets corresponds to the cell labelled N_{22} in Table 8.

The cells labelled N_{12} and N_{21} correspond to the remaining intersections. The information in the contingency table can be used to test whether Group 1 is more (or less) coherent than Group 2, in the sense that it is (or not) more often "in synch" than Group 2. McNemar offers the scaled difference $(N_{12}-N_{21})^2/(N_{12} + N_{21})$ as a suitable test statistic for which a χ^2 distribution is suggested (provided that numbers are large enough). Bovi points out that a continuity correction (due to Sheskin (2002)) may also be applied (the statistic becomes $(|N_{12}-N_{21}| - 1)^2/(N_{12} + N_{21})$). In principle, the test can also be applied, *mutatis mutandis* to the information in the leading diagonal cells, which we have done here as a check on the main results. Whilst the attraction of the approach is that it can be applied to groups of countries, it can also be applied to individual countries or to groups that are represented by a single aggregate number—it is just that in these cases the country in question (or the aggregate) can only ever be typified as being "in synch" with itself. If a single country or aggregate takes the place of group 1 (2) in the formula, then the cells N_{22} (N_{12}) and N_{21} (N_{22}) are null. There is also a problem in comparing groups of unequal size in that it is "harder", other things equal, for a large group to be in synch with itself than for a smaller group. Here we have made the ad hoc adjustment that in comparisons of groups of unequal size, only 80% of the members of the larger group need to be in synch for the group as a whole to be regarded as such; clearly this is an arbitrary adjustment. For these reasons the clearest comparisons are those between the "core EMU" and the "Anglo" group—which happen to be the focus of Bovi's attentions in his original papers.

In the current application we recognize at first pass nine groups, two individual countries and one aggregate. The groups are: Core EMU (Germany,

Table 9. Bovi-McNemar test statistics, full sample 1970–2003.

	Core EMU	Non EMU	EU15	EU15*	G7	ROW	OECD	USA	ANGLO	DEU	EMUUK	NAMU
EMU	0.33	0.20	–	92.25	1.29	–1.64	3.86	100.15	0.17	92.25	–	–1.09
Core EMU		0.00	0.09	90.27	0.57	–2.46	5.26	98.15	0.00	85.72	0.09	–1.96
Non EMU			0.06	95.34	0.53	–2.91	5.76	96.33	0.00	95.34	0.06	–2.88
EU15				89.29	0.31	–3.52	6.55	95.34	0.05	87.72	–	–2.91
EU15*					95.04	–107.04	110.04	0.07	–99.04	–	–89.29	–108.00
G7						–9.00	13.24	84.25	1.33	91.35	0.31	–6.37
ROW							–	102.54	4.57	109.00	3.52	0.09
OECD								105.53	9.31	112.00	6.55	1.60
USA									88.17	0.07	–95.34	–98.19
ANGLO										97.15	0.05	–
DEU											87.72	–108.00
EMUUK												–2.91
NAMU												

Notes:
critical values $\chi^2(1)$ at 1% = 2.71 / at 5% = 3.84 / at 10% = 6,63
Clusters of countries:
EMU : all EMU countries; coreEMU : FRA,DEU,ITA; nonEMU : GBR,SWE,DNK; EU15 : all EU countries; G7 : USA,CAN,JPN; ROW : all non EU countries; OECD : all OECD, not EU; ANGLO : only USA,CAN,GBR; EMUUK : EMU with UK included; NAMU : USA and UK
Single countries: USA; EU15*; DEU : Germany

France and Italy); EMU (all current members of EMU except Greece, and Luxembourg for which data are not available); non-EMU (Denmark, UK, Sweden), EU 15 (all except Greece and Luxembourg); the G-7; the rest of the world (ROW)—all countries listed in Table 1 (i.e OECD) minus the groups already mentioned; the OECD (all countries in Table 1 minus the EU countries; "Anglo"—the USA, UK and Canada, EMUUK—the EMU plus the UK and NAMU, the US and UK. Two individual countries are shown—the US and Germany and one aggregate—that for the EU 15, denoted EU15*.

Table 9 gives a first set of results. For their interpretation, bear in mind that in terms of the formulae quoted above, the countries reported in the column heads are group 1 whilst those reported in the rows are group 2. This means that a positive and significant value of the figure reported would indicate that the group defined in the column is more coherent than that reported in the row, whilst a significant negative figure would have the opposite implication. Bearing in mind the critical values listed at the foot of the table, it is clear that rather little is significant that does not involve one of the individual countries

Table 10. Bovi-McNemar test statistics, sample 1970–1985 (upper side) / 1985–2003 (lower side).

	Core EMU	Non EMU	EU15	EU15*	G7	ROW	OECD	USA	ANGLO	DEU	EMUUK	NAMU
EMU	-	–	–	44.31	1.33	–	–	48.00	0.40	43.31	–	–
Core EMU	–	–	–	41.33	0.09	–1.33	–2.27	43.09	–0.09	37.23	–	–1.33
Non EMU	0.33	0.69	–	48.00	1.33	–	–	46.08	–	45.08	–	–
EU15	–	–	–0.09	42.32	0.33	–	–	44.08	–	39.71	–	–
EU15*	48.02	49.00	47.61	47.03	–44.00	–49.00	–50.00	–	–46.00	–	–42.32	–49.00
G7	0.25	0.53		0.06	–51.07	–	–	38.72	–	39.34	–0.33	–
ROW	–1.92	–1.14	–3.27	–2.57	–58.06	–	–	45.30	–	48.00	–	–
OECD	–3.77	–3.00	–5.40	–4.57	–60.06	–	–	46.30	–	49.00	–	–
USA	52.27	55.07	50.28	51.27	–	45.56	57.25	59.24	–40.69	–	–44.08	–45.30
ANGLO	0.08	–0.33	–0.08	–	–53.07	–	–	–47.52		43.09	–	–
DEU	49.00	48.49	50.28	48.02	–	52.07	61.00	63.00	54.07		–39.71	–48.00
EMUUK	–	–	–0.09	–	47.03	–0.06	2.57	4.57	–51.27	0.08		–48.02
NAMU	–1.14	–0.69	–3.00	–1.92	–59.00	–3.60	–	–	–52.94	–	–60.00	–1.92

Notes:
critical values χ²(1) at 1% = 2.71 / at 5% = 3.84 / at 10% = 6,63
Clusters of countries:
EMU : all EMU countries; coreEMU : FRA,DEU,ITA; nonEMU : GBR,SWE,DNK; EU15 : all EU countries; G7 : USA,CAN,JPN; ROW : all non EU countries; OECD : all OECD, not EU; ANGLO : only USA,CAN,GBR; EMUUK : EMU with UK included; NAMU : USA and UK
Single countries: USA; EU15*; DEU : Germany

or the EU15 aggregate. The main exception is that some of the figures in the OECD column border acceptable levels of significance. But significance here means that there is a difference in the coherence of the groups compared. On this basis there is little to support the view that there is a distinctive coherent European grouping—only the EU15-OECD pairing might suggest otherwise (the same can be said at a lower level of significance for Core EMU and non-EMU pairings with OECD here). Clearly, though, the pairings that involve an individual country or the EU15 in aggregate tell a different story—which seems to suggest that individual countries are more idiosyncratically different than any grouping: but recall that key entries for these entities are null.

An attraction of the Bovi–McNemar methodology is that it allows one to examine the movement of the measure of relative coherence over time. Unfortunately, our sample is rather too short to allow this, but for what it is worth we tried splitting the sample. In table 10 we concentrate exclusively upon the groups (dropping the individual countries and the EU15 aggregate), split the sample into two equal-sized sub-samples and introduce a continuity correction. Not too surprisingly, as the results show, the sub-samples are too small to support much reliable inference, and there is little that can even be tested, and of that little that is significant except for some of the comparisons involving the OECD. But these comparisons do not involve EMU or core-EMU.

Conclusions

The object of the paper was to see whether measures of business cycle synchronization or coherence support the view that there are "business cycle clubs". We had particularly in mind that it might be possible to detect the emergence of a "European business cycle". The results we have obtained seem to show that whilst some business cycle groupings can be detected for periods of time, only a few of these are reasonably persistent. The presence of a persistent—or growing—"European" grouping seems particularly hard to detect, perhaps surprisingly given the common implicit acceptance of the contrary view. Among the possible explanations for this must be counted the following: changes in the relative frequency of global versus regional or national-idiosyncratic shocks; changes in the interrelationships between economies (to put it loosely, the growth of "globalization"), and the habit of examining the European cycle by starting with Europe and looking at its development, so to speak from the inside out. In acting in this way there is a clear risk of failing to distinguish globalization from Europeanization. Something must be added also to account for differences in the results that may be obtained, on the one hand by working with industrial production data or by working with GDP data.[4]

Acknowledgement

The author wishes to acknowledge the helpful research assistance of Peter Claeys of the EUI and, as well, the hospitality of the European Commission (DG-ECFIN) during a stay as Research fellow there during the month of May 2004, when work on this paper was advanced.

References

Andrews, D. and M. Kohler (2005) "International Business Cycle Co-Movements through Time", *mimeo*, Reserve Bank of Australia.

Artis, M.J., (2003) "Is There a European Business Cycle?", *Ces-ifo Working papers*, No 1053, October

Artis, M.J. (2004) "Is There a European Business Cycle?", in (ed.) Siebert, H.: *Macroeconomic Policies in the World Economy*. Heidelberg: Springer.

Artis, M.J., Krolzig, H.M. and J.Toro (2004), "The European Business Cycle", *Oxford Economic Papers*, 56, 1–44

Artis, M.J. Marcellino, M. and T. Proietti (2002) "Dating the EuroArea Business Cycle", *CEPR Discussion Papers*, No.3696. London: CEPR.

Barrell, R and M. Weale (2003) "Designing and Choosing Macroeconomic Frameworks: the position of the UK after Four Years of the Euro", *Oxford Review of Economic Policy*, 19, 132–148.

Baxter, M. and A.C. Stockman (1986) "Business Cycles and the Exchange Rate Regime", *Journal of Monetary Economics*, 23, 377–400.

Baxter, M. and R.G.King (1999) "Measuring business cycles: approximate band-pass filters for economic time series", *Review of Economics and Statistics*, 81, 575–93.

Bovi, M (2003) "A non-parametric analysis of international business cycles", ISAE Working Papers, No. 37.

Bovi, M (2004) "Economic Clubs and European Commitments. A Business Cycles Race", available at http://www.sigov.si/zmar/conference/2004/papers/Bovi.pdf

Camacho, M., Pererz-Quiros, G. and L.Saiz (2004) "Are European Business Cycles close enough to be one?", paper given at the conference on "EMU enlargement to the East and West", Budapest, 24/25 September.

Harding, D. and A. Pagan (2001) "Extracting, Analysing and using Cyclical information", *mimeo*

Harding, D. and A. Pagan (2002) "Synchronization of Cycles", *mimeo*

Harvey, A.C. and A.Jaeger (1993) "Detrending, Stylized facts and the Business Cycle", *Journal of Applied Econometrics*, 8, 231–47.

Harvey, A.C. and T.Trimbur (2003) "General Model-based filters for extracting trends and cycles in economic time series", *Review of Economics and Statistics*, 85, 244–255.

Kaufmann, S. (2003) "The Business Cycle of European Countries. Bayesian Clustering of country-individual IP growth series", *Working Papers of the National Bank of Austria*, No 83.

Kaufman,L. and P.J. Rousseow (1990) *Finding Groups in Data*. New York: John Wiley and Sons, Inc

Massmann, M. and J. Mitchell (2002) "Have UK and European Business Cycles become more correlated?", *National Institute Economic Review*, no. 192, 58–71.

McNemar, Q (1947) "Note on the sampling error of the difference between correlated proportions or percentages", *Psychometrika*, 12, 153–157

Sheskin, D.J. (2000) *Handbook of Parametric and Nonparametric Statistical Procedures*, 3rd edition. Boca Raton: Chapman and Hall/CRC Press.

Notes

1 See Harding and Pagan (2001, 2002) for a discussion of the stylized facts of the business cycle.
2 Bearing Australia in mind, it can be seen that for this country the only high correlation is with Canada. This feature is among those explored in Andrews and Kohler (2005).
3 The Netherlands and Switzerland are more constant companions for Germany.
4 A paper that is close to this one, both in its problem set and in its methodology is that by Camacho et al (2004), which works entirely with industrial production data.

2

South Australia's Regional Innovation System: Findings from the Australian Bureau of Statistics' 2003 Business Innovation Survey

Richard Blandy

University of South Australia

Introduction

Theoretical ideas about innovation go back at least to Adam Smith's view (Smith, 1776) that increased productivity was associated with specialisation and the division of labour, implying technological advances in processes and organisation. Alfred Marshall (Marshall, 1890) saw specialisation and progress arising out of the external economies associated with the rise of specialist suppliers of goods and services used as inputs in other firms in particular industries giving rise to growing agglomerations. The idea of collaboration among firms (at least as suppliers and demanders) starts to emerge as an element in innovation. Michael Porter (Porter, 1990) gave a spatial dimension to this idea seeing *regional* industry clusters emerging as a result of externality-driving innovations produced and introduced by firms in *local* supply chains. Philip Cooke, Mikel Landabaso and others from the 1990s to the present (for example, Cooke, 1992; Landabaso, Oughton and Morgan, 1999; Cooke, 2001) developed the regional dimension in innovation to propose the existence of regional innovation systems (RISs) and learning regions. Henry Etzkowitz (Etzkowitz, 1997) proposed the evolution of a "triple helix" of interacting players (enterprises, universities and government) sharing and exchanging functions in a knowledge-based economy and society. Recently, Philip Cooke and Loet Leydesdorff (Cooke and Leydesdorff, 2005) introduced the opportunity for low-cost, *long distance* interactions as well as in regional networks leading to the development of "constructed advantage" for a region.

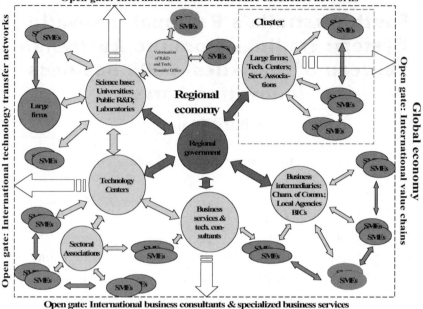

Figure 1. *Constructed Advantage: An Externally-Connected Regional Innovation System in a Knowledge-Based Economy and Society.*
Source: Landabaso, Oughton and Morgan (1999, p. 7)

This idea can be illustrated by a diagram from Landabaso, Oughton and Morgan (1999, p. 7).

In Figure 1, the regional innovation system is depicted as comprising a regional economy made up of a regional government interacting with a regional science base, large firms, technology centers, sectoral associations and SMEs in clusters, business intermediaries, business services and consultants, with each part of this regional innovation system open to global options. Choices made between local and global options give rise to the regional advantage that is *constructed* locally.

These ideas—the identities of the various elements in the regional innovation system, their interactions, and options for local or global sourcing—underpin the identification of useful data that can be collected. This theoretical structure underpins the guidelines for collecting and interpreting technological innovation data known as the *Oslo Manual*, first published in 1993 and now in its third edition (OECD and Eurostat, 2005).

The ABS's 2003 Business Innovation Survey

The Australian Bureau of Statistics' 2003 Business Innovation Survey (ABS, 2003) is based on the concepts and standard questions in the *Oslo Manual*, although it adopts a smaller minimum size of firm and wider industry coverage than has been used in Europe, and also pioneered questions on non-technological innovation (a matter that has now been taken up in the 3rd edition of the *Oslo Manual*). The ABS survey data and results, with appropriate adjustments for these factors, can be compared with the Eurostat Community Innovation surveys and results, therefore.

The sample was 8500 businesses employing four or more people (with all firms employing 200 or more people included). The sample was stratified by industry, state/territory and firm size (number of employees). The main reference period was 2001–2003, but sometimes the reference period was 2003, and on a few occasions was fiscal 2003. The survey was undertaken by mail (with response being required by law, as is standard for ABS surveys).

After cleaning the results (eliminating firms chosen from the ABS's database that were non-functioning, for example), 6195 weighted responses were available for analysis nationally, including 401 weighted responses available for South Australia. Using the SPSS statistical package, descriptive frequency and cross-tab presentation of the data were possible, as well as statistical testing of differences in measures of central tendency and variance, and multivariate analyses like analysis of variance and regression analysis (including logistic regression).

Three measures of innovation are identified in the survey:

- the introduction of new goods or services (Yes or No)
- the implementation of new operational processes (Yes or No)
- the implementation of new organizational or managerial processes (Yes or No).

In addition, any combination of positive responses to the above three questions is classified as an "innovator".

Other variables on which data were collected in the survey are:

- Length of operation at 12/03 (4 groups)
- Percentage of foreign ownership at 12/03 (4 groups)

- Number of employees at 12/03
- Collaborations (10 types)—within 100 km
- Collaborations (10 types)—up to global
- Sources of ideas and information (13 types)
- Methods of acquiring knowledge or abilities—up to global and excluding higher ed. and research institutions (6 types)
- Methods of acquiring knowledge or abilities—from Australian higher ed. and research institutions (8 types)
- Methods of acquiring knowledge or abilities—from global higher ed. and research institutions (8 types)
- Key business drivers for innovation (9 types)
- Skills and capabilities sought in new staff (7 types)
- State or Territory (7 variables)
- Industry (1–4 digit ANZIC code)
- Postcode of location (HQ)
- Sources of innovations (3 sources)
- Degrees of novelty of innovations (3 degrees)
- Impact of innovation on 2003 turnover (%)
- Degrees of export focus of innovations (%)
- Formal methods to protect IP in 2003 (4 methods)
- Informal methods to protect IP in 2003 (4 methods)
- Factors hampering innovation (13 factors)
- If new location, reasons for shifting(11 reasons)
- Where business searches for people for innovation (8 places)
- Expenditure in last financial year (A$'000)
- Expenditure on innovation activities (8 categories, A$'000)
- Expenditure on innovation by State or Territory (7, %)
- Expenditure on innovation by funding (7 sources, %)
- Gross income of business (A$'000)
- Operating profit or loss (A$'000)

These variables are all candidates for inclusion in descriptions and analyses of South Australia's Regional Innovation System.

Some Descriptive Outcomes of South Australia's Regional Innovation System

South Australia possesses a far greater proportion of innovative firms than any other State in Australia. Forty-six per cent of South Australian firms are "innovators", while the next highest proportion is 36 per cent in New South Wales. The corresponding figure for Australia is 35 per cent (ABS, 2003, p. 14). This gap exists whichever of the four survey measures of innovation is adopted (ABS, 2003, p. 15).

After adjusting the data to make them comparable with European survey data, *Australian* businesses ranked *seventh* in a comparison with businesses in various countries of the European Union (ABS, 2003, p. 12). If one were to make the same adjustment to South Australia's score as to Australia's, *South Australian* businesses would rank in *equal first* position (with Germany).

Most innovations in Australian firms occur in firms undertaking more than one form of innovation, in fact, as shown in Table 1, below.

Table I. Combinations of Types of Innovations, Australian Firms, 2003.

Type of Innovation	Only this type	All innovation combinations with this type included	Only this type/ All combinations (%)
Goods and services	233	1027	22.7%
Operational processes	404	1419	28.5%
Organisational/managerial	359	1326	27.1%
All three types	996	3772	26.4%

Source: Author's computations using SPSS on unit record data from ABS, 2003.

In Table 1, only 26.4 per cent of all innovations occur as isolated "single type" innovations—73.6 per cent of innovations occur in firms undertaking more than one form of innovation. Only 22.7 per cent of innovations in goods and services occur as isolated "single type" innovations—77.3 per cent of new goods and services occur in firms undertaking more than one form of innovation. Similar figures apply to innovations in operational processes and in organisational and managerial processes.

Innovation in Australian (including South Australian) firms can be seen from these data as a broad ranging, ongoing activity within enterprises, not as isolated acts of product or process creation. This result confirms the main conclusion of an important study undertaken into innovation in Australian businesses by the Business Council of Australia in 1993 (Carnegie *et al*, 1993).

South Australian innovative firms are also more successful than South Australian firms generally. They have survived slightly longer (5.8 years compared with 5.4 years overall). The innovative firms are slightly larger: average employment size is 10 persons compared with 9 persons overall, while average turnover is 2.6 million compared with $1.4 million overall. The innovative firms are more profitable: *mean* operating profit is $653,000 compared with $237,000 overall, while *median* operating profit is $96,000 compared with $70,000 overall.

The industries in South Australia with the highest proportions of innovative firms are manufacturing, business services, and accommodation, cafes and restaurants. Fifty-three per cent of South Australia's manufacturing firms are classed as innovative, compared with 46 per cent, nationally. Fifty-two per cent of South Australia's business services firms are classed as innovative, compared with 32 per cent, nationally. Fifty-one per cent of South Australia's accommodation, cafes and restaurants are classed as innovative, compared with 27 per cent, nationally.

Comparing South Australian innovative firms with Australian innovative firms, on average,

- South Australian innovators have survived slightly longer,
- are approximately the same size in employment terms, but smaller in terms of average turnover,
- are less profitable in term of mean profit, but more profitable in terms of median profit,
- are more innovative in manufacturing, business services, finance and insurance, retail trade, and accommodation, cafes and restaurants,
- are similarly distributed across industries, but
- are *less collaborative.*

This latter finding is something of a surprise, because collaboration is hypothesised theoretically as a key element in making firms innovative. Indeed, this is borne out in the data in that 21 per cent of South Australia's innovating firms are classed as collaborators, compared with only 10 per cent of South Australia's firms, generally; while 27 per cent of Australia's innovating firms are classed as collaborators compared with 12 per cent of Australian firms, generally. The surprise lies in more Australian innovators being classed as collaborative compared with South Australian innovators. There must be something else at work explaining innovativeness in South Australian firms than collaborativeness.

Causes of Innovativeness in South Australian Firms

To examine causes of innovativeness in South Australian firms, a model of innovativeness was used in which whether a firm was an innovator or not was made a function of other variables on which data was collected by the ABS in its 2003 survey. Since the dependent variable ("innovator or not") is a categorical variable, the appropriate regression model to use is "logistic" regression.

The model was regressed in stepwise fashion against all of the variables on which data was collected by the ABS except:

- Length of operation at 12/03 (4 groups)—considered to be an outcome
- Industry (1–4 digit ANZIC code)—not available at the time the regressions were run
- Postcode of location (HQ)—not available at the time the regressions were run
- Degrees of novelty of innovations (3 degrees)—considered to be an outcome
- Impact of innovation on 2003 turnover (%)—considered to be an outcome
- Degrees of export focus of innovations (%)—descriptive, not considered to be causal
- Factors hampering innovation (13 factors)—responses considered to be unreliable
- If new location, reasons for shifting(11 reasons)—considered to be an outcome

- Expenditure in last financial year (A$'000)—considered to be correlated with other firm size variables
- Expenditure on innovation activities (8 categories, A$'000)—considered to be a scale variable

A stopping rule was adopted for the stepwise procedure that continued to add explanatory variables to the regression equation while the χ^2 for included variables remained significant (at the 5% level), up to the equation specification that yielded the *least significant* value on the Hosmer and Lemeshow χ^2 test.

This procedure yielded the following model of the causes of innovativeness in South Australian firms (Table 2, below):

Table 2. Causes of Innovativeness in South Australian Firms, 2003: Stepwise Logistic Regression Results.

	B	S.E.	Wald χ^2	d.f.	Sig.	Exp(B)	95.0% C.I. for EXP(B)	
							Lower	Upper
New corporate strategies	3.297	0.598	30.428	1	.000	27.028	8.377	87.210
High turnover on non-innovative products	0.087	0.026	11.594	1	.001	1.091	1.038	1.148
Uses secrecy re IP	2.497	0.649	14.819	1	.000	12.144	3.406	43.299
Price competition in product markets	1.980	0.548	13.063	1	.000	7.244	2.475	21.199
Seeks IT skills . and capabilities	2.084	0.621	11.278	1	.001	8.037	2.382	27.119
Spends on innov. in SA	0.097	0.031	9.708	1	.002	1.102	1.037	1.172
Uses borrowing to fund innovation	0.055	0.027	4.066	1	.044	1.056	1.002	1.114
Constant	−3.730	0.434	73.996	1	.000	.024		

Source: Author's computations using SPSS on unit record data from ABS, 2003, where B is the regression coefficient for the variable, S.E. is the standard error of the regression coefficient, Wald χ^2 is the χ^2 value for the regression coefficient, d.f. is the number of degrees of freedom for the χ^2 value, Sig. is the significance of the χ^2 value, Exp(B) is the odds ratio corresponding to the regression coefficient (B), and 95.0% C.I. for EXP(B) is the 95 % confidence interval for EXP(B). The odds ratio EXP(B) should exceed 1.0 if the impact of the variable on whether a firm is innovative or not is to be greater than 50/50, i.e., pure chance.

Model tests:
- All variables are significant @ 5% level of significance.
- Hosmer and Lemeshow test: $\chi^2 = 6.149$ with 5 d.f., significance = 0.292
- Nagelkerke $R^2 = 0.880$
- 93% of innovators and 98% of non-innovators are correctly forecast by the model.

The model tests indicate that this model fits the data well. All variables are significant, the (alternative) hypothesis that the model explains the values of the dependent variable cannot be rejected, the value for Nagelkerke's pseudo-R^2 is high, and a high proportion of innovator firms and non-innovator firms are both correctly identified by the model.

Putting the figures in Table 2 into words yields the following conclusions about what distinguishes an innovative firm from a non-innovative one. An innovative firm

- has developed new corporate strategies (very important),
- uses secrecy to protect its intellectual property (very important),
- looks for skills and capabilities in IT to support its new processes (important),
- faces price competition for the goods or services it produces (important),
- spends on innovative activities within SA,
- has a higher turnover from non-innovative goods or services, and
- spends on innovative activities using borrowed funds.

It seems unlikely that a firm will be innovative unless it has developed some new strategies as a business—why would it be innovative if it sees a future that is not different from the past? An innovator is more likely to be aware than a non-innovator that it has intellectual property to protect and is more likely to try to protect it by means that are not only inexpensive but also that do not advertise the fact that it has intellectual property to protect. Innovators are more likely to be reliant on IT skills and capabilities than non-innovators, and are more likely to face greater price competition for the goods and services that they produce than non-innovators are. South Australian innovators are more likely to spend on innovative activities *within* South Australia, rather than on innovative activities elsewhere. Firms introducing innovations in a particular year are likely to have a *smaller* proportion of their turnover attributed to innovations introduced in earlier periods than non-innovators are. What this means is that there appears to be a limit on the risk that firms are willing to run in introducing new products and services. Innovative firms are more likely than non-innovative firms to borrow because their need for funds exceeds their own funds or because of a desire to spread risk.

To check these results, the regression model was tested using the same candidate variables against data for Australia as a whole, rather than only for South Australia. This procedure yielded the following model of the causes of innovativeness in Australian firms (Table 3, below):

Table 3. Causes of Innovativeness in Australian Firms, 2003: Stepwise Logistic Regression Results.

	B	S.E.	Wald χ^2	d.f.	Sig.	Exp(B)	95.0% C.I. for EXP(B)	
							Lower	Upper
Buys new equip and tech	1.200	0.119	101.37	1	.000	3.321	2.629	4.196
Responsive to customer needs	0.771	0.094	66.599	1	.000	2.161	1.796	2.601
Seeks skilled people	1.089	0.133	67.544	1	.000	2.973	2.293	3.855
New corporate strategies	1.396	0.132	111.63	1	.000	4.041	3.118	5.235
Collaborative	1.231	0.142	75.152	1	.000	3.426	2.593	4.526
Uses res facilities of Aust res institutes (non higher ed.)	4.100	0.651	39.657	1	.000	60.368	16.848	216.302
Uses own funds for innovation	0.134	0.032	17.994	1	.000	1.143	1.075	1.216
Uses borrowing for innovation	0.057	0.008	49.041	1	.000	1.059	1.042	1.076
Constant	−2.811	0.078	1308.2	1	.000	.060		

Source: Author's computations using SPSS on unit record data from ABS, 2003, where B is the regression coefficient for the variable, S.E. is the standard error of the regression coefficient, Wald χ^2 is the χ^2 value for the regression coefficient, d.f. is the number of degrees of freedom for the χ^2 value, Sig. is the significance of the χ^2 value, Exp(B) is the odds ratio corresponding to the regression coefficient (B), and 95.0% C.I. for EXP(B) is the 95 % confidence interval for EXP(B). The odds ratio EXP(B) should exceed 1.0 if the impact of the variable on whether a firm is innovative or not is to be greater than 50/50, i.e., pure chance.

Model tests:
- All variables are significant @ 5% level of significance.
- Hosmer and Lemeshow test: $\chi^2 = 11.670$ with 4 d.f., significance = 0.020
- Nagelkerke $R^2 = 0.746$
- 76% of innovators and 99% of non-innovators are correctly forecast by the model.

The model tests indicate that this model does not fit the data as well as the model fits the South Australian data, but fits the data moderately well, nevertheless. All variables are significant, but the (alternative) hypothesis that the model explains the values of the dependent variable can be rejected at the 2 per cent level of significance, the value for Nagelkerke's pseudo-R^2 is moderately high, and a moderately high proportion of innovator firms and a high proportion of non-innovator firms are correctly identified by the model.

Putting the figures in Table 3 into words yields the following conclusions about what distinguishes an innovative firm from a non-innovative one. An innovative firm

- uses the research facilities of Australian (non higher education) research institutes to acquire knowledge (very important),
- has developed new corporate strategies (important),
- is classed as collaborative (important),
- acquires new equipment and technology, from any source, including overseas (important),
- seeks skilled people of all kinds (important),
- is driven by a desire to be more responsive to customer needs (important),
- spends on innovative activities using its own funds,
- spends on innovative activities using borrowed funds.

Innovative firms in Australia, generally, are more likely to make use of *Australian* non-higher education research institutes to acquire knowledge. It is curious and disturbing that they are not more likely to make use of Australian higher education research institutes. As in South Australia, it also seems unlikely that a firm will be innovative unless it has developed some new strategies as a business. As found earlier, innovative firms are more likely to be collaborative than non innovative firms. As seems intuitively obvious, innovative firms are more likely to acquire new equipment and technology than non innovative firms are. Innovative firms are more likely to seek skilled people of all kinds than non innovative firms are. Innovative firms are more likely to be driven by a desire to be more responsive to customer needs. Innovative firms are more likely to need either their own or borrowed funds to finance their innovative activities than non innovative firms are.

Conclusions for Innovation Policy for the South Australian Government

The results of this analysis of the Australian Bureau of Statistics' 2003 Business Innovation Survey can be presented as things that the South Australian government might do to increase the rate of business innovation in the State, that is, to enhance South Australia's Regional Innovation System.

The policy would read something like this:

1. Target well-established firms with messages about
   - the need to respond to a rapidly changing, and highly competitive, world
   - by being responsive to customer needs, particularly through
   - process innovation and product differentiation,
   - using new equipment and technology and
   - a highly skilled work force.
2. Encourage research institutes to meet the needs of innovating firms.
3. Facilitate the protection of intellectual property.
4. Ensure an adequate supply of IT skills for the support of new production processes.
5. Encourage local spending by firms on their innovative activities.
6. Support collaboration between firms.
7. Create a financial climate where innovative firms have access to more funds (both loans and equity).

References

ABS (2003), *Innovation in Australian Business*, Cat. No. 8158.0, ABS, Canberra.

Carnegie, R., M. Butlin, P. Barratt, A. Turnbull and I. Webber (1993), *Managing the Innovating Enterprise: Australian companies competing with the world's best*, The Business Library in association with Business Council of Australia, Melbourne.

Cooke, P. (1992), "Regional innovation systems: competitive regulation in the new Europe", *Geoforum*, 23, pp. 365–382.

Cooke, P. (2001), "Regional innovation systems, clusters and the knowledge economy", *Industrial and Corporate Change*, 10, pp. 945–974.

Cooke, P. and L. Leydesdorff (2005), "Regional development in the knowledge-based economy: the construction of advantage", http://users.fmg.uva.nl/lledesdorff/constructed_advantage.

Etzkowitz, H. and L. Leydesdorff (1997), *Universities and the Global Knowledge Economy: A Triple Helix of University-Industry-Government Relations*, Pinter, London.

Landabaso, M., Oughton, C. and K. Morgan (1999), "Learning regions in Europe: theory, policy and practice through the RIS experience", 3rd International Conference on Technology and Innovation Policy, Austin, USA, September.

Marshall, A. (1890), *Principles of Political Economy*, Macmillan, London.

OECD and Eurostat (2005), *Oslo Manual: Guidelines for Collecting and Interpreting Innovation Data*, 3rd ed., OECD Publishing, Paris.

Porter, M. (1990), *The Competitive Advantage of Nations*, The Free Press, New York.

Smith, A. (1776), *The Wealth of Nations*, Edinburgh.

3

Employees as Creditors: Protecting their Claims

Kevin Davis

Melbourne Centre for Financial Studies

Introduction

The failure of a firm has significant implications for its employees, most obvious of which is loss of employment and the economic and social consequences thereof. An additional cost is the financial loss arising from claims of the employee on an insolvent employer, which are unable to be met due to insufficient assets of the failed firm. These claims arise from accrued entitlements to (annual or long service) leave, redundancy payments triggered by insolvency which result from legislative provisions, or pension fund claims where, for example, contributions have been reinvested in the employing firm.

Losses to employees arising from employer insolvency have led to public policy intervention designed to protect employees against such loss. Underlying such intervention is recognition that some form of failure exists in the "market" for employee entitlements. While that can provide the rationale for intervention, it does not identify which (if any) of several potential policy remedies is appropriate.

Unfortunately, policy interventions sometimes occur as an initial response to urgent social and economic problems and become entrenched, even though they have not been subjected to a rigorous cost-benefit assessment against alternatives. It is argued here, that the current Australian approach to protecting employee entitlements falls into this category.

That current approach involves, primarily, an *ex post*, taxpayer funded, compensation scheme (GEERS) for lost entitlements of employees of failed firms. It was introduced in 2001 (amending a similar scheme introduced the previous year). *Ex ante*, it is an explicit government guarantee to a specific group of creditors (employees) to businesses, provided free of charge.

Such a policy approach has not generally found favor in other credit markets where market failure is perceived to exist. It has, for example, been used in crisis situations in banking markets to protect depositors, but few would argue that it is preferable to available alternatives as a permanent approach.

In banking, those alternatives include such things as explicit, industry funded, deposit insurance schemes, minimum capital requirements, depositor priority/preference (over other claimants), and asset portfolio restrictions. Employee entitlements are quite different to bank deposits, and the debtors (businesses and banks respectively) operate quite differently, but there is merit in considering whether similar alternatives are preferable to, or could complement, the GEERS compensation scheme.[1]

In this paper, some alternative mechanisms for protecting employee entitlements are analyzed and compared. It is argued that the costs of the approach adopted in Australia, involving a tax-payer government guarantee scheme, could be considerably reduced by simultaneous implementation of several alternative mechanisms. It is argued that the costs of these alternatives are much less than commonly perceived, and less than the benefits which would arise from their introduction.

Underpinning the argument is recognition that employees are, to some degree, involuntary creditors of their employers and unable to assess or easily manage the credit risk associated with this status. The policy options examined in this paper can be seen as alternative (although not mutually exclusive) methods for reducing the credit risk faced by employees.

In Section 1 of this paper, some background to the nature of employee entitlements and problems arising from company failures is given. Section 2 elaborates on the notion of employees as creditors to their employer and the sources of market failure. Section 3 suggests a number of alternative (or complementary) policy approaches which might be adopted. Section 4 provides information on the cost of alternatives (or complements) to the GEERS scheme, and Section 5 concludes.

1. Employee Entitlements and Company Failures

Employee entitlements consist of claims on the employer for amounts such as unpaid wages, unused annual or long service leave entitlements, as well as contingent claims such as redundancy payments which do not accrue until the workers' employment contracts are terminated at the point of insolvency.[2] These amounts and the risk involved can be substantial from the perspective of the employee, particularly since any loss occurring through employer insolvency occurs simultaneously with loss of employment.

Several large company failures at the start of the millennium made unpaid employee entitlements a political issue of importance. The collapse of Ansett Airlines left some 16,000 employees with an estimated $670 m worth of employee entitlements unpaid (DPL, 2002). Other notable failures at around the same time included OneTel (with 1,400 employees owed a total of $19 m in accrued entitlements), Australian mining giant Pasminco, insurance company HIH and retailer Harris Scarfe[3].

But the problem is not confined solely to large corporate collapses. It has been estimated that up to 20,000 workers lose their jobs every year because of failed businesses and that, in total, employees would face about $140 m a year in unpaid entitlements (DPL, 2004).

Through employee entitlements, employees provide (perhaps unwillingly) credit to their employer as a form of working capital at an implicit interest rate unrelated to the credit risk involved (Davis and Burrows, 2003).

For most employers, the amount of funding derived from this source is a relatively small proportion of the total funding of the company, although in aggregate the amount involved exceeds $50 billion (Davis and Burrows, 2003). Table 1 illustrates for an illustrative sample (and gives average figures for a large sample) of Australian listed companies using 2003 annual report data. For some labor intensive companies, employees are very significant creditors while, on average, employee entitlements are around 5 per cent of total debt claims.

2. Employee Entitlements as a Form of Credit

The finance provided to companies by employees by way of entitlements involves risk, return and governance considerations. Consider the case of a firm which at some date has accrued obligations to employees of, for example, long

Table 1. Employee Entitlements and Company Financial Structure
Selected Australian Companies: 2003.

ASX Code	Company Name	Employee Entitlements as % of			Secured Debt/ Market Value
		Secured Debt	Total Debt	Market Value (Debt + Equity)	
Selected companies					
CML	Coles Myer	51%	12%	4%	8%
TLS	Telstra	23%	4%	1%	5%
RIO	Rio Tinto	49%	7%	2%	4%
BHP	BHP Billiton	21%	6%	2%	8%
FOA	Foodland	5%	3%	1%	28%
AMC	Amcor	14%	5%	2%	13%
TEM	Tempo	87%	26%	12%	14%
TOL	Toll	26%	11%	3%	11%
CCL	Coca Cola Amatil	10%	5%	2%	19%
WHS	Warehouse Group	152%	7%	2%	1%
RIN	Rinker	6%	3%	1%	13%
BLD	Boral	323%	7%	3%	1%
SKE	Skilled Group	169%	26%	7%	4%
Sample of 244 listed companies					
Mean		19.7%	6.5%	2.1%	10.6%
Median		11.0%	3.3%	1.1%	9.6%

Source: Davis and Lee (2005)

service leave. Because that leave will not be taken until some future date, employees are providing credit to the company. The implicit, promised, rate of return on the credit provided is the rate of wages growth (since the dollar value of entitlements when paid is calculated by multiplying days accrued by the current salary level). This is unlikely to appropriately reflect the credit risk faced by the creditor employee.

There are several reasons to believe that there is "market failure" in this credit market. First, employees are to some degree "involuntary creditors", and do not have complete flexibility in adjusting the amount of credit provided, to the employer by way of accrued entitlements. Second, employees have limited ability to assess the credit risk of their employer. Third, optimal wealth allocation would be unlikely to lead to employees voluntarily holding significant financial wealth in the form of loans to their employer because default on those loans will occur simultaneously with loss of wage-income following company failure.[4] Fourth, corporate financing of this form does not involve capital market discipline or monitoring.

3. Alternative Policy Responses

Faced with market failure in a credit market, there are a number of alternative policy responses which warrant comparison using (at least an implicit) cost-benefit analysis.

The current policy approach is primarily an *ex post* one of dealing with the symptoms of the market failure. Employee-creditors are eligible for compensation from a taxpayer funded scheme (GEERS) if their employer becomes insolvent and unable to meet its obligations. (Upper limits are placed on the amount of compensation which can be claimed.) GEERS becomes a claimant on the assets of the insolvent company, in place of the employee creditors to whom compensation has been paid.

Two other planks of policy are, however, also relevant, and aim to reduce the ultimate cost of claims made on the scheme. The first is the *Corporations Law* prohibitions on companies trading while insolvent (and thus running down assets available to meet creditor claims), together with the *Corporations Law Amendment (Employee Entitlements) Act 2000* which makes it an offence to take actions (such as transferring assets between related companies) designed to avoid payment of employee entitlements. The second is the granting of *preferential unsecured creditor* status to (and ranking of priority between different types of) employee entitlements.

Despite such measures, the cost of GEERS to the taxpayer is substantial. Recoveries by GEERS from the assets of failed businesses appear to be less than 10 per cent of the amount of compensation paid to claimants, which exceeded $60 million in 2002–3. (DPL, 2004). Moreover, legal complexities abound through financial engineering by creditors which may have the effect of thwarting the objectives behind granting of preferential unsecured creditor status. Floating charges over company assets which crystallize into a fixed (secured) charge upon insolvency are a case in point.[5]

One possible modification to the GEERS approach, consistent with what is commonly advocated for bank depositor protection schemes, would be to implement a user pays charge for the insurance protection provided by the scheme. In practice, administrative costs and difficulties in estimating fair insurance premiums appear to make such an approach infeasible. Taxpayer funding is then required, but at the cost of eschewing the opportunity to provide appropriate incentives to, and discipline of, employers through price signals (insurance premiums) based on estimates of credit risk. Similarly, inappropriate distributional consequences result with employers which are high credit risks not facing appropriately higher funding costs for employee provided credit.

Alternative *ex ante* approaches are possible, which tackle the problem prior to the event of failure and reduce or eliminate the "loss given default" faced by employees when an employer fails. One such possibility is to require that claims of employees are secured against risk free assets held by the employer. Another is to elevate the priority status of claims of employees above that of other creditors of the employer (the maximum priority proposal).

These alternative approaches have been implicitly or explicitly rejected by government on the apparent grounds that they impose excessive costs on companies through increases in the cost of debt finance. In the subsequent section it is argued that the costs of such approaches are much less than commonly argued and that they warrant consideration as a complement to a compensation scheme.

4. Assessing the Cost of Some Alternatives

In this section, an assessment of the cost of two alternative approaches to protecting employee entitlements will be made. The *Deferred Benefit (DB) Account* and the *Maximum Priority Proposal (MPP)* can both be seen as mechanisms for reducing the *Loss Given Default (LGD)* faced by employee creditors in the event of company failure. Because each reduces, but does not completely eliminate, credit risk, they are better seen as complements rather than alternatives to a GEERS style scheme. Their merit is that the cost to taxpayers of GEERS would be reduced, and that they would also improve credit market discipline over employers.

The DB Account

The *DB Account* (Davis and Burrows, 2003) envisages employers maintaining balances at least equal to reasonable aggregate provisions for entitlements in designated DB accounts at financial institutions. In the event of insolvency, employee entitlement claims would be paid from that account.

Administrative costs of such a scheme would be very small. The apparent drawback of such a scheme is that it appears to involve an increase in funding costs to employers, since the "free" working capital provided by employee entitlements must be replaced by other sources. In some cases that may be the case, but (as will be argued below) that is where employees are currently subsidizing high risk employers by involuntary provision of credit at a rate of return which does not reflect the credit risk involved.

Table 2 provides a highly simplified balance sheet for an employer. Panel A depicts the situation in the absence of the *DB Scheme*, while Panel B assumes that such a scheme has been implemented. The difference arising from the introduction of such a scheme is the addition of an equal value of assets and liabilities (corresponding to the size of employee entitlements) to both sides of the balance sheet. (For simplicity, it is assumed that no changes in working capital requirements occur). The liability of employee entitlements (of amount X) is secured against the asset of the *DB Account* (of amount X). Additional debt funds (of amount X) must be raised from the capital markets to replace the funds now tied up in the *DB Account*.

Table 2. Balance Sheet Effect of the Deferred Benefit Scheme.

Panel A				**Panel B**			
Before				After			
Assets		**Liabilities**		**Assets**		**Liabilities**	
Physical	K	Debt	D	Physical	K	Debt	D + X
Financial	F			Financial	F		
		Provisions for Employee Entitlements	X	DB Account	X	Provisions for Employee Entitlements	X
		Equity	S			Equity	S

In a perfect capital market, where employees were receiving an appropriate, credit risk related return on funds provided by way of employee entitlements, this would have no effect on company value. Employee entitlements, now being free of credit risk, would receive a rate of return equal to that paid on the *DB Account*, against which they are secured. The additional debt funds raised would have the same cost as the employee entitlement credit being replaced.

In practice new debt finance raised may cost significantly more than the funds being replaced. However, where that reflects capital market based assessment of the borrower's credit risk, the implication is that the employer was previously being subsidized by the employee-creditor who was not receiving an appropriate risk related return on funds provided. The employer now faces a cost of funds appropriately related to the credit risk involved and is exposed to capital market monitoring and discipline.

Ultimately, the economic case against adopting such an approach appears to rely on administrative costs, problems associated with compliance, and capital market imperfections which create additional (non-risk related) costs for companies forced to raise additional funds to replace those currently received from employee-creditors. While such costs and problems do exist, it is not apparent that they are of sufficient size to prevent consideration of such a scheme, at least as a complement to a GEERS style compensation fund.

The Maximum Priority Proposal (MPP)

The MPP was announced by the Prime Minister on 14 September 2001. It envisaged employee entitlements being elevated in priority above secured creditors. However, as part of its stock-take of Corporate Insolvency Laws, the Parliamentary Joint Committee on Corporations and Financial Services recommended: "that the maximum priority proposal not be adopted." (PJCCFS), 2004). Acceptance of finance industry assertions about the adverse effects of the MPP on the corporate credit market appeared to be significant in reaching this conclusion. Unfortunately, little (if any) empirical evidence has been provided to support such assertions.

Davis and Lee (2005) provide some such empirical evidence, drawing on credit risk modeling techniques commonly used in financial markets. Those techniques utilize option pricing theory, and were initially popularized as a method of assessing credit risk by the work of Merton (1974). Credit spreads (the margin paid by the borrower over the risk free rate) are estimated by noting that a holding a risky debt security issued by a company can be modeled as equivalent to holding a risk free debt plus writing a put option over the assets of the debt issuer (with the strike price of the option equal to the promised debt payment). Consequently, credit spreads can be estimated once the leverage of the company and volatility of its asset value are known.

The option pricing approach can be applied to estimate credit spreads for both first ranking debt and for more junior debt. The effect of the *MPP* can thus be assessed by calculating the change in credit spread required by secured lenders if their first ranking status is downgraded to second ranking behind employee entitlements.

Some intuition behind the results derived from such an approach can be gained by noting that the credit spread on a debt security will be driven by the two key parameters of expected *Loss Given Default (LGD)* and *Probability of Default (PD)*. The expected return on a debt security (r^e) which has a contractual rate of r_q can be written as:

$$1 + r^e = (1 - PD)(1 + r_q) + PD(1 + r_q)(1 - LGD) = (1 + r_q)(1 - PDxLGD) \quad (1)$$

Consequently, to maintain a given expected return, increases in the probability of default and in the loss given default must be accompanied by increases in the quoted interest rate (and thus the credit spread over the risk free rate).

Consider a company which has secured debt obligations of D and employee entitlements of X (and no other liabilities) outstanding. It will become insolvent if assets fall below $(D + X)$, and PD is the probability of this event occurring. Suppose that A is the expected value of assets available to meet creditor claims if the company becomes insolvent, and that $A < D$. For secured creditors, the loss given default is then $(D - A)$, and employees would receive nothing. If employee entitlements are placed ahead of secured creditors under the *MPP*, secured creditors now have a higher loss given default of $(D - (A - X))$.[6] Because of the increase in *LGD*, the credit spread on secured debt will increase, but the extent of the increase will depend upon the size of X relative to D. If employee entitlements (X) are small compared to secured debt (D), the increase in *LGD* for secured debt will be small. If the probability of default (PD) is also small then, from equation (1) the increase in credit spread will be small.

The option pricing approach enables estimates of the increase in credit

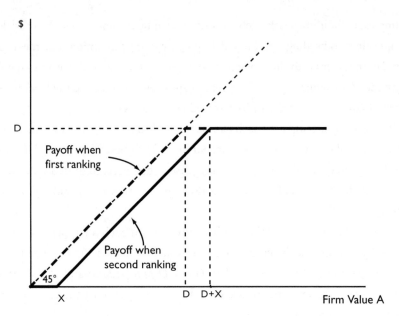

Figure 1. *Change in Secured Debt Payoff under the MPP.*
The solid line shows the payoff to secured creditors who are owed D when they rank ahead of other claimants (employee entitlements) who are owed X. The dashed line shows the secured creditor payoff when ranked behind the other claimants under the MPP. (For firm asset values A > D + X, the firm is not insolvent and secured creditors receive D in both cases).

spread from the *MPP* to be estimated for companies with differences in overall leverage, relative importance of employee entitlements, and underlying business risk (as measured by asset volatility). Figure 1 provides a depiction of the payoffs for secured creditors (owed *D*) both before and after the introduction of the *MPP*. Before the *MPP*, the payoff as depicted is equivalent to that from holding a risk free debt, promising *D*, and writing a put option over the assets of the firm with a strike price of D. The Merton model for estimating the credit spread uses this equivalence, since to prevent arbitrage profits, the current market value of the risky claim of *D* due at time T (at the risky interest rate r_q per cent) must equal that of the risk free claim of *D* (at the risk free rate of *r* per cent) less the market value of the put option *P*, which is calculated using the Black-Scholes option pricing equation. Thus, using the arbitrage relationship:

$$De^{-rT} - P = De^{-r_qT} \tag{2}$$

the credit spread ($r_q - r_f$) can be derived as:

$$r_q - r = -\ln[N(d_2) + N(-d_1)/L]/T \tag{3}$$

where $N(.)$ is the cumulative normal distribution function, $L = De^{-rT}/V$ is a "quasi-leverage" ratio (where V is the firm's current value), σ is the volatility of firm value, and

$$d_1 = [\ln\left(\frac{V}{D}\right) + \left(r + \frac{1}{2}\sigma^2\right)T]/\sigma\sqrt{T} \tag{4}$$

and

$$d_2 = d_1 - \sigma\sqrt{T} \tag{5}$$

Under the *MPP*, the payoff to secured creditors (who rank behind employee entitlements promising X) is now equivalent to that from: (a) holding a risk free debt, promising D, (b) writing a put option over the assets of the firm with a strike price of $D + X$, and (c) buying a put option over the assets of the firm with a strike price of X. (This is also equivalent to buying a call option with a strike price of X and selling a call option with a strike price of $D + X$). Using this equivalence, the credit spread for secured creditors under the *MPP* is now

$$r_q^{\#} - r = -\ln\{m[N(d_2^*) - N(d_2^{\#})]/L + N(d_2^*) + [N(d_1^{\#}) - N(d_1^*)]/L\}/T \tag{6}$$

where the ratio of employee entitlements to firm value is given by $m = Xe^{-rT}/V$, and

$$d^{\#}_1 = [\ln\left(\frac{V}{X}\right) + \left(r + \frac{1}{2}\sigma^2\right)T]/\sigma\sqrt{T} \tag{7}$$

$$d^{\#}_2 = d^{\#}_1 - \sigma\sqrt{T} \tag{8}$$

$$d^*_1 = [\ln\left(\frac{V}{D+X}\right) + \left(r + \frac{1}{2}\sigma^2\right)T]/\sigma\sqrt{T} \tag{9}$$

and

$$d^*_2 = d^*_1 - \sigma\sqrt{T} \tag{10}$$

Davis and Lee (2005) provide estimates of the change in credit spread $(r_q^{\#} - r_q)$ for a range of realistic parameter values of volatility and leverage ratios for Australian companies. Note that (in addition to asset volatility) the key parameters are the ratios of secured debt to assets and of employee entitlements to assets. (Unsecured debt, and thus the more traditional leverage ratio of total debt/assets is not directly relevant, since unsecured debt ranks behind both secured debt and employee entitlements. Insolvency may occur if total assets fall below total debt but, if there is significant unsecured debt, not involve any shortfall for secured creditors and employees).

Based on a sample of 244 listed companies, almost 50 per cent of companies have secured debt/assets of less than 20 per cent and employee entitlements/assets of less than 1.5 per cent. For realistic assumptions about asset volatility, the probability of default (PD) of such companies is quite small, and the change in the expected loss given default for secured creditors arising from the *MPP* is also relatively small. Consequently, the estimated change in credit spreads is extremely small, in the order of 2 basis points p.a. for five year debt (when asset volatility of 30 per cent p.a. and a risk free interest rate of 5 per cent p.a. is assumed).

For a group of more highly levered companies (secured debt/assets >40%, employee entitlements/assets > 2.5%), the estimated increases in credit spreads are as high as 50 basis points, although only around 2 per cent of companies in the sample used fall into this category. While high, significant changes such as this indicate that employees (or, through GEERS, taxpayers) are currently bearing credit risk of those firms for which they are not compensated.

Based on these results, it appears premature to conclude that the maximum priority proposal would involve significant disruption to credit markets. For most companies the effect on credit spreads would appear to be negligible. For a small group of companies, there may be significant increases in the cost of secured debt, but those are the ones benefiting from a subsidized cost of debt at the expense of employees and/or taxpayers.

5. Conclusion

This paper provides some initial steps towards an informal cost-benefit comparison of various policy approaches to dealing with the problem of default on employee entitlements in the event of employer insolvency. It has been argued that the approach currently adopted, of a taxpayer funded, ex post, compensation scheme, is at variance with policy approaches favored in other credit markets where investor protection is deemed to be an important issue. Given the specific nature of the credit market for employee entitlements, the political pressures arising when newly unemployed workers face additional financial hardship through employer insolvency, and the fact that other policy approaches do not provide 100 per cent protection, there is a case for continuation of such a compensation scheme. (The desirability of rapid and cost effective payment of entitlements in such situations also prompts a role for a compensation scheme as a component of the insolvency process).

There are strong grounds for complementing the GEERS scheme with other policy measures, such as those outlined here. Both the *Deferred Benefits Scheme* and the *Maximum Priority Proposal* would reduce the cost of GEERS to the taxpayer by reducing the credit risk of employee entitlements. In addition, higher credit risk companies would no longer receive implicit subsidies from employee-creditors and would face enhanced credit market discipline.

References

Davis K and G Burrows, (2003) "Protecting Employee Entitlements" *The Australian Economic Review*, June, Vol. 36 No. 2, pp. 173–80.

Davis K and J Lee (2005) "Employee Entitlements and Secured Creditors: Assessing the Effects of the Maximum Priority Proposal", *mimeo*, Department of Finance, The University of Melbourne,

DPL (2004) "Corporate Insolvencies and Workers' Entitlements" Department of the Parliamentary Library, E-Brief: Online Only, issued Date August 2001; Updated 15 September 2004
http://www.aph.gov.au/library/intguide/econ/insolvencies.htm

Merton R, (1974) "On the Pricing of Corporate Debt: The Risk Structure of Interest Rates" *Journal of Finance* pp. 449–470

PJCCFS (2004) *Corporate Insolvency Laws: a Stocktake*, Parliamentary Joint Committee on Corporations and Financial Services June 2004, Commonwealth of Australia 2004, ISBN 0 642 71400 2, Senate Printing Unit, Parliament House, Canberra.
http://www.aph.gov.au/Senate/committee/corporations_ctte/completed_inquiries /2002-04/ail/report/ail.pdf

Tyndall F, (2005) "UK ruling could help Walter's workers" *Australian Financial Review*, 27 July, p. 9.

Notes

This paper draws on material in Davis and Burrows (2003) and Davis and Lee (2005).

1 One additional policy measure has been to accord employee entitlements priority status over other unsecured creditors in the event of insolvency, but behind secured creditors.
2 In Australia, superannuation entitlements of employees participating in a company scheme are protected separately.
3 Other notable insolvencies include Patrick Stevedores, Exicom, the Sizzler Chain, Braybrook Manufacturing, Coogi and Cobar Mines.
4 In theory, if not in practice, employees could seek implicit compensation for the risk borne on finance provided via deferred benefits through higher wage rates.
5 The priority of such floating charges over employee entitlements was the subject of a recent U.K. court case (Tyndall, 2005) which determined that priority lay with employee entitlements.
6 This assumes A > X. If available assets (A) are less than employee entitlements (X), the LGD for the secured creditors under the MPP would be D.

4

Oligopsony, Monopsony and Collective Bargaining in the Victorian Broiler Chicken Industry: The Dominance of Doctrine over Performance?

Joe Isaac

University of Melbourne

Abstract

While collective bargaining has been a longstanding feature of the Australian labour market, in recent years a new area of collective bargaining has developed between entities commonly referred to as "small businesses" and firms which buy their goods and services. A significant feature of these areas of collective bargaining is that the buyers are big and few in number and are able to exercise market power. To enable such collective bargaining to take place without offending the Trade Practices Act on grounds of collusive behaviour requires authorisation from the ACCC, which lays down certain requirements to ensure that the public benefit from collective bargaining would outweigh any public detriment from the anti-competitive element of the arrangement. One such area in which authorisation has been the Victorian broiler chicken industry. Following a review under the National Competition Policy commissioned by the Victorian Government, the Victorian broiler chicken growing industry was deregulated and subject to a determination by the Australian Competition and Consumer Commission authorising a form of collective bargaining. This paper analyses the Review and the Authorisation related to this industry in some detail to show their questionable analyses and conclusions, and argues that doctrine rather than evidence of economic performance appears to have dominated their determination of "public benefit". It concludes that if a return to the regulated system is not possible, there is strong case for the collective bargaining process of the broiler chicken growing industry (and similarly placed industries) to be processed under state industrial relations laws with appropriate immunity from the Trade Practices Act.

It is generally accepted that if an industry in an unregulated market is subject to forces that prevent it from achieving optimal public benefit in terms of economic efficiency and/or certain social objectives, such "market failure" justifies government intervention in order to advance the "public benefit".[1] The sources for such failure are well known. They include chiefly pockets of market power on the part of sellers and/or buyers arising from lack of competition (monopoly/monopsony/oligopoly/oligopsony), public goods, transaction costs, externalities, and incomplete information.[2]

The Victorian broiler chicken industry provides an interesting case study[3] of the rejection of a regulated system following a review ordered by the State government under the National Competition Policy and the determination of the Australian Competition and Consumer Commission (ACCC, the Commission). The rejection was based less on evidence of economic performance and more on a narrow view of "competition" and the "market" in which it operates. The logic behind the finding of the Review and the determination of the Commission are worthy of note. This issue is of importance to several other industries[4]—including lorry drivers, TAB agents, newsagents, dairy farmers, and sugar cane growers—in which lopsided bargaining power prevails. Although policy in this area of activity is generally determined on the basis of competition, restrictive trade practices, microeconomics and law, this paper argues for a labour market/collective bargaining approach to the issues involved.

The background

Broiler chickens[5] are grown by farmers ("growers") under special contracts with firms ("processors") that, among other things, dress, package and whole-sell broilers in Australia. It is a comparatively new industry in its present form, its main development dating back to the 1960s. The unbalanced market power between the growers and processors has been a source of conflict between them on the appropriate fee for growing chickens. In Victoria, a breakdown in negotiations in 1968 led to an interruption in supplies for over four months, causing the State government to intervene and enact the Uniform Broiler Contract Act 1968. This turned out to be ineffective when another breakdown occurred in 1974. On this occasion, the government appointed an independent arbitrator who determined the growing fee based on certain principles on which modifications have been built over the years to encourage dynamic productivity. The likelihood of a further breakdown in negotiations following the end of the 1974 contract period, led the government to bring down successive legislation to regulate the industry. It established a tripartite body, the Victorian Broiler Industry Negotiating Committee (VBINC), to provide the basis of negotiation on the determination of growing fee and various operational requirements for the industry. A series of amendments to the Act relating to the structure and procedure of the VBINC followed, culminating in the Victorian Broiler Chicken Industry Act 1991 and the Broiler Chicken Industry Regulations 1992.

The enactment of the Competition Policy Reform Act 1995 and the associated Competition Principles Agreement emanating from the recommendations of the Hilmer Report in 1993, obliged governments to review arrangements that restricted competition. In the circumstances, the Victorian (Kennett) Government responded to its obligations under the Competition Principles Agreement to review the Broiler Chicken Industry Act and the Regulations relating to it. Under the Agreement, legislation restricting competition should not be undertaken unless it can be established that:

> the benefits of the restriction to the community as a whole outweigh the costs; and
> the objectives of the legislation can only be achieved by restricting competition.[6]

KPMG was commissioned by the Victorian Government to undertake the Review. An important principle of this Review was "that there must be a presumption against statutory intervention and the onus should be on the proponent of intervention to establish the case."[7] The Review found that the existing arrangements could be in breach of the Trade Practices Act (TPA) and concluded that "The Act and Regulations should be repealed because the case for the retention of the broiler chicken legislation is not established by its proponents."

Following the Review, Marven Poultry Pty Ltd for itself and on behalf of Victorian Chicken Meat Processors and Chicken Growers, duly sought the necessary authorisation (A90750) from the ACCC to engage in processor-based collective bargaining for the purpose of fixing the growing fee and other terms of growing chickens. Authorisation was also sought for an elaborate Code of Conduct dealing with the procedural aspects of negotiations. Such authorisation is necessary to protect the parties from any risk of prosecution under the TPA. Based on submissions from the processors and growers, the ACCC responded on 28 June 2001 with the *Marven Poultry* Determination authorising collective negotiations on certain conditions backed substantially by a Code of Conduct submitted by the processors.[8]

The Victorian Farmers Federation (VFF), on behalf of the growers, challenged the validity of the authorisation. The challenge succeeded on technical grounds,[9] after an appeal to a Full Court of the Federal Court.[10] Following the Review, although the 1991 Act, was not repealed, the VBINC ceased to operate because the appointment of its membership had lapsed. This left the industry in a state of uncertainty with fees being fixed in an ad hoc fashion by groups of growers. When the growers failed in their attempts to persuade the (Bracks) Government to restore VBINC, they proceeded in May 2004, through the VFF, with their second best option of applying to the ACCC for authorisation to conduct processor-based collective negotiations[11] on certain conditions, including the right to "collectively boycott processors", that is, refuse to take delivery of day-old chickens.[12] The Commission granted its authorisation on 2 March 2005.

This paper will examine successively the following—the structural characteristics of the Victorian broiler chicken growing industry; the nature and history of the regulated industry; an assessment of the KPMG Review and the basis of two ACCC's Determinations in the industry. It goes into some detail on the Review and the Determinations in order to expose their line of reasoning on an activity that fits uncomfortably in the restrictive trade practices jurisdiction.

Basic features of the industry[13]

The nature of competition in the chicken broiler industry is determined by the industry's structural, technical and economic features. Although there is, in general, common ground between the parties on the basic features of the

56

industry, different inferences have been drawn from them in support of one or other arrangement for determining the terms on which growers' services should be compensated. The following features are central to the issues which follow:

- The supply of growing services is drawn from some 210 growers (nearly 90% are members of the VFF) who supply labour, management and capital in the form of land, sheds, power and equipment connected with the growing of chickens. It is estimated that the financial capital outlay for the farms range between $0.5m and $5m depending on location and size and number of sheds. The physical capital is specific to the chicken growing operation and cannot be turned to other economic activities. Much the same can be said of the processors' plant and equipment.

- There are five processors[14] based in Victoria, three of which conduct fully vertically integrated production operations, with chick breeding farms, hatcheries, feed mills, growing farms and finally, processing operation to supply the wholesale consumer market with chicken meat. However, only 10% of the chicken supply in Victoria is grown in the processors' own farms; the rest is outsourced by the processors to private growers. The trend has been for processors to sell off their farms. One of the processors also operates in Griffith (New South Wales) and supplies chicken meat to Victoria, New South Wales and South Australia. At this location, the growing process is undertaken in the processor's own farms. Less than 10% of chickens are imported from other States while overseas imports are negligible.

- It is important to note that the number of processors has fallen despite the substantial growth in output.

- The growing cycle of a batch is between seven and eight weeks. The processors have substantial control of the growing process—they supply the day-old chicks of a particular genetic stock, feed and medication, and impose detailed technical requirements on their particular group of growers on how the chickens should be raised to maturity. They also provide transportation of chicks, materials and the grown chickens.

- The practice has been for groups of growers to be tied to particular processors for a 3-year contract period with the likelihood of an indefinite rollover arrangement, subject to a 6-month termination notice. This arrangement provides substantial continuity and stability favoured by both parties.

- Grower entry into the industry is limited. It depends on securing a contract with a processor in advance of establishing the required infrastructure of a farm. In their recent application to the ACCC, the growers have sought a 5-year contract because it would provide them with greater security and encourage expansion to a more optimal farm size. Most of the invested capital is specific to the industry[15] and needs to meet the start-up requirements of the processors before entering into a growing agreement. There is little mobility of growers between processors, growers being liable to incur costs in adapting sheds to the particular requirements of another processor. The evidence suggests that processors do not poach on each other's growers but there are occasions when a processor would "borrow" growers tied to other processors to supplement their stock of broilers, sometimes without notifying the growers concerned. A further point to note is limit on grower entry resulting from strict regulations imposed by local authorities on the setting up of farms.

- Processor entry into the industry is also limited by the barrier of relatively high start-up costs (approximately $5–6 million) and the uncertainty of gaining either new growers and/or growers from other processors. Further, the supply of chicks is limited by licensing requirements of the two genetic types used, these licenses currently being held by only three processors.

- Although the "market" for growing services under consideration is within Victoria, for purposes of understanding the issues in contention, that, for technical and economic reasons[16], the growers are clustered within about 80 km of the processors. As a result, there are effectively three relevant regional markets, reflecting a greater concentration of demand that might be evident by considering Victoria as a whole. Thus:

- the Bendigo market has a single processor, a monopsonist.
- the Geelong market has a single processor, a monopsonist.
- the Melbourne market is spread out although mostly in the Mornington Peninsula east of Melbourne in close proximity to each other, with three processors, one of whom takes up about half the output. Although this market may be characterised as oligopsonistic, it is arguable that it is close to monopsonistic insofar as each group of growers is effectively tied to a particular processor.
- Market concentration on the demand side is also reflected in the fact that the two largest processors take up about half the market share of the Victorian chicken output[17] and use the services of more than 70% of growers; while the corresponding figures for the three largest processors are about three-quarters and 80%. The three largest processors have access to supply from other States, thus increasing their bargaining power in relation to their Victorian growers. Further, two processors supply chicks of the required genetic stock to the other processors. As noted earlier, the supply of chicks is limited by licence of two genetic stocks Thus, processors are interlinked by the supply of chicks and, in some cases, also by the supply of feed.
- The growing fee represents 15% of the cost of live birds, 8% of the wholesale cost of birds, and 6–8 % of the retail price of chicken meat. The effect of changes in the growing fee on the retail price of chicken meat is therefore likely to be relatively small.
- The retail market for chicken meat is highly concentrated. Nearly 70% of the Victorian retail market is taken up by two retailers.

These basic features of the chicken growing industry in Victoria raise the question of the nature of competition in this industry. It is now well established that in determining whether or not competition exists, the first task is to identify the "relevant market".[18] This involves identifying the nature of the relevant *service* market and the *geographical* extent of that market have to be identified.[19] In this case, the relevant service market is the growing of chickens; while three of the relevant geographical markets are the specific locations in Bendigo, Geelong and a particular area of Melbourne.

In each of the first two markets, the growers face a single buyer (processor) for their services, and both groups of growers are locked into dealing only with their respective single buyers by virtue of the location of the buyers' plant, the growers' location, and the specificity of the growers' plant and equipment. Entry is restricted on the side of both supply and demand—in the former, by the buyer's control on the engagement of growers and on the side of demand by the difficulties of entry by another processor in those markets. Further, the growers are unable to move to another processor or to exit to another activity. Under these conditions, it is clear that the processors as monopsonists have "undue market power", this situation being the antithesis of competition, in the sense that the processors can—they have the "discretion"[20]—to manipulate the price at which the services of the growers can be obtained.[21] The growers, on the other hand, must not only run their business strictly in accordance with the specifications of their buyer, but are singly unable to dictate the size of their growing fee and must take what is dictated by their processor short of a fee level which force growers to exit the market.

So far as the Melbourne market is concerned, there are three processors. Each group of growers is tied to one processor, again because of their and the processors' location and the specificity of their plant and equipment Here again entry is restricted on the side of supply and demand. Although in terms of the broader market, this can be regarded as oligopsonistic, there is a strong monopsonistic element in terms of the narrower market in which each processor effectively operates. Moreover, although there are three processors, one of them takes up half the output of chickens in the area, they are linked by the supply of chicks and the supply of feed, and do not poach on each other's growers, whose movement between processors is rare. These factors interlink the interests of the processors and limit any constraints on their market power.

This situation derives essentially from the economies of scale and vertical integration on the part of the processors. It is important to note that these features are not a reflection of the earlier regulated arrangements of the industry. Rather, the nature of the industry and the undue market power favouring the processors, derived from the oligopsonistic/monopsonistic character of the relevant markets, led to the industry being regulated.

Procedures and principles under the VBINC regulated regime

Since 1968, a number of Acts relating to the broiler chicken industry have applied in Victoria. The one of particular relevance to this paper is the Broiler Chicken Industry Act 1978 as amended in 1991 and the Broiler Chicken Industry Regulations 1992. At the time of the Review, the former had not been revoked but the latter had lapsed. The Act established the Victorian Broiler Industry Negotiating Committee (VBINC) "to improve Stability in the Broiler Chicken Industry, and for other purposes." The determinations of the VBINC were binding on the growers and processors, and penalties were pre-scribed for offences against the terms of the determinations.

The three objectives of the (VBINC) as laid down by the Broiler Chicken Industry Act 1978[22] were:

(a) to create an environment and develop processes that facilitate agreements between growers and processors; and

(b) to determine process and recommend terms and conditions that would apply under fair and competitive conditions; and

(c) to ensure the exploitation of growers does not occur.

These objectives implicitly recognise the inherent structure of the industry and the difficulties arising therefrom in settling on the growing fee and other terms. The Regulations specify the terms and conditions that may be inserted in contracts and prescribes the form of the contract. The VBINC was made up of an independent chair, four representatives each of growers and processors, and two independent members with "commercial expertise", all with voting rights.

How objective (b) is to be achieved is not specified by the Act but it was at the forefront of VBINC's considerations when determining fees and other terms of the contract. This concern is reflected in the elements of the formula used to determine fees. An essential feature of this formula were the produc-tivity or efficiency inducements built into the system on both the demand and supply side and expressed in the Growing Fee Model. These formed the frame-work into which were built various cost items relevant to the growing process (materials, labour, management, depreciation and an imputed normal profit margin, made up of the Bond rate plus 1.5% for risk). These essential elements were incorporated in the Growing Fee Model.[23]

In order to encourage economies of scale, the Growing Fee Model was related to farm size and cost items on a standard of efficiency at which the industry aimed as a kind of optimum standard, rather than the average performance operating at the time. Thus, at the time of the Review, the Model was based on a newly built farm with 120,000 birds per batch capacity, operating at the optimum 5.1 batches per year and with a shed size of 60,000 sq ft. This compares with the 1999 average contract farm with about 90,000 birds per batch and shed size of just over 46,000 sq ft, while 32% of farms took less than 60,000 chickens per batch. On this approach, the contract conditions provide incentive for economies of scale and improved performance. Further, the factors underlying the Model are not static. They are changed from time to time to generate further improvements. There is also flexibility in the way the terms are applied to meet the needs of the processors. The progressive expansion of the growing capacity of existing growers by the addition of their shed capacity shows the effectiveness of the incentive to greater efficiency.

Although there was a Standard Growing Fee (SGF), that fee was not necessarily paid by any processor. A margin of 3% above and below the SGF was prescribed, depending on the efficiency of the processor as reflected in the quality of the chicks and feed, bird density and mortality and the batch rate, all of which were under the control of the processor. A higher fee was paid to the grower as a penalty for the processor's lower efficiency in connection with these items and as an inducement for greater efficiency. However, by agreement between a processor and its affiliated growers, the margin could exceed 3%, a reflection of the flexibility of the system

An additional spur to competition and efficiency on the growers is through the operation of the "pool" system[24] for determining the entitlements to individual growers. The individual grower's fee could range between plus or minus 5% and 12.5% of the SGF, depending on the grower's performance. The grower's incentive to maintain high performance was also sustained by the processor's right to terminate its contract with a grower whose efficiency was below 90% (full cost basis) and 95% (feed conversion ratio basis)[25] of the average performance in four successive batches.

The existence of processors' farms and the scope for processors to increase the output of such farms at the expense of private growers' output and the entry of new growers must also be included as a competitive element in the industry. Although much of increased demand was met by the growth of existing farms to tap economies of scale, a course favoured by processors, new growers accounted for more than half of new shedding capacity between 1989 and 1998. In recent years processors have chosen to close down their own farms.

The results of the regulated system speak for themselves. The real growing fee per bird fell by 27% between 1976 and 1999. The real growing fee *per kilogram* fell significantly more than the real growing price *per bird* since 1983 because of the increase in the average size of birds. At the time of the Review, the Victorian growing industry was said to be the most cost-efficient in Australia, the growing fee per bird and by weight being 5.6% and 8.6% respectively below the national average.[26] The Australian growing industry has been rated second only to Denmark in an international benchmarking comparison of technical efficiency. A further reflection of the efficiency of the independent farms is their ability to hold their own against processor farms whose share in total output had fallen over the last decade. It is significant in this connection, that the processor did not bring any evidence to either the Review or the Commission, to compare the performance of their farms with that of the private farms. Further, the VBINC procedures did not call for resort to boycott/strike action and kept transaction costs to a minimum by its effective built-in mediation processes.

The National Competition Policy Review

The Review provides an interesting insight on how a blinkered competition doctrine in pursuit of Competition Policy can take precedence over economic performance presumably because the latter is associated with a regulated regime. As mentioned above, the Review was conducted by KPMG. It included, among other matters, a comparison of cost/benefit of the previous regulated system with a counterfactual unregulated system. It concluded that the Act and Regulations should be repealed. Its conclusion rested on the following:

For government intervention in a market to be justified on economic grounds, a market failure must be evident or likely and the costs of government intervention must be less than the benefits to society at large. Intervention may also occur to achieve social or other objectives the government wishes to pursue. Our examination of the broiler industry legislation indicates that the legislation:

- does not address market failure in the relevant market;
- has the implicit objective of changing power relations between grower and processors and redistributing income to the growers;
- creates restrictions on competition that are not necessary to achieve the stated objectives; and
- imposes costs on the community that are likely to exceed any benefits.

The broiler chicken industry legislation was introduced in 1975 and has remained largely unchanged since 1978. The legislation takes no account of the existence of the TPA and its application as that has evolved over the last 25 years. The introduction of the unconscionable conduct provisions of the TPA is a recent development in general competition law that is particularly relevant to assessing the continuing need for the industry-specific legislation. This development is one of several changes in the context of the Act which has not been taken into account. *Collectively, those developments alone are such as to fundamentally question the continuing need for the legislation, even without the NCP legislative review framework.*[27]

Consider the main points raised.

That the legislation does not address market failure and is concerned with changing power relations.

While it is arguable that the legislation may have been prompted more by social/equity/political considerations than by pure economic considerations related to market failure, the circumstances which gave rise to the legislation arose essentially from an industry exhibiting the sources of market failure. The Review defines market failure as "a situation in which economic efficiency is unable to be achieved by the normal operations of the market mechanism."[28] It identifies the following "major causes" of market failure—

externality, natural monopoly, public goods and information asymmetry. The first three do not apply to the industry under consideration. As for the last, the Review may be overstating somewhat the situation in maintaining the differences between the parties are not "sufficiently profound" as to cause a serious misallocation of resources.

However, more seriously, the Review underplays other elements of market failure related to market power that are well recognised in the economics literature and in Australian case law. Given the structure of the industry in Victoria, the point made by the Review that "Price competition is integral to vigorous competition" (p.91), and, by implication, that deregulation would bring about "vigorous competition" in the segmented chicken-growing market is only valid on the supply side—the growers—of the market. But this does not consider the relevant regional *markets* or whether deregulation would lessen market failure. Furthermore, there are impediments to the entry and particularly to the exit of growers because of the specificity of their plant and equipment. The effect of the "more vigorous" competition would simply mean that in the circumstances of low elasticity of supply, growers would be put in a weaker bargaining position and be forced to accept lower fees. The continued small number of processors despite the substantial growth of the industry also suggests that entry on the side of processing is very limited. Moreover, the Review seems to treat the "market" as constituting the whole of Victoria[29] rather than broken up in several distinct areas.

The existence of competition in the chicken *meat* market is not sufficient justification for neglecting the demand side of the chicken *growing* market, on the assumption that lower growing fees would be passed on to the consumer and would add to the public benefit. This may or may not be the case, especially as the chicken meat market is highly concentrated in Victoria and Australia-wide and presents a situation in which there are a small number of sellers and buyers. However, the Review (and the Commission later) failed to consider in any detail the nature of the chicken meat market and the extent to which the cost of growing chicken could be passed on to that market. Moreover, the proportion of the growing fee is only around 6–8 % of the retail price of chicken meat. Any change in the growing fee, even if passed on to the retail market, could be expected to result in little, if any, substitution of other meats.

It is important to note that the financial statements of the processors, which are private companies, were not opened to scrutiny by the Review to establish the profitability of their processing operations and the extent to which increased growing costs would impinge on oligopsonistic/monopsonistic profits.

The Review makes light of the unbalanced market power, regarding it as "not uncommon" in commercial relationships. It maintains that there "is no evidence that in an unregulated market the processors will enhance their bargaining power through restrictive agreements and practices".[30] However, the more relevant consideration is whether they have the potential to do so. In reviewing the pre-legislation history of the industry, the Review maintains that collusive behaviour by processors on fees "may have been possible but unlikely".[31] No explanation is given for this assertion. While no overt collusion may have taken place, such collusion could have been tacit. Given the interdependence between the processors in the Victorian market and the low elasticity of supply, the processors would find it to their financial interest not to compete with each other and to drive fees up. Further, a price leadership situation could be expected to arise. No communication between the processors would be necessary for such a situation to eventuate. The same restraint would exist among processors in "poaching" growers from each other. It is not contradicted that movement of growers between processors is rare.[32]

The Review regards the interdependence between the growers and processors as providing the "basis for reasonable contract terms and conditions". (p. 72) This mutual dependence is undeniable but it does not mean that the processors may not exercise their greater bargaining power in determining the terms of the contract.

That the VBINC system creates restrictions on competition not necessary to achieve its objects

Instead of resorting to legislation, the Review suggests that other courses are available to the growers to prevent processors abusing their market power. It mentions potential ACCC authorisation of processor-based enterprise collective negotiations, the TPA's "unconscionable conduct" provisions, and "voluntary market based measures such as advisory and assistance by the VFF" as alternatives to regulation.[33]

The case for the ACCC's authorisation of enterprise collective negotiations will be considered below and is, in any case, at variance with the Review's contention that there is no evidence the processors' bargaining power is enhanced in an unregulated market. The value of resorting to the TPA's unconscionable conduct provisions is of doubtful value for growers—the likely length, difficulty of proof, cost and uncertain outcome of such litigation would discourage action by aggrieved growers. As for advice and assistance from the VFF, the proscription on common advisers under the ACCC authorisation discussed below would effectively deny such assistance. Considered against the principles and procedures of the regulated system, the last two alternatives are unsatisfactory band-aids reflecting the shortcomings of the recommended deregulated system.

That the VBINC legislation imposes costs on the community that are likely to exceed any benefits

The Review asks whether there should be less concern about the existence of a restriction on competition "if the fees determined under it approximated competitively-set fees".[34] Its answer is in the negative because "It is the existence of an anti-competitive element itself, not merely its effect at a particular time that is of fundamental concern". *Such an answer suggests that doctrine rather than an established performance record and its analytical basis under regulation should determine policy.* Again, this focuses on the "anti-competitive" element on the supply side and downplays those inherent on the demand side by the prevailing features of the relevant market.

In its assessment of costs and benefits of the present system as against a counterfactual deregulated system, the Review comes out in favour of the latter. The basis of this conclusion is that the regulated fees could be higher than the fees which would operate under "competitive conditions", by which the Review means a deregulated market. It also assumes that the higher fee would be largely passed on to the consumer. This conclusion draws on the processors submission of two factors—the existence, under the prescribed fees system, of super-normal profits based on goodwill or economic rent, which, it is assumed, would be eliminated under deregulation;[35] and also on greater productivity which would result from deregulation. As argued in the Appendix, there is no substance in both points submitted.

Overall, by its faulty understanding of the features of a "competitive market" and what may be inferred as a doctrinal opposition to regulation regardless of efficiency outcomes, the Review failed to make a cogent economic case for a deregulated system in preference to the VBINC system.

The ACCC's response to the processors application for authorisation of processor-based collective bargaining

Following the Review, Marven Poultry and other processors sought authorisation from the ACCC (A90750) for processor-based collective bargaining agreements. On 20 June 2001, the ACCC issued its Determination and supporting arguments. Although the conclusions of the KPMG Review were based on a comparison of the regulated system with a counterfactual unregulated system while the ACCC came to its Determination based on a comparison between two counterfactual systems—an unregulated system and processor-based collective bargaining—there was much common ground between them. In substance, ACCC approved the form of authorisation sought by the processors which it said represented a compromise between the existing regulated arrangement and a fully deregulated system. The authorised system was to be backed by guidelines incorporated in a "Code of Conduct" prescribing guidelines on procedures for negotiations, the content of contracts and dispute settling.

The Commission showed full awareness of the structure of the industry and, unlike the Review, also of the significant lopsided bargaining power in favour of the processors. However, it rejected industry-wide collective bargaining as a basis for settling the growing fee and other terms because

> While collective negotiations on an industry wide basis would provide growers with a greater degree of bargaining power, the Commission considers that such industry wide collective negotiations would also be likely to have a far greater detrimental effect on competition than the proposed arrangement. [36]

Accordingly, to reinforce this objection to industry wide collective negotiations, the Commission also refused to authorise a common adviser to represent growers in negotiations in the different grower groups because:

There is a real likelihood that negotiations would result in a set of identical prescribed contracts across the industry, similar in place under the current regulated system. Common, industry wide representation would increase the potential for an industry wide price fixing arrangement and have a much greater detrimental effect on competition than would collective negotiation at the individual [grower group] level without a common industry negotiator. **This outcome would be inconsistent with the intent of industry deregulation and could negate the public benefits of easing the transition to a deregulated market identified by the Commission ...'**[37]

Further, the transitional phase would enable the growers to acquire the necessary skills to negotiate efficiently. Therefore, there is "some public benefit in facilitating the transition to deregulation".[38] The Commission noted that in other cases where it has authorised a similar transitional arrangement, it has required "that industries demonstrate a clear commitment and movement towards operating in a deregulated market."[39] Such an expectation is also in the present authorisation.[40]

On the matter of transaction costs, the Commission admitted that while

the proposed arrangements are likely to increase transaction costs relative to the current regulated system, there are likely to be considerable savings in terms of time and labour for both the processors and growers if each processor is able to negotiate growers' fees and conditions through [the grower groups] (be it single or more than one) rather than individually with, in some instances, up to 60 growers.[41]

However, as will be seen later, it did not include this finding in making its Determination.

It will be convenient to analyse this Determination along with a subsequent Determination of the Commission in connection with the growers' applications (A40093 and A90931) for authorisation to be discussed next.

Further ACCC authorisations

As mentioned above, the refusal of the Victorian government to return to a regulated system and restore the VBINC, and the successful legal challenge of the

Commission's authorisation of the processors' application, resulted effectively in a deregulated industry. In December 2003, the processors applied for authorisations (A90901, A90902, A90903, A90904 and A90905) on terms substantially the same as those sought in 2001. This was granted to three of the five applicants. The growers, led by the VEF, anticipating that the Commission would not accede to an industry-wide collective bargaining arrangement, applied for an authorisation of a system of processor-based collective bargaining on somewhat different terms from those sought earlier by the processors. In essence, five grower groups would bargain with the respective processors for whom they were and had been growing chickens. There would be "uniform contractual cycles" for growers each lasting five years. In other words, contracts would terminate on a common date for all the parties and the negotiations between each of the five growers groups and their respective processors for a new contract periodically, would take place at the same time at the end of five years. The elements of the built-in productivity concept of the regulated system outlined earlier would continue to apply but would be subject to periodic negotiations. As part of the process, should contract negotiations break down, the growers concerned would have the right to boycott their processor by refusing to accept chicks for growing. Such boycott could only be exercised after negotiations for a period of six months and, should mediation prove unsuccessful, 28 days thereafter.

The VFF supported its application by relying essentially on the case for countervailing bargaining power in favour of the growers in a oligopsonistic/monopsonistic industry, the minimisation of transaction costs and the continuing improvement in productivity that could be expected to accrue under such a system. The ACCC issued its final Determination on 2 March 2005, granting substantially the terms sought by the growers but it refused to prescribe certain procedural provisions preferring that these be negotiated between the parties.

There were certain common elements as well as significant differences between the reasoning underlying the two Determinations.

Transition to a de-regulated system

In coming to its Determinations, the Commission rejected any form of industry-wide negotiation. It said that such a system "would be inconsistent with the intent of industry deregulation and could negate the public benefits of easing the transition towards a deregulated market ..."[42] It also said it required industries to "demonstrate a clear commitment and movement towards operating in a more competitive environment."[43] The Commission also believes that because growers had operated in a highly regulated arrangement and have limited experience in "commercial contract negotiations" the transitional arrangement would help them to acquire the necessary skills to "negotiate efficiently".[44]

It is difficult to understand how the Commission could believe that the industry could be expected to move to a deregulated system of individual bargaining. Such an expectation is unrealistic and confusing, and sits uncomfortably alongside its findings on the nature of the industry and its view that "processors will continue to maintain a high degree of control over the growers with or without collective bargaining arrangements".[45] The ACCC clearly recognised the nature of the industry in several parts of both Determinations. Thus, in the second Determination[46] it said that the imbalance in bargaining power arises from:

- the limited opportunity for growers to switch production from chicken growing given the significant capital investment and the specific nature of capital (in particular growing sheds)
- the limited opportunity for growers to switch processors given the location of processors and the switching costs arising from the specific growing requirements of each processor
- the direct control over growing operations by processors through the provision of day old chickens, growing specifications and the provision of other necessary inputs such as feed and veterinarian services
- the reliance of growers on processors as their sole source of income and
- the often limited bargaining expertise of growers in comparison to generally larger and more experienced processors.

These features are hardly likely to change significantly in the foreseeable future. If anything, the trend has been in the opposite direction, spurred by the economies of scale and vertical integration. Nor would greater skill in bargaining make any difference to the structure of the industry.[47] Moreover, by suggesting a transition to complete deregulation, the ACCC has introduced an unnecessary element of uncertainty into the investment expectations of the growers.

There was no rigorous examination of the VBINC system

Although the Commission does make references and comparisons with industry-wide collective negotiations, it is fair to say that it does not examine and evaluate in any systematic and rigorous way, the operation and performance of the regulated industry. It simply asserts that there is less competition under the regulated arrangements than would exist under the authorised arrangements. In the first Determination (A90750), the ACCC explained its limited approach as follows[48]:

> The Commission is required to assess the public benefits and detriments of the proposal before it, not the benefits and detriments of existing legislation. The counterfactual situation that the Commission has to consider in assessing the application is one where the arrangements were not in place. Given all parties[49] accept that the existing legislation is in breach of the TPA, the Commission does not consider it reasonable to use the legislation as the counterfactual[50] situation is assessing the proposed arrangements.

The fact that existing legislation were in breach of the TPA should not have stopped the Commission from weighing the public benefits of this arrangement against other arrangements and opening the door to the VBINC arrangement being authorised by appropriate state legislation. This self-imposed narrow interpretation of its task has led the Commission to what on the evidence is arguably a second-best determination from the point of view of the public benefit. It needs to be emphasised that *processes* should not be taken to be synonymous with *outcomes*. Performance rather than the institutional arrangement as such, must be the ultimate test of the public benefit. This is after all the remit of the ACCC in determining authorisation applications. It should not be about rejecting a regulated system *per se*.

The Determination refers at various points to industry-wide negotiations and to the VBINC regulated arrangements as if they are synonymous. Further, it appears to characterise the Standard Growing Fee as a common or uniform fee. This is a superficial and misleading basis for judging the present system. The VBINC regulated system is not simply an industry-wide negotiating arrangement, but one intermediated by a composite tribunal in which the independent members have generally had the determining voice on outcomes. It was noted above that as laid down by the Broiler Chicken Industry Act, the VBINC is bound by the objectives of balancing the market power of the contending parties in an oligopsonistic/monopsonistic market and attempting to determine prices "that would apply under fair and competitive conditions". Although reaching this objective calls for judgment, it is manifest in the formula for determining growing fees in which flexibility and productivity-generating factors are built into the formula to simulate competitive elements in the system. Moreover, the fact that the contract is imposed uniformly for the whole industry should not be taken as detrimental to efficiency or to a competitive outcome. In an industry with oligopsonistic and monopsonistic structures, the outcome of a regulated system of the kind which applied in Victoria could well be closer to a competitive outcome than what might eventuate from the authorised arrangement. This is an issue which the Commission deliberately did not examine and must be regarded as a major deficiency in its task to consider and to determine what could be expected to advance public benefit most.

There is another puzzle in the Commission's reasoning. On the one hand, it admits the current lack of competition for growers services because of the structure of the industry.[51] On the other, it considers this to be "to a large degree a result of the lack of incentives under the current arrangements"[52]; and that the removal of "this impediment" under the proposed authorisation "will greatly enhance the scope for competition among processors for growers' services."[53] The existence of incentives on both growers and processors inherent in the Standard Growing Fee formula was noted earlier and was acknowledged by the Commission. No explanation is given why and how greater incentives would operate under the authorised arrangement. Given the small number of processors and the consequences of the strong likelihood of interdependence of their policies on fees, their negative attitude to "poaching" of growers and, as the ACCC itself has noted, the discouragement to greater grower mobility between processors because of costs in adapting sheds to the requirements of the processor, the self-interest of the processors may very well minimise or thwart the realisation of the potential for greater competition.

The performance of the Victorian industry under the regulated regime was noted earlier. It would have been desirable for the ACCC to establish valid grounds for concluding that a less centralised arrangement, free from the procedures and rules of the VBINC, would provide the means to better performance and greater public good. Its failure to do so leaves it open to being regarded as doctrinally opposed to regulation regardless of considerations of merit on public interest grounds. The ACCC says that the growers failed "to provide conclusive evidence to support their claim that the processors are earning supra-competitive profits."[54] Why should the onus be on the growers to establish this point? Does the ACCC not have the power to examine the financial accounts of the processors on a confidential basis?

The ACCC's concept of competition

Here and there, the ACCC compares the extent of competition between three situations—the processors bargaining with individual growers, its authorised system of enterprise collective negotiations, and industry-wide collective negotiations. However, it gives the concept of "competition" an unusual meaning and significance, colouring its approach on a number of issues. Instead of following the procedure established by case law noted above in determining the relevant *market* and its competitive characteristics, it looked at supply in isolation from demand to decide on whether there was more or less competition. Thus, by its curious logic, any increase in the bargaining power of growers has a detrimental effect on competition and, consequently, damages public benefit. It follows from this that competition is greatest and public benefit is maximised in a deregulated system where processors bargain with individual growers, and that the "detrimental effects" of reduced competition is greater under industry-wide collective bargaining than under its authorised system of segmented collective bargaining.[55] Hence, before granting authorisation, to maximise the public benefit, it considers factors that would offset the detrimental effects of reduced competition.[56]

It says all this while admitting that the ability of the growers to exploit any increase in bargaining power under the authorised arrangement is limited because of the various factors which lead to a low elasticity of supply[57]. Since there is very little movement of growers between processors, greater competition under the authorised system could occur only within groups of growers on the side of supply. Moreover, in another part of its Determination[58] on the difference in the degree of competition, the ACCC modified its argument somewhat. Conceding that in the absence of authorisation

> the nature of the industry, and the relationship between processors and growers, is such that generally speaking, if individual negotiation was to occur, growers in each grower group would most likely be offered standard form contracts ... Consequently, the difference between the level of competition amongst growers with or without the proposed arrangements would be small.[59]

In the circumstances, can it be said, that there would be greater competition, in a meaningful sense, under a deregulated system than the authorised arrangement in the three chicken growing *markets*?[60] The demand side is unchanged. There will continue to be a small number of processors, three at the most in Mornington Peninsula market, and one only each in the Bendigo and the Geelong areas, demand in the State being concentrated in two processors, as well as a high degree of interdependence in growing fee decision-making of the processors. Processors are further inter-linked by the supply of chicks, and in some cases, by the supply of feed. While the processors have argued that this inter-linking is a matter of commercial expediency, it, nevertheless, increases the interdependence between them.

The significance of such interdependence has been commented on above. The processors would find it in their interest not to compete against each other to drive fees up, especially as the chicken meat market is competitive as against other meats and the wholesale market for chicken meat is dominated by two firms. To pass on increased fees might be difficult in the circumstances. This would be so under the authorised arrangement no less than under a deregulated system.

It would appear that concealed in the Commission's notion of competition and public benefit is an implicit concern for the risk of increases in the price of chicken meat to the consumer arising from increased bargaining power to the growers. It may be inferred from this that the Commission criterion of increasing public benefit is increasing consumer welfare[61] rather than increasing total welfare, which includes growers' welfare and is, therefore, consistent with Pareto optimality.[62] However, even on the consumer welfare criterion, its Determination is inconsistent with its own findings. Thus, in granting authorisation to the processor-based collective bargaining system, the Commission conceded that the anti-competitive elements of such authorisation would be limited by the low level of competition between members of grower groups, by pressure from "powerful downstream purchasers of processed chicken meat" against the passing on of any fee increases, and by the fact the growing fees make up only 6–8% of the retail price of chicken meat.[63] Moreover, the Commission neglected to consider the medium/long term investment incentive and consequential productivity effects of a shift in income from processors to growers. Such productivity growth would of course add consumer welfare.

These considerations throw doubt on the existence of the "detrimental effect of greater competition" in the authorised arrangement as compared with a system of individual bargaining.

Comparing the detrimental effects on competition of industry-wide collective bargaining and the authorised arrangement

The unusual meaning and significance given to "competition" and its alleged "detrimental" effects have also influenced the ACCC's assessment of industry-wide collective bargaining as compared with its authorised processor-based collective bargaining. It maintains that while industry-wide bargaining would give growers more bargaining power, it would also be likely to have a **far greater** detrimental effect on competition than the proposed arrangements. The Commission has consistently opposed industry wide collective negotiation across a number of industries due to concerns regarding the detrimental effect on competition of such arrangements.[64]

It said further that the separation of bargaining units into "discrete groups would act to reduce the overall anti-competitive effect of the conduct compared to a situation where there was a single Victoria-wide bargaining group."[65]

It is possible, but unlikely, that the bargaining power of the growers, particularly those in the Bendigo and Geelong regions would be greater under industry-wide bargaining because they would otherwise be confronted by a single buyer. But why should this cause "far greater" detrimental effects on competition in the Victorian chicken growing market as compared with a situation in which all five processors faced 210 growers in collective bargaining?

As noted above, in granting authorisation to the segmented collective bargaining, the Commission conceded that the anti-competitive elements of such authorisation would be limited, that there would be difficulty in passing increased fees to the consumer, and by the fact the growing fees make up 6–8% of the retail price of chicken meat.[66] Would these factors be any less applicable under industry-wide collective bargaining?

It is unlikely that breaking the industry up into separate market groups would weaken the degree of interdependence between the processors. Nor could there be any movement of growers between the three regions because they are locationally fixed. Further, there are no significant differences in product or production methods between the different regions as to warrant separate bargaining units. The authorised arrangement would establish the basis substantially not of greater competition as compared with industry-wide collective bargaining but of non-competing pockets effectively of bi-lateral monopoly. The interdependence on the demand side would continue to prevail with the likelihood of the segmented negotiations resulting in similar settlements. Given the dominance of two processors in a group of five processors, pattern setting within the industry is likely to prevail.

Connected with its view about the greater anti-competitive element of industry-wide bargaining compared to the authorised segmented system of bargaining, is the requirement under the authorisation that there should not be "common representation" or adviser in collective negotiations across two or more groups.[67] Such common representation, it is said, would "significantly" increase the anti-competitive effect of the arrangement.[68] It would appear that the Commission regards forces that result in uniform terms and conditions as being against the public benefit, despite the fact that the three regions produce the same product in much the same way. A contrary and more persuasive view would be that under something closer to perfect competition, a free flow of information would result in fairly uniform terms and condition in a market. In practice, it would be surprising if the terms being negotiated between one group of growers and a processor would not be known throughout the industry. It would also be surprising if the terms of the different agreements would vary significantly between the different bargaining groups. This is all the more likely because under the authorised arrangement, negotiations for a new round of contracts would commence at about the same time. It was noted above that in its comparison of unregulated individual bargaining and the authorised system of processor-based collective bargaining, the ACCC conceded a standard contract form would largely prevail.[69]

Insufficient weight to transaction costs of the authorised arrangement compared to industry-wide collective bargaining

Consideration of the burden of transaction costs played an important part in the Determination. Despite the ACCC's conclusion that the authorised system would be more anti-competitive than a completely deregulated system, one of its justifications for authorising processor-based collective contracts is that it would involve lower transactions costs than would result from individual grower contracts. The lower transaction costs would flow to the public benefit.[70] Further, as noted above, the Commission regards the authorised arrangement as a transitional phase to individual bargaining. This, it said, would relieve growers of having to face "the considerable costs and difficulties adapting to a deregulated market",[71] who would in time acquire the "skills to be able to negotiate efficiently".[72] Putting this element of cost saving into the balance of public benefits is no more persuasive than the expectation that the authorised system can be regarded realistically as a transition to individual bargaining.

However, in its rejection of industry-wide collective bargaining, and by implication the VBINC regulated system, the ACCC failed to weigh the lower transactions costs of these centralised arrangements, which it conceded, against the costs of its alleged detrimental effects of reduced competition. Several sources of increased transactions costs can be distinguished in the authorised arrangement as compared with the VBINC regulated industry-wide system. Thus, separate collective bargaining groups are bound to add to cost of contract determination, probably by a factor of five, especially as a common adviser is not allowed. By the processors own admission, the costs of negotiations are high.[73] The provision of individual bargaining with growers who are not part of any group would add further costs. The possible delays and associated costs of the authorised dispute settling and boycott provisions are also relevant additional cost items in operating the authorised system. Thus, apart from dubious concern about anti-competitive detrimental effects, the ACCC has authorised a system, which by its own admission,[74] is bound to have higher transaction costs than the VBINC industry-wide arrangement. However, it did not include this element in its balancing of cost-benefit considerations.

Collective boycott

It is well established in the industrial relations literature that without the *right* to coercive economic action in the form of a strike or lockout, no pressure would exist for collective bargaining in good faith. The party unwilling to concede a benefit, being in a better position to weather the passage of time without a settlement, could simply stall and allow negotiations to drag on. The existence of this right may be expected to speed up the resolution of a dispute, generally without the need to exercise it, since the side initiating a strike or lockout would also suffer from an interruption in production.

The application by the growers to have the right to refuse to accept day-old chickens from the processors in the event of a stalemate in their negotiations and failure of mediation, marked a new element in the Commission's consideration of collective bargaining authorisation. Referred to as "collective boycott" but in effect similar to strike or lockout, it follows one of the recommendations of the Dawson Report[75] relating to collective bargaining between small and big business. It is noteworthy that in its submission to the Dawson Review, the Commission, reflecting its assumption of the anti-competitive effect of boycotts, expressed itself against immunity being available in such collective bargaining.[76]

In relation to the growers' application for authorisation to include the right to boycott as part of the negotiation process, the Commission maintained that it "could significantly increase the anti-competitive effects of the proposed collective bargaining arrangements."[77] This right would, of course, strengthen the bargaining power of the growers by allowing them to apply pressure on the processors to bargain in good faith. However, as in other cases where the growers' bargaining power is strengthened, the Commission regards it as anti-competitive rather tan as producing a more equal balance of bargaining power, a reflection of its unwarranted neglect of the demand side of the market. The Commission agreed to give this right to the growers on the basis that certain public benefits would accrue from it to offset the "anti-competitive detriments".[78] However, in its concern to minimise the "anti-competitive detriments" of the right to boycott, it has imposed procedures that would in effect water down this right. Thus, it has required the growers intending to apply this right to give their respective processor 21 days notice of this intention[79] in order that the processors may better prepare themselves for the event; and that any batch of chicken being grown at the time a boycott becomes available, must be completed before the boycott is applied.[80] Further, additional restrictions apply to reduce the incidence of a boycott taking place affecting more than one grower group. In substance, these restrictions aim at avoiding an industry-wide boycott.[81]

The Commission laid down these restrictions while admitting (Ibid para 12.9) that the growers, in their concern to avoid the loss they would sustain from the boycott, would apply it as a last resort, following at least seven months of negotiations and 28 days of mediation thereafter. Underlying these restrictions on the boycott powers of the growers is the ACCC's concern to minimise the risk and extent of interruption to the supply of chickens in the interest of the consumer. This is understandable but not justifiable since the inconvenience and any rise in price to the consumer as a result of chicken meat shortage would be transitory. Further, it is inconsistent with the ACCC's recognition of the greater bargaining power of the processors and the ability of the main processors to draw from their operations in other states during a boycott in Victoria.

It was noted above that the VBINC regulated system avoided the need for a boycott provision because under its processes, in the event of disagreement, it could impose a binding award on the parties. No stoppages occurred in the industry, a situation fairly regarded as industrial harmony and relevant to transaction costs, prevailed while the system operated. The Commission failed to put this point in the balance of public benefits in its Determination.

However, even the limited boycott provision allowed by the Commission was overturned on appeal by the processors to the Australian Competition Tribunal.[82] Although admitting that the processors have significant market power, the Tribunal rejected the boycott provision on the grounds that the likely cost of boycotts would be unduly high while, with the growth of demand over time, the processors' market power is likely to weaken.

Given the structure of the industry, both grounds are highly speculative and are in substance contradicted by the admission that there "is no empirical evidence of the effect of collective boycotts" (para 438) and that it is highly uncertain' (para 451) how the growers would exercise their boycott power. The tribunal gave no consideration to the very limited degree of collective boycott allowed by the ACCC in speculating on the cost of the boycott. It would have been more appropriate in the circumstances, given the existence of significant market power, to allow the boycott provision and to see how it works over time. Should the concerns of the Tribunal be realised, it would then be open to the processors to bring the matter back to the Tribunal. It is surprising that the Tribunal did not impose the onus of establishing the likely cost of the boycotts on the appellants.

A further puzzling aspect of the Tribunal's reasoning is reflected in its statement that "In the thirty two years of the life of the Act, the ACCC and its predecessor have never before authorised a collective boycott." (para 442) This is obviously true, but the Dawson Committee had only recently considered the situation and had issued a recommendation that there should be a right to collective boycott. The Tribunal's remark is in effect a denial of the Dawson Committee's recommendation.

It is arguable that, by its reasoning, the Tribunal has unwittingly made a strong case for a regulated system. If a collective boycott is not allowed and a situation of bilateral monopoly is found by the Tribunal to exist (para 451), surely the public (consumer) interest is best protected by something like the VBINC.

Concluding observations

The history of the Victorian chicken broiler industry as analysed above raises a number of worrying conclusions. First that the Review under the Australian Competition Policy should be so lacking in analytical rigour. Second that in embracing the National Competition Policy, the Victorian government should appear to take a doctrinaire approach and be against a regulated system regardless of the public benefit evidence in favour of it. The Victorian government may also have been unwilling to risk losing the National Competition payments from the federal government for refusing to abide by the findings of the Review. Third, that the Commission's Determination should leave a critical gap in its evaluation of the public benefit. It is true that in terms of advancing the public benefit, the authorised arrangement, by establishing in the Victorian industry, effectively, pockets of collective bargaining with the right to boycott, does provide a more even balance of bargaining power between the growers and the processors than would prevail under individual bargaining. Nevertheless, obstructed by its unusual concept of "competition", by its unrealistic expectation of the industry's transition to a deregulated system, and by giving inadequate weight to transaction costs, the Commission does not go far enough in advancing the public benefit: its authorisation refused industry-wide collective bargaining and minimised the boycott powers of the growers. By denying itself a close examination of the VBINC regulated system, the Commission did not allow the performance of this system and the benefit to the public to be assessed.[83] All this is surprising in view of the Commission's clear grasp of the structural features of the industry.

Finally, in the light of the above considerations, if a regulated system is ruled out, there is strong case for the collective bargaining claims of similarly placed small businesses to be processed under state industrial relations laws with appropriate immunity from the Trade Practices Act. This would avoid the contentious balancing of public benefit/detriment elements under hypothetical counterfactual situations. It would also be less expensive to the parties and the public purse than the existing arrangement. Moreover, there is surely a close analogy with a number of issues central to industrial relations—individual bargaining, enterprise collective bargaining, industry (multiple-employer) collective bargaining, and the right to strike. There is also a close analogy between the provision of *physical* capital by growers in discharging their chicken-growing services and the application of *human* capital by skilled labour in the supply of their services. Although the ACCC has asserted that the growers are independent contractors and not employees (para 9.41), the legal test distinguishing one from the other is not entirely clear and depends on the particular circumstances of each case. This issue has not been tested for this industry. However, a primary legal test is that the persons concerned (in this case, the growers) are required to do not only what should be done, but also how it should be done. There is little doubt that this particular test is satisfied in this industry. The decision of the High Court (Hollis v Vabu Pty Ltd, 2001, HCA 44) adds weight to this point, although the Courts may impose additional tests.[84] The analogy between growers and clothing out-workers is also persuasive.[85] Legislation "deeming" such businesses to be employees would dispel any legal doubts.

Acknowledgements

I am indebted to Maureen Brunt, John Clarke, Graeme Ford and Rhonda Smith for helpful comments. However, I am solely responsible for what appears in this paper.

Notes

1   M Brunt, "The Australian Antitrust Law after 20 Years—a Stocktake", *Review of Industrial Organization* (1994) 9 505

2   M R Baye, *Managerial Economic and Business Strategy*, 3rd Edn,. 2000, McGraw-Hill, Boston, Ch.13

3 The industry in the other States are broadly similarly structured but have not proceeded along similar lines. Study of these States is in process.

4 See ACCC, *Authorising and notifying collective bargaining and collective boycott issues paper*, July 2004. p.8; and Rhonda L Smith, "Authorisation and the Trade Practices Act: More about public benefit" (2003)11 CCLJ 31.

5 Under the Broiler Chicken Industry Act 1978, broiler chicken is defined as "chicken which is being grown or has been grown under intensive housing conditions specifically for consumption as poultry meat after processing".

6 Clause 5(1) of the Competition Principles Agreement. Review, quoted in Department of Natural Resources and Environment, *National Competition Policy Review of the Broiler Chicken Industry Act 1978* (referred to in this paper as the KPMG Review) p. 1.

7 Victorian Government's *Guidelines for the Review of Legislative Restrictions in Competition*, quoted in KPMG Review, at p. I

8 The Commission had earlier granted similar authorisations to the industry in South Australia and Tasmania.

9 The VFF could have challenged the Determination before the Australian Competition Tribunal on the basis of the ACCC's application of competition principles but it chose not to do so.

10 Jones v Australian Competition and Consumer Commission (2003) FCAFC 164.

11 This is analogous to enterprise-based collective bargaining in industrial relations terminology.

12 The term "boycott" is somewhat unusual in a situation where there is collective withdrawal of services. The word "strike" would seem to be more appropriate.

13 These were drawn from the KPMG Report and the submission of the VFF. Some of the figures relating to the number of processors and their shares of growers have changed since the matter went to the ACCC. But the differences are not significant for purposes of the arguments in this paper.

14 Inghams, Bartter, Baiada, La Ionica and Hazeldene. At the time when the VBINC was functioning, there were six processors, two of which have since amalgamated into the present Baiada.

15 It may be argued that the growers could switch to growing other birds—turkey or duck, for example. This is a problematic option because location near to processor is critical to efficiency.

16 The chickens lose weight and condition if they are transported to the processors for a distance of more than an hour' s drive.

17 They take up 70% of the total Australian chicken meat market

18 Dean, J. in *G & M Stephens Cartage Contractors Pty Ltd* (1997) ATPR 40-042 at 17,460

19 *Howard Smith Industries Pty. Ltd. and Adelaide Steamship Industries Pty. Ltd.* (1997) ATPR 40-023 at 17,336

20 Maureen Brunt, *Economic Essays on Australia and New Zealand Competition Law*, (2003) Kluwer Law International, The Hague, p. 194

21 *Queensland Co-operative Milling Association and defiance Holdings Ltd.* (1976) ATPR 40-012 at 17,246

22 Section 8A inserted by No. 35/1988, s. 13

23 The details are set out in the VFF Submission (Section 3) to the Review in some detail and in the Review Final Report (section 4.2).

24 A "pool" is a group of growers who at any one time receive a batch of day-old chicks.

25 These are efficiency measures. The former is derived by dividing the weight of feed used in the growing period by the live weight of the chickens collected at the end of the growing period. The latter is the sum of the full cost of chicks, feed and processor standard growing fee across the pool batch, divided by the live weight of birds collected. See The Victorian Farmers Federation, Chicken Meat Group, submission to the Review,1999: 24.

26 The Victorian Farmers Federation, Chicken Meat Group, *The National Competition Policy Review of the Broiler Chicken Industry Act* 1978, para 4.2, henceforth referred to as the VFF Submission.

27 KPMG Review, para 5.1. Underlining added.

28 KPMG Review, para 3.4.3.

29 See, for example, Appendix 4 of the KPMG Report

30 KPMG Review para 3.4.5.4)

31 Ibid para 3.4.4

32 The following summary quotation, although concerned with oligopoly, could also apply to oligopsony: "Any realistic theory of oligopoly must take as its point of departure the fact that when market concentration is high, the pricing decisions of sellers are interdependent, and the firms involved can scarcely avoid recognizing their mutual interdependence. Perceptive managers will recognize that their profits will be higher when cooperative policies are pursued than when each firm looks only after its own narrow self-interest. As a consequence, even in the absence of any formal collusion among firms, we would expect tightly oligopolistic industries to exhibit a tendency towards the maximization of collective profits, perhaps approaching the pricing outcome associated with pure monopoly. However, oligopolistic rivalry is played out in an uncertain, ever changing environment. While the evolution of this environment permits managers to learn about rival intentions, it also poses the constant danger that a rival will undercut the existing pricing structure in search of a competitive advantage. Coordination of pricing policies is not easy." (F M Scherer and David Ross, *Industrial Market Structure and Economic Performance*, (3rd Edition), (1990) p. 226. The close links between the processors in the Victorian industry could be expected to greatly reduce the prospect of the kind of rivalry and the associated self-damaging tit-for-tat process mentioned in this quotation. See also Roger D Blair and Jeffery L Harrison, *Monopsony: Anti-Trust Law and Economics*, (1993), Princeton University Press. Empirical studies of the effective exercise of oligopsonistic and monopsonistic power are discussed in Hanson, Phillip and

Simmons, Phil, "Measures of Buyer concentration in the Australian Wool Market", *Review of Marketing and Agricultural Economics*, (1995) Vol. 63, pp. 304–310; and Schroeter, J R and Azzeddine Azzam, "Marketing Margins, Market Power and Price Uncertainty", *American Journal of Agricultural Economics*, (1991). 73, pp. 990–99.

33 Ibid p. 104

34 Ibid p. 91

35 It is interesting that the Review attempts to measure super-profits of the growers but not inspect the books of the proecssors to assess their super-profits, if any.

36 A90750 para 9.38

37 Idem para 9.39: emphasis added.

38 Idem para 9.81

39 Idem para 9.74

40 Idem para 9.39

41 Idem para 9.68

42 A90750 para 9.39; A40093, A90931: para 12.15

43 A40093, A90931: para 11.39

44 ACCC, *Authorising and notifying collective bargaining and collective boycott issues paper*, July 2004, p. 14.

45 A40093, A90931 para 10.60

46 Ibid para 11.8. Similar points were made in A90750 paras 9.2, 9.53, 9.28, 9.29.

47 R L Smith "Authorisation and the Trade Practices Act: More about public benefit" (2003)11 CCLJ 37.

48 para. 9.6

49 This is hardly an argument against looking closely at the effects of the regulated arrangement. After all, the enterprise collective bargaining system it determined was in breach of the TPA and needed authorisation to ensure its immunity from the TPA. The VFF and its grower members did not accept that the legislation was in breach of the TPA, rather that it *may* be in breach. VBINC operated under State legislation and there is a strong case for believing that it is immune from the TPA. Nor should any weight have been given to the expressed opposition of the Victorian Government to the regulated system.

50 The VBINC regulated industry can hardly be regarded as a counterfactual in the same sense that deregulated or segmented collective bargaining system are. It is an *actual* historical situation on which there is data.

51 A90750 paras 9.26 and 9.53

52 Ibid para 9.85

53 Ibid para 9.86

54 A40093, A90931 para 11.30

55 Ibid paras 10.25, 12.1, 12.2, 12.3.

56 Ibid para10.62.

57 A90570 para 9.23

58 A40093, A9093

59 Idem paras 10.19, 10.20.

60 It is interesting to note that the in the earlier application (A90750), the Commission agreed with the Review that the relevant market for chicken growing to consider is the whole State. When it came to the latter applications (A40093 and A90931), it said that "it was arguable" that the market in Victoria is "a more limited regional market". (para 8.14)

61 R Officer and P Williams "The Public Benefit Test in an Authorisation Decision", in M Richardson and P Williams (Eds), *The Law and the Market*, The Federation Press, Sydney, 1995, p.163

62 For a fuller discussion, see Rhonda L Smith, n.37, at 23 *et seq*.

63 A40093 and A90931 para 12.2

64 A90570 para 9.38: emphasis added

65 A40093, A90931 para 10.25

66 Idem para 12.2.

67 Idem para10.28

68 A similar constraint was placed in relation to the authorisation of A90750 where a "common adviser" could be used across grower groups. (para 9.159)

69 A40093, A90931 para 10.19.

70 A90750 para 9.231. See also A40093, A90931 at paras 11.42–46

71 A90750 para 9.80

72 A90750 para 9.81

73 A90750 para 6.5

74 Idem, para 9.68

75 *Review of the Competition Provisions of the Trade Practices Act*, July 2004

76 Responding to this submission, the Dawson Report (p. 120) noted that "collective bargaining by its very nature, may involve a collective boycott and the Committee would not favour such a restriction. Whether, in the circumstances, a particular form of boycott might be in the public interest, would be for the ACCC to assess after notification. Such an arrangement could, of course, be the subject of an application in authorisation."

77 A40093 and A90931 para 12.7

78 Ibid para 12.19

79 Ibid para 12.25

80 Ibid para 12.25

81 Ibid paras 12.9, 12.22

82 Re VFF Meat Growers Boycott Authorisation [2006] ACompT (21 April 2006)

83 It has been argued that "the best solution to the problem of a durable monopoly or monopsony will be a form of regulation, rather than anti-trust exemption". (Roger G. Noll, *Antitrust Law Journal*, 72, 2005, 619.

84 See C. Fox, W. Howard and M. Pittard, (1995) *Industrial Relations in Australia: Development, Law and Operation*

85 See the Australian Industrial Relations Commission, *Clothing Trades Award 1982*, Print G8966, 7 April 1987, p. 22

86 KPMG Review p 11

87 Ibid p. 131

Appendix

In the course of Review, the processors maintained and KPMG largely accepted, that the growers were earning super-normal profits that would be eliminated by deregulation. They based this argument on the presumption of the existence of rent or goodwill element reflected on recent resale values of farms by comparison with their cost of replacement. This shows that the resale values of the growing facilities of the particular farms (excluding land and house) were much higher than their cost of replacement. This goodwill or economic rent is said to be the capitalised value of the super-normal profit built into the existing price and so making it higher than would exist under competitive conditions. Taking an average of two unrepresentative existing farm models, the Review provided a middle estimate of the present growing fee per bird exceeding the assumed "competitive" price by about 7 cents.

Apart from the unrepresentative selection of farms, the mistaken notion that, given the structure of the industry, an unregulated chicken growing market equates to a more competitive market than the VBINC regulated system, has been commented on above, namely, a market is not competitive in a meaningful sense if only one side—the supply side—is competitive while the demand side remains oligopsonistic/monopsonistic. The assumption of the existence of economic rent in the prescribed fee can be given no credible endorsement as providing a case for deregulation especially as the profit rate built into the Growing Fee Model is an average Bond rate plus 1.5% for risk. First, although the Review was not able to provide an indication of the magnitude of the excess above a competitive fee level because of data limitation, it was prepared to conclude that on balance the costs to the community of the legislative restrictions are likely to exceed benefits.[87] Second, to regard an *unrealised notional capital gain*, which may or may not accrue on the sale of the present farms at some indeterminate future date, as being a source of super-profits and an addition to an assumed competitive price, is a highly artificial rationalisation of the case for the deregulation of an industry whose inherent features are inconsistent with the requirements of a competitive market. In any case, the inflation of land values can occur regardless of the economic activity carried out on it, and should not be regarded as a profit element of that activity.

Third, even assuming there is a goodwill element which may be realised on the sale of farms, given the nature of the industry, there is no reason to believe that the problems of entry, of both processors and growers, are likely to be significantly easier under deregulation; bearing in mind especially the difficulty of obtaining permits for growers in location within acceptable distance from processing plants. In the circumstances, it would be unrealistic to expect that the goodwill element would be eliminated under deregulation.

The other element in the Review's calculations of costs and benefits arises from the assumption of a productivity increase that would ensue following deregulation. On this matter, the Review states that "improvements in productivity are critical to the benefits from a removal of the fee-setting process."[88] The assumption of higher productivity arising from a deregulated market rests on two arguments advanced by the processors, the first one of which was substantially accepted by the Review, and the second, on which the Review was neutral.

The first argument is that the contract under the regulated system required any expansion in output desired by the processor to be drawn from the most efficient smallest grower in the group. This, it is argued, slows down productivity growth because the smallest growers "may not" be as efficient as the largest growers. (p. 65) A number of points arise in this connection. In practice, this requirement is infrequently resorted to by the processors. As noted above, the industry has grown from new entries, from a substantial growth in average size of farms, and from an increase in the output of processors farms. Further, while a large farm may show a higher average product than a small farm, this may not be true for their marginal products, which are the more relevant consideration in the argument. No figures were submitted by the processors to substantiate their argument and it is difficult to place any weight on this point.

Nor can much weight be placed on the Review's unsupported opinion that "it is reasonable to assume that the current arrangements, which do not readily permit development of grower/processor relations specific to the individual needs of each processor's business, operate to improve efficiency. Accordingly, it follows that freeing up these arrangements could lead to significant improvements in efficiency." (p. 109) If this means that the processors, by virtue their stronger market power, could dictate to the individual grower terms to their liking, than that implies a situation not of competition but of greater monopsony/oligopsony power. In which case, regulation, by limiting such power, would bring the industry closer to competitive outcomes. The flexibility of the regulated system to meet the special needs of particular processors was noted above. Furthermore, the VBINC had the power to consider the needs of particular processor and growers on merit.

The second argument advanced by the processor is that the present system generates disincentives for productivity improvements through technical changes; or, in the words of the Review, there is a loss of "dynamic efficiency". (p. 72) No evidence is given to support this assertion. And it cannot be taken seriously given the productivity inducements in the growing fee formula and the task of the VBINC in this connection.

5

Green National Accounting: The Good, the Bad, and the Ugly

Philip Lawn

Flinders University, Adelaide

1. Introduction

Green national accounting has been a topic of conjecture ever since it emerged from the "limits to growth" debate of the early 1970s. As a response to concerns about the environmental impact of a growing economy, green national accounting has evolved considerably and now exists in a variety of forms. In the majority of cases, it exists as a simple environmental cost adjustment to Gross Domestic Product (GDP). In more recent times, however, green national accounting has been broadened to include such economic indicators as the Index of Sustainable Economic Welfare (ISEW) or Genuine Progress Indicator (GPI), and a stock-based indicator called Genuine Savings (GS) that is now the centrepiece of World Bank sustainability studies. At the same time, increasing interest in the concept of ecological sustainability has led to the inclusion of biophysical indicators such as the Ecological Footprint (EF) and measures of "critical natural capital".

Despite many criticisms, most observers regard green national accounting as an important and justifiable reporting development. Indeed, environmental reporting is now included in the United Nations System of National Accounts albeit in the form of environmental satellite accounts to complement rather than supplant the more traditional use of Gross Domestic Product as a measure of national income (UN, 1993). While very few countries are currently reporting the environmental impact of a growing economy directly in their national accounts, many have established stock and flow accounts for specific environmental assets. Furthermore, countries such as Australia have developed a national balance sheet framework to incorporate the value of environmental assets in the calculation of a nation's net worth (see ABS, 1995).

Given the rapid developments in green national accounting over the last thirty-odd years, my aim in this paper is to outline some of these developments, to discuss some of the on-going controversies, to reveal the results of past studies, and to pass judgment on the practices being adopted generally by green national accountants. It is perhaps worth pointing out from the beginning that one of the greatest weaknesses of green national accounting is the regular failure on the part of proponents to develop theoretical foundations to support national accounting revisions. Because many national accounting adjustments are often made on a purely arbitrary basis, the nature of some of the revisions and the valuation methods used have led to false and misleading results. Moreover, they have led to erroneous policy conclusions.

2. Green GDP (Sustainable Net Domestic Product)

2.1. Theoretical issues

As I have just mentioned, green national accounting began in the early 1970s with adjustments to GDP to reflect the environmental cost of a growing economy. For obvious reasons, revised measures of GDP were initially referred to as "green GDP". Invariably where green GDP has been calculated, the adjusted measure of national income is lower than GDP itself. Nonetheless, values of green GDP have exceeded raw measures of GDP in instances where environmental adjustments have been made on the basis of changing resource stocks and where stocks have increased either through the cultivation of renewable resources or the discovery of additional non-renewables (see Repetto et al., 1989; and Young, 1990). There is considerable criticism of this approach and I will return to this debate when I later consider some of the valuation issues associated with green GDP.

Although there are a few commentators arguing against green adjustments to GDP, there is considerable agreement that natural resource depletion represents the consumption of income-generating capital, not income. However, early attempts at measuring green GDP were rather ad hoc and almost exclusively constructed around simple accounting identities that involved GDP as a base item from which the cost of resource depletion was subtracted.

In view of the disquiet surrounding the initial makeshift approaches to green national accounting, it quickly became clear that adjustments to GDP needed to reflect a more appropriate definition of national income. With this in mind, accounting identities were formulated as per the Hicksian concept of income—i.e., that national income should reflect the maximum quantity of goods and services a nation can consume in the present without undermining the capacity to consume the same quantity of goods and services in the future (Hicks, 1946). In this sense, it was universally agreed that a proper measure of national income should be premised on the need to keep income-generating capital intact. Since natural capital depletion, as well as human-made capital depreciation, is not reflected in measures of national income, it was widely accepted that GDP overstated a nation's "true" income.

Still dissatisfied with the national accounting identities emerging within the green accounting literature, Weitzman (1976) employed a dynamic optimisation approach to show that a natural expression for green GDP could arise from a utilitarian maximisation perspective.[1] In doing so, Weitzman argued that measures of green GDP or Hicksian income were best generated from a dynamic optimal growth model. Furthermore, Weitzman demonstrated that shadow prices could be derived to appropriately value the cost of resource depletion and environmental degradation.

Weitzman's approach was a significant departure from early green accounting attempts for a number of reasons. First, it revealed that market prices are not shadow prices if there are imperfections and distortions within the economy. Consequently, the widespread practice of using of market or surrogate prices to value the cost of resource depletion appeared dubious. Second, it highlighted that investment could be treated as discounted future consumption and, as a consequence, be counted as current income. Finally, it formalised green GDP, or what might be referred to as Sustainable Net Domestic Product (SNDP), as the equivalent to the interest generated by an appropriately managed stock of income-generating capital (see also Solow, 1986; and Hartwick, 1996).

While the practice of using simple accounting identities to calculate SNDP has continued since the release of Weitzman's paper, a number of environmental economists believe that Weitzman's dynamic optimisation approach is far superior (e.g., Common, 1990; Hartwick and Olewiler, 1998; Hartwick, 2000; Asheim, 2000). Having said this, the Weitzman approach to green national accounting has not gone uncriticised. One of its glaring weaknesses is that it assumes that the national product—namely, the quantity of goods and services annually produced by domestically located factors of production—is an appropriate indicator of social welfare and something that ought to be maximised (Daly, 1996). By confining the nation's welfare to its consumption of the annual net product, many welfare-related arguments are excluded from the social utility function that is maximised in the dynamic optimisation problem. As a consequence, the shadow prices derived are not entirely accurate.

Another criticism of the Weitzman approach has recently been made by Dasgupta and Maler (2000). They insist that green national accounting must apply to the economy's realised path as opposed to its optimal path. That is, the theory underpinning green adjustments to GDP must be applicable to any feasible economic path so that a more accurate picture is provided of what is actually occurring as opposed to what should be occurring. This leads to two important conclusions. First, while Weitzman's dynamic optimisation approach can valuably inform us of the desirable future pathways of a national economy, it maybe of little use as the basis for a green national accounting methodology. Second, despite distorted market prices leading to potentially undesirable decisions, they are, nonetheless, the signals upon which "actual" resource allocation decisions are made. Hence they can still be used to value the cost of resource depletion and environmental degradation should the aim of green national accounting be one of measuring "what is" rather than "what ought to be" (Cairns, 2002). Thus, while measures of SNDP based on simple accounting identities are imperfect indicators of Hicksian income, they remain useful if their properties and limitations are appreciated and understood (Cairns, 2000 and 2002).

According to England and Harris (1998), what constitutes the most important aspect in terms of calculating SNDP is that the accounting identities used are strictly in keeping with the Hicksian concept of income and subsequent adjustments are based on appropriate valuation techniques. One of the popularly accepted accounting identities for measuring SNDP is that put forward by Daly (1996):

$$SNDP = GDP - HCD - NCD - DRE \tag{1}$$

where:
- SNDP = Sustainable Net Domestic Product
- GDP = Gross Domestic Product
- HCD = human-made capital (producer goods) depreciation
- NCD = natural capital depletion
- DRE = defensive and rehabilitative expenditures

The rationale for the subtractions from GDP in equation (1) is this: could a nation consume its entire GDP in the current year and be in a position to consume the same level of output in the following year? The answer is, of course, no. At the very least, a more accurate measure of a nation's Hicksian income requires the estimated value of human-made capital depreciation to be subtracted from GDP. By human-made capital I mean producer goods such as plant, machinery, and equipment. This, in turn, enables one to obtain a measure of Net Domestic Product (NDP) as per equation (2):

$$NDP = GDP - \text{human-made capital depreciation} \tag{2}$$

For some economists, this depreciation allowance serves as an adequate adjustment to GDP to obtain a proper measure of national income. However, in view of the Hicksian concept of income, a further question remains—that is, could a nation continue to consume its annual NDP without impoverishing itself? Many economists believe not and therefore argue that NDP as well as GDP is not an adequate measure of Hicksian national income.

There are two main reasons why a number of environmental economists believe NDP is an inadequate measure of Hicksian income:

1. NDP fails to make an allowance for natural capital depreciation (depletion)—it only makes an allowance for human-made capital depreciation. Yet if a nation continued to deplete its natural capital by: (a) extracting renewable resources at a rate exceeding their natural

regenerative capacity; (b) failing to invest enough of the proceeds from non-renewable resource depletion to establish renewable resource substitutes; and (c) generating waste levels that exceed the environment's waste assimilative capacity, it could not continue to sustain a level of consumption equal to the NDP. As previously mentioned, natural capital depletion of this kind represents the consumption of income-generating capital, not income.

2. NDP includes a range of regrettable defensive and rehabilitative expenditures that are necessary for a nation to defend itself from the unwanted side-effects of economic activity. These such expenditures, and the goods and services produced, enable a nation to maintain its productive capacity over time (e.g., vehicle repairs, medical procedures following industrial accidents, and salt-water interception and evaporation dams on the Murray-Darling Basin). Consumption of the entire NDP would leave nothing for a nation to set aside for defensive and rehabilitative purposes.[2]

2.2. Valuation issues

Perhaps the two biggest controversies surrounding environmental cost adjustments to GDP relate to the means by which the environmental costs are calculated and whether they should be deducted at all. There are some commentators, such as Rymes (1992), who argue that environmental costs are already taken into account in micro decision-making and reflected to a significant extent in final measures of GDP. To then calculate the aggregate environmental cost *ex post* and deduct it from GDP is tantamount to double-counting or, more accurately, double-deducting.

Others point out that deducting environmental costs is justified given that the lack of markets for environmental services results in the failure or inability of decision-makers at the micro level to take the loss of such services into account. I believe this controversy simply highlights the importance of internalising unpriced environmental services—something that continues to take a back-seat in public policy—which would not only improve decision-making at the micro level, but also result in a more accurate measure of national income at the macro level. In other words, as imperfect as NDP would remain, it would better resemble Hicksian income than at present since the "what is" would more closely approximate the "what ought to be".

Of course, this still leaves open the question as to what proportion of the total environmental cost should be deducted from GDP. Clearly, there is logic in the opposing arguments posited by both Rymes and the green national accountants advocating an environmental cost adjustment. At first thought, it would seem that the solution comes down to estimating the extent to which market prices fail to reflect the full cost of depleted natural capital. This would no doubt remain a point of conjecture and another area of long-running debate.

There is, however, one aspect related to natural capital depletion that ought not to be controversial. Let's assume that the previously mentioned stock accounts for specific environmental assets revealed that a nation was continuing to consume its income-generating natural capital. This would suggest that rational decisions at the micro level might not, when aggregated, be equating to rationality at the macro level of sustainability.[3] Indeed, it could be argued that the extent to which market prices are failing to incorporate the cost of depleted natural capital might closely reflect the extent to which income-generating natural capital is being consumed rather than being maintained. For example, the greater is the extent to which market prices fail to incorporate the cost of environmental damage, the more likely it is that income-generating natural capital would be consumed. Thus, it could be argued that an adjustment to GDP to reflect the consumption of income-generating natural capital would effectively capture the macro sustainability impact of having only some portion of all environmental costs reflected in market prices and, therefore, incorporated into micro decisions.

The need for some sort of adjustment aside, there is considerable debate surrounding the methods used to value the cost of resource depletion. As I mentioned earlier, a number of green GDP studies have involved an adjustment based on annual changes in the market value of stocks of natural resource assets. Two high profiled examples of this approach include the study on Indonesia by Repetto et al. (1989) and another on Australia by Young (1990). In the Indonesian case, the oil price hike of the early 1970s plus the discovery of additional oil reserves resulted in an absurdly high 52.9% rise in Indonesia's

NDP for 1974 (NDP being the term used by Repetto et al. for green GDP).[4] Indonesia's real GDP rose by only 8% in the same year. The subsequent stabilisation of oil prices and a revision of known oil reserves saw the NDP fall to something just exceeding the 1973 figure in 1975. In the same year, real GDP increased by 4.6%.

As for the Australian study, NDP increased from 1980 to 1988 by an average annual rate of 5.4% while real GDP increased over the same period by an average of 3.4% per annum. Despite deductions for land degradation, pollution-related defensive expenditures, and habitat loss due to forestry, their combined impact was overwhelmed by the often large positive change in the value of Australia's mineral deposits. Results of this nature have led El Serafy (1993, 1996a, 1996b, and 2006) to question the use of the changing stock valuation approach. Indeed, according to El Serafy (1993, p. 14):

Since resource stocks are normally much larger than annual extraction rates, re-estimation of their [physical] size, as well as incorporation of changes in value … following price fluctuations, can dwarf the adjustment specifically due to extraction.

Because of the enormous potential for radical changes in green GDP, El Serafy believes the stock valuation approach renders the resulting measures "erratic and economically meaningless" (El Serafy (1993, p. 22). After all, it is possible for a resource-rich country to experience a period of non-renewable resource discoveries yet be consuming its reserves at a very rapid and unsustainable pace. Over the discovery period, the nation's SNDP could be rising—suggesting an increase in sustainable productive capacity—even though it would be clearly operating in an imprudent and unsustainable manner.

The apparent superiority of accounting for the cost of resource depletion over the practice of adjusting GDP for changes in resource stock values leads us to the next main valuation controversy. While there are some observers who argue that the entire cost of natural capital depletion should be deducted from GDP, others do not. According to a group of green national accountants, led by El Serafy (1989, 1996a, 1996b, and 2006), there is a fundamental difference between resources that exist *in situ* and resources that have been extracted for production purposes. The availability of the latter compared to the current unavailability of the former means that the resource extraction process is a value-adding process like any other economic activity. What's more, resource extractors deserve to earn profits as a reward for their contribution to the economic process.[5] However, when resources are made available in the present, they are no longer available for future production purposes. Thereby, only a certain portion of the resource extraction profits should be classed as true income. The remainder, which is very much like a "user cost" in the Keynesian tradition (Keynes, 1936), should be invested to establish suitable replacement assets. It is the user cost that El Serafy believes should be deducted from GDP when calculating Hicksian income. Unfortunately, many green national accounting exercises have wrongly subtracted the full cost of natural capital depletion, thereby ignoring the contribution made by the resource extractive sector (e.g. Repetto et al., 1989; Young, 1990; Van Tongeren et al., 1993; Sorensen, 2000; DGBAS, 2002; ABS, 2002).

Exactly what should be classed as income and what should be deducted from GDP can be ascertained through the use of the following user cost formula (El Serafy, 1989):

$$X / \Pi = 1 - \frac{1}{(1+r)^{n+1}} \tag{3}$$

where:

- X = true income (resource rent)
- Π = total net receipts (gross receipts less extraction costs)
- r = discount rate
- n = number of periods over which the resource is to be liquidated
- $\Pi - X$ = user cost or the amount of total net receipts that must be set aside to establish a replacement asset to ensure a perpetual income stream.

The two key parameters in the determination of the income and user cost components are the number of periods over which the resource is to be liquidated and the chosen discount rate. The greater are the values of these two parameters, the more substantial is the income component and the smaller is the amount that needs to be set aside each period to ensure a perpetual income stream.

The number of periods over which the resource is to be liquidated is relatively easy to estimate and, in the majority of cases, depends on the size of a non-renewable resource deposit as well as expected future resource prices. The major difficulty lies in determining the most appropriate discount rate. According to El Serafy, the chosen discount rate should reflect prudent behaviour on the part of the resource liquidator.

It is at this point that the views on the discount rate depend upon two different schools of thought. The first school of thought—the advocates of the so-called "weak sustainability" position—argue that human-made capital is a near perfect substitute for natural capital. From a sustainability perspective, it matters little if natural capital is in decline so long as the stock of human-made capital expands sufficiently to offset the loss. To achieve sustainability, it is only necessary to maintain a combined stock of natural and human-made capital. Thus the discount rate used in equation (3) should simply reflect the interest rate generated by the replacement asset, whether it be an item of human-made capital or a cultivated renewable resource.

"Strong sustainability" advocates, on the other hand, believe that natural and human-made capital are more or less complements and, as such, sustainability requires the two forms of capital to be non-declining. This means it is necessary to ensure a depleted non-renewable resource is replaced by a renewable resource substitute. It also means that the discount rate used to determine the user cost of resource depletion must equal the interest rate generated by the cultivated renewable resource asset. This, of course, is equivalent to its natural regeneration rate.

What does the choice of discount rate mean in terms of the deduction made for the depletion of natural capital? If a weak sustainability approach is adopted, where it is common for the replacement asset to be a form of human-made capital, the chosen interest rate is usually six or seven per cent. This will almost certainly be higher than the interest rate used if a natural capital asset is established as per the strong sustainability approach. Indeed, for most renewable resources, the natural regeneration rate is approximately two to three per cent and therefore considerably lower than the rate of return on human-made assets (although strong sustainability advocates will point out that the return on a human-made capital asset is entirely dependent on the availability of natural capital, but not vice versa).

Consider, then, a non-renewable resource with a mine life of thirty years. At a discount rate of two per cent, the user cost constitutes 54% of depletion profits (i.e., 46% constitutes income in the Hicksian sense). However, at a discount rate of seven per cent, the user cost constitutes just 12% of depletion profits (i.e., 88% constitutes income). Clearly, the user cost deducted in the calculation of SNDP will be much higher when the strong sustainability stance is embraced. SNDP will be correspondingly lower.

I must confess that I am a strong sustainability advocate for the following reasons. First, human-made capital is nothing more than transformed natural capital. Indeed, to exist, human-made capital requires the presence of natural capital and the low entropy matter-energy it provides.[6] This is a defining condition of complementarity, not substitutability. Second, if human-made capital is a near perfect substitute for natural capital, why has humankind spent so much time and energy accumulating human-made capital when it was clearly endowed with the supposed substitute in such abundance? The answer is twofold:

1. We are better able to transform natural capital into service-yielding goods when equipped with human-made capital than with natural capital alone. This is because human-made capital embodies human know-how that is not naturally embodied in natural capital. However, this only makes human-made capital the "efficient" cause of production, not the "material" cause of production, the latter being a quality that rests solely with natural capital.

2. Human-made capital enables humankind to add value to natural capital. For example, we use manufacturing equipment to convert timber into furniture because a chair is more comfortable to sit on than a raw log. But in the process of increasing the service-yielding qualities of natural capital, human-made capital does not serve as a physical substitute for natural capital. Indeed, the machinery and equipment used to manufacture wooden chairs are totally unproductive unless there are timber logs (natural capital) entering the furniture factory.[7] Of course, it maybe possible to increase the

service yielded by production and consumption activities and therefore sustain the same level of consumer satisfaction from a smaller quantity of resource-providing natural capital. But this involves switching the attention to welfare and away from sustainable productive capacity. It is only the latter which SNDP is designed to measure. More on welfare indicators shortly.

A third reason why I belong to the strong sustainability school of thought is that, again, from a purely physical perspective, any improved technology embodied in human-made capital merely reduces the high entropy waste associated with the transformation of natural capital to goods and services. Naturally, while technological progress continues in this direction, more output can be produced from less resource input (i.e., a greater proportion of the matter-energy embodied in resources ends up in final goods and services while a smaller proportion ends up as immediate production waste). The improvement in the efficiency of production resulting from technological progress can be denoted by the following:

$$E = Q/R \tag{4}$$

where:

- E = the technical efficiency of production
- Q = the matter-energy embodied in final output
- R = the matter-energy embodied in resource inputs.

Unfortunately, there are thermodynamic limits to the reduction of production waste. For this reason, there are limits to the increase in E. Why is this so? The first law of thermodynamics—the law of conservation of energy and matter—dictates that the quantity of matter-energy embodied in the resources used to produce a particular good cannot be less than the matter-energy embodied in the final product. In fact, it must always be a little more thanks to the second law of thermodynamics—the so-called Entropy Law. Together these two laws ensure that 100% production efficiency and the 100% recycling of matter is impossible.[8] It also means that E must be less than a value of one (i.e., $E < 1$) (Lawn, 2003a). As a consequence, any given amount of output requires a minimum irreducible quantity of resource input, as illustrated by Figure 1.

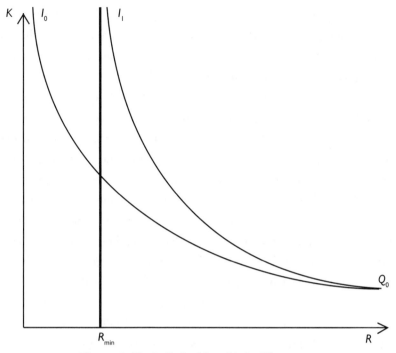

Figure 1: *Physically feasible and infeasible isoquants.*

The two axes in Figure 1 represent the two major categories of production inputs—namely, human-made capital (which might include human labour) and low entropy resources (K and R). In a world where production is hypothetically unconstrained by the first and second laws of thermodynamics, isoquant I_0 represents the different (K, R) combinations capable of producing a given amount of output Q_0. In this Garden of Eden situation, the extremities of isoquant I_0 asymptotically approach the respective K and R axes. However, in a world where *real* production activities take place, the isoquant for the same quantity of output (I_1) confronts a resource asymptote (R_{min}) that exists at the thermodynamic limit of $E = 1$. Clearly, all the (K, R) combinations to the left of R_{min} as represented by I_0 are physically infeasible.[9] To sustain Q_0 over time, it is necessary to ensure the existence of a sufficient stock of natural capital so as to provide nothing less than the minimum resource flow of R_{min}.

All up, it is not possible to keep producing more and more output from less and less resource input. Furthermore, the apparent substitutability between natural and human-made capital resulting from the reduction in production

103

waste is merely a case of "implied substitutability" (Lawn, 1999). It is not a case of substitutability in the strict sense of human-made capital "taking the place of" natural capital. Hence, any continued decline in resource-providing natural capital implies less output at some stage in the future.

It should also be remembered that natural capital provides more than just resources for human-related production and consumption purposes. It serves as a sink for wastes and provides essential life-support services that human-made capital cannot replicate. While the loss of natural capital during the past two hundred years may not have entirely compromised a nation's sustainable productive capacity (indeed, it may have increased it given there was an initial need to accumulate human-made capital), there comes a time when this situation is overturned. Estimates are now emerging that humankind is currently appropriating at least 40% of the world's net primary photosynthetic product for its own purposes (Vitousek et al., 1997). Taking into account the needs of other species to maintain the planet's ecological integrity, this amounts to a human consumption rate of 1.3 Earths (Wackernagel et. al, 1999). In other words, the current rate of global resource consumption exceeds the Earth's capacity to generate a maximum sustainable resource flow by a factor of 30%. It would appear, therefore, that a strong sustainability stance now needs to be adopted and an assumption be made that any depletion of natural capital constitutes a decline in a nation's long-run sustainability. Adjustments to GDP should accordingly reflect this.

2.3. Previous green GDP studies

I have already referred to two past green GDP studies in the case of Repetto et al. (1989) and Young (1990). Other green GDP exercises include studies on Mexico (Van Tongeren et al., 1993), Sweden (Skanberg, 2001), USA (Cobb and Cobb, 1994), Taiwan (DGBAS, 2002), China and Japan (Akita and Nakamura, 2000), and two further studies on Australia (Hill and Hill, 1999; and ABS, 2002). Surprisingly, very few green GDP studies have been undertaken over the last thirty years. Most attention has been given to the concept of green accounting and the theoretical and valuation issues involved. Hence, there has been more talk about green national accounting than practical action. While it is true that the compilation of stock and flow accounts for various resource types is a common practice in most countries, many researchers and national statistical bureaus are far more reticent about taking the additional step of deducting resource depletion costs from GDP.

In view of the different approaches involved in green national accounting, it is very difficult to make international comparisons of green GDP. However, it is clear that the greatest variation in green GDP and standard GDP occurs amongst resource-rich countries with a heavy dependence on the sale of resources for export revenue.

I have previously indicated that the stock valuation approach to green GDP adjustments and the failure to recognise the contribution made by the resource extraction sector can lead to potentially meaningless results. Furthermore, I have argued that adjustments should reflect the strong sustainability position on natural capital depletion. I would therefore like to finish this section on green GDP by reworking the results from the exercise conducted on Indonesia by Repetto et al. (1989). To recall, the Repetto et al. study involved the use of the stock valuation approach to estimate environmental adjustments to GDP. In Table 1, the results of Repetto et al.'s study are revealed (NDP1) plus the results I have derived using El Serafy's user cost approach under weak and strong sustainability conditions (NDP2 and NDP3).

It should be pointed out that Repetto et al.'s exercise included no deduction for human-made capital depreciation or defensive and rehabilitative expenditures. Hence, the final figure for NDP involved just one of the adjustments included in equation (1). In addition, the resource coverage of the Repetto et al. exercise was confined to petroleum, forestry, and soil assets.

To determine the user cost of resource depletion under weak and strong sustainability conditions, as per equation (3), I have assumed that the exhaustion time of each resource type at any point in time is thirty years. I have also assumed that the relevant discount rates under weak and strong sustainability conditions are seven and two per cent respectively. As I indicated earlier, this means that the percentage of the resource rent to be deducted from GDP is 12% under weak sustainability conditions and 54% under the strong sustainability scenario.

Figure 2 shows how the adjustment to GDP using the user cost approach (NDP2 and NDP3) produces a more meaningful result than the method used

Table 1. Indonesia's GDP versus NDP from 1971 to 1984: Repetto et al. (NDP1), El Serafy - weak sustainability (NDP2), El Serafy - strong sustainability (NDP3).

Year	Unadjusted		Repetto et al. (1989)						El Serafy (weak sustainability: 7% discount rate)						El Serafy (strong sustainability: 2% discount rate)					
	GDP	% change	Petrol-eum	Forestry	Soil	Net change	NDP1	% change	Petrol-eum	Forestry	Soil	User cost	NDP2	% change	Petrol-eum	Forestry	Soil	User cost	NDP3	% change
	a	b	c	d	e	f (c+d+e)	g (a+f)	h	j	k	m	n (j+k+m)	p (a+n)	q	r	s	t	u (r+s+t)	v (a+u)	w
1971	5,545		1,527	-312	-89	1,126	6,671		-33	-37	-11	-81	5,464		-148	-168	-48	-364	5,181	
1972	6,067	9.4	337	-354	-83	-100	5,967	-10.6	-57	-42	-10	-110	5,957	9.0	-257	-191	-45	-493	5,574	7.6
1973	6,753	11.3	407	-591	-95	-279	6,474	8.5	-71	-71	-11	-154	6,599	10.8	-321	-319	-51	-691	6,062	8.8
1974	7,296	8.0	3,228	-533	-90	2,605	9,901	52.9	-154	-64	-11	-229	7,067	7.1	-694	-288	-49	-1,031	6,265	3.4
1975	7,631	4.6	-787	-249	-85	-1,121	6,510	-34.2	-147	-30	-10	-187	7,444	5.3	-660	-134	-46	-841	6,790	8.4
1976	8,156	6.9	-187	-423	-74	-684	7,472	14.8	-152	-51	-9	-212	7,944	6.7	-686	-228	-40	-954	7,202	6.1
1977	8,882	8.9	-1,225	-405	-81	-1,711	7,171	-4.0	-174	-49	-10	-233	8,649	8.9	-784	-220	-44	-1,047	7,835	8.8
1978	9,567	7.7	-1,117	-401	-89	-1,607	7,960	11.0	-161	-48	-11	-220	9,347	8.1	-726	-217	-48	-991	8,576	9.5
1979	10,165	6.3	-1,200	-946	-73	-2,219	7,946	-0.2	-166	-114	-9	-288	9,877	5.7	-747	-511	-39	-1,298	8,867	3.4
1980	11,169	9.9	-1,633	-965	-65	-2,663	8,506	7.0	-259	-116	-8	-383	10,786	9.2	-1,167	-521	-35	-1,723	9,446	6.5
1981	12,055	7.9	-1,552	-595	-68	-2,215	9,840	15.7	-301	-71	-8	-380	11,675	8.2	-1,353	-321	-37	-1,711	10,344	9.5
1982	12,325	2.2	-1,158	-551	-55	-1,764	10,561	7.3	-216	-66	-7	-288	12,037	3.1	-970	-298	-30	-1,298	11,027	6.6
1983	12,842	4.2	-1,825	-974	-71	-2,870	9,972	-5.6	-254	-117	-9	-379	12,463	3.5	-1,141	-526	-38	-1,705	11,137	1.0
1984	13,520	5.3	-1,765	-493	-76	-2,334	11,186	12.2	-243	-59	-9	-312	13,208	6.0	-1,095	-266	-41	-1,402	12,118	8.8
Ave. annual growth rate		7.1						4.1						7.0						6.8

Note: Except for percentage changes, all values are measured in billions of Rupiah at 1973 prices

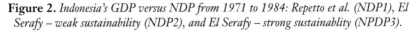

Figure 2. *Indonesia's GDP versus NDP from 1971 to 1984: Repetto et al. (NDP1), El Serafy – weak sustainability (NDP2), and El Serafy – strong sustainablity (NPDP3).*

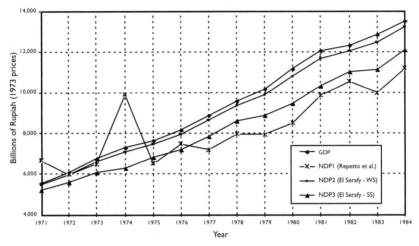

by Repetto et al. (NDP1). The massive rise in NDP1 in 1974 occurs in a year where: (a) the depletion of oil stocks was much larger than 1973 and 1975 (in fact, 1974 was one of the largest depletion years during the study period); (b) when the rate of harvesting and logging damage was also relatively high; and (c) when the rate of soil erosion was the fourth highest of the fourteen years over the study period. One can safely conclude that the radical variation in NDP1, particularly between 1971 and 1978, fails to provide any meaningful information to policy-makers about the annual change in Indonesia's net product. Nor does it serve as a guide to Indonesia's environmental and natural resource use policy.

Conversely, NDP2 and NDP3 are more stable indicators of Indonesia's net product. Despite significant oil discoveries and large oil price increases in 1974 and 1980–81, neither are erroneously reflected in the measure of Indonesia's NDP. As expected, there is a much greater impact on the final measure of NDP in the case of the strong sustainability adjustment which, as I outlined, accounts for the excessive conversion rate of natural capital to final goods and services as well as the lack of sufficient investment in replacement natural capital assets. Above all else, NDP3 is a much better approximation of Indonesia's Hicksian income than NDP2 and especially NDP1.

3. Genuine Savings (GS)

3.1. The shortcomings of SNDP

While SNDP provides a better measure of Hicksian income than GDP, some observers have questioned whether it serves as an adequate indicator of long-run sustainability. This is an important consideration because one of the main reasons for establishing green national accounts is to determine whether a nation's economy is operating on a sustainable pathway and, should it not be, what it means in terms of both future consumption and welfare.

We have seen that the main premise behind Hicksian income and SNDP is the need to keep income-generating capital intact. Let's assume that national accounting adjustments have been made as per equation (1) and the final measure of SNDP for a particular year is lower than GDP. Does the final figure for SNDP indicate a level of output that can be consumed indefinitely? Not necessarily. If a nation continues down the same unsustainable path by consuming its capital assets, it is unlikely that the SNDP calculated for a particular year will be consumable at some point in the future.[10]

So what does SNDP actually indicate? In the end, SNDP merely approximates the output level that would currently be available for consumption if appropriate steps had been taken over the previous year to move the economy onto a sustainable pathway (i.e., had the necessary stocks of capital been maintained). Whether this level of output can be consumed in the long-run depends upon a nation actually taking the appropriate action. Despite this, SNDP is still a very useful statistic, although I agree with Hamilton (1994) that SNDP does not readily translate into a policy signal about the long-run sustainability of a nation's economy. Consequently, SNDP cannot, by itself, be used to develop a national sustainability policy.

It is because of this fact that attention has recently been directed towards a nation's capital stocks. As has already been argued, long-term sustainability ultimately depends on the maintenance of income-generating capital. To accommodate concerns raised by Victor (1991) over the long-run effect of declining capital stocks, Pearce and Atkinson (1993) put forward a savings rule as a potential indicator of sustainable development. Based on earlier work by Hartwick (1977) and Solow (1986), the original savings rule has continuously undergone a rigorous refining process. It is now commonly referred to as Genuine Savings (GS) following the work of Hamilton (1994).

In a nut-shell, GS measures the stock of income-generating capital by comparing the depreciation of a nation's capital stock with its investment in all forms of capital. The use of the term "genuine" was coined by Hamilton to reflect the fact that an appropriate savings rule must include natural capital, not simply human-made capital. There are many equations available to calculate GS (Pearce and Atkinson, 1993; Hamilton, 1994; Pearce et al., 1996; and Dietz and Neumayer, 2006). For the purposes of this paper, GS can be represented by the following:

$$GS = HCI - NFB - HCD - NCD + q.\Delta EHI \qquad (5)$$

where:
- GS = Genuine Savings
- HCI = investment in human-made capital (producer goods)
- NFB = net foreign borrowing
- HCD = human-made capital (producer goods) depreciation
- NCD = natural capital depletion
- $q.\Delta EHI$ = value of environment's augmented/diminished life-support function (q = marginal value of ecosystem health; ΔEHI = change in the ecosystem health index) (Costanza, 1992).

Presumably, long-term sustainability is denoted by a non-negative measure of GS. As with Hicksian income, the value of GS depends very much on how the cost of natural capital depletion is calculated. Assuming that the El Serafy user cost approach is the most appropriate means for deducting depletion costs, a higher value is subtracted if the strong sustainability stance to capital maintenance is adopted relative to the weak sustainability position. Not unlike the calculation of Hicksian income, a number of GS studies have involved the 100% deduction of resource rents which, according to Dietz and Neumayer (2006), results in the underestimation of GS.

This aside, Dietz and Neumayer (2006) believe the plethora of GS investigations has generated two significant green accounting benefits. In the first instance, it has led to the development and subsequent compilation of an extensive database on resource extraction rates, prices, and extraction costs. Second, it has accelerated the theoretical development of the GS concept and brought about more advanced methods to estimate resource rents and the amount to deduct when calculating GS. This latter development has also benefited green GDP calculations.

3.2. Previous GS studies

For whatever reason, there has been a much greater desire to calculate GS than green GDP. Since the first GS study was conducted by Pearce and Atkinson (1993), further investigations have been undertaken by Kunte et al. (1998), Hamilton and Clemens (1999), Neumayer (2000a and 2003), Hamilton (2003), and Dietz and Neumayer (2006), just to name a few.

In the first GS study by Pearce and Atkinson, estimates were derived for eighteen countries from the developed and developing world. Employing their own savings rule, Pearce and Atkinson found that eight of the surveyed nations were sustainable (i.e., net savings were positive). Two nations were found to be marginally sustainable, while the remaining eight nations—all from the developing world—were deemed as having unsustainable economies.

While Pearce and Atkinson have continued to be at the forefront of GS studies, the GS responsibility has been largely taken up by the World Bank. Drawing from United Nations statistics, the World Bank regularly publishes GS measurements for over 150 countries (see World Bank, 2004). Figure 3 reveals the recently released GS estimates of the world economy plus six nation categories. The World Bank typically calculates its GS figures as a percentage of Gross National Product (GNP). The figure shows that the GS of the global economy was positive between 1976 and 2000, as it also was for East Asia, South Asia, and OECD countries. The Caribbean and Latin America experienced negative GS in the mid-1980s, while the GS of Sub-Saharan Africa was negative for most of the study period.

The worst performing nations were those of North Africa and the Middle East. This group of countries collectively experienced negative GS for the entire study period—presumably a result of the failure of many oil-rich Middle Eastern countries to invest a sufficient portion of oil depletion profits into replacement capital assets. Apart from countries that are severely impoverished or rely heavily for income upon the exploitation of non-renewable resources, the remainder of the world appears to be operating sustainably. Of course, this

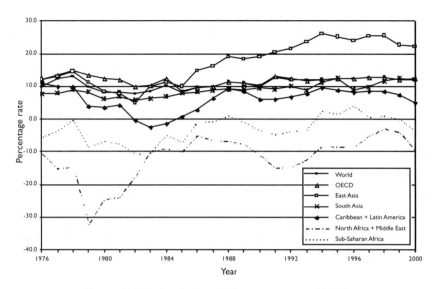

Figure 3. *Genuine Savings (GS) as a percentage of GNP.*

depends on whether World Bank estimates of GS are adequate indicators of long-run sustainability. As we shall soon see, this may not be the case.

Like many previous GS studies, the World Bank calculates the cost of natural capital depreciation by multiplying the volume of resource extraction (R) by the difference between the resource price (P) and the average cost (AC) of extraction:

$$\text{Cost of natural capital depletion} = (P - AC) \times R \tag{6}$$

As in the case of many Hicksian income studies, this method of computation ignores the contribution that the resource extractive sector makes in providing resources to produce and accumulate human-made capital. Hence, the World Bank tends to overestimate the deduction for resource depletion and, as a consequence, underestimate the value of GS.

Neumayer (2000a) has responded by employing the El Serafy user cost method to recalculate the GS of the supposedly unsustainable and marginally unsustainable nations of Sub-Saharan Africa, North Africa, and the Middle East. At no stage did Neumayer seek to use different discount rates to reflect the strong and weak sustainability positions on capital maintenance. Instead, Neumayer applied a blanket discount rate of 4%. What Neumayer discovered was that the two worst performing regions no longer had negative GS. Indeed, the GS of most individual nations within these regions also moved from a negative to a positive value. Moreover, the countries that continued in negative GS territory failed to preserve their stock of human-made capital. Hence, the depletion of natural capital was incidental to the negative GS these countries experienced.

It is interesting to note the comment by Dietz and Neumayer (2006) that the El Serafy and World Bank methods closely converge if the discount rate adopted for the user cost calculations is lower than 4%. This suggests that, as inaccurate as the World Bank estimates of GS might be, they are much closer to strong sustainability measures of GS than those of Neumayer (2000a). If so, a number of countries, albeit a minority of them, have unquestionably operated in an unsustainable manner.

3.3. The shortcomings of GS

Not unlike SNDP, the concept of GS has a number of deficiencies. First, using optimisation principles, it has been shown that a positive value for genuine savings is a necessary but insufficient condition for achieving sustainability (Asheim, 1994; Pezzey and Withagen, 1995). Second, Dietz and Neumayer (2006) have revealed a range of theoretical weaknesses associated with GS. I will not go into details here except to say that these deficiencies relate to the impact on the GS model of exogenous shocks such as technological progress, terms-of-trade effects, and a non-constant discount rate over time.

Finally, despite the strong sustainability approach involving a more austere estimation of the user cost of natural capital depletion, it is still possible for natural capital to decline—which denotes unsustainability—and for GS to be positive.[11] For example, assume that the strong sustainability-based user cost method is employed to calculate GS. Assume, also, that the stock of human-made capital has increased while the stock of natural capital has declined. Should the value of the former exceed the value of the latter, GS will be positive. However, since the maintenance of both human-made and natural capital is necessary to achieve sustainability under strong sustainability conditions, the positive value for GS is misleading.

In the end, a measure of GS simply measures the value of the combined stock of capital if steps had been taken to keep both human-made and natural capital intact. But, like a measure of SNDP, a positive value for GS does not indicate long-term sustainability if a nation fails to introduce the necessary policy measures to ensure appropriate capital maintenance. Hence, regardless of what stance is taken in relation to the user cost calculation of resource depletion, a positive value for GS is only meaningful in the weak sustainability sense.

Alarmingly, an increase in GS in the presence of declining natural capital also points to an excessive rate of conversion of natural to human-made capital since, along with the output generated, neither can be sustained into the future. Economic logic dictates that a nation should maximise the productivity of the limiting factor of production and invest in its increase (Daly, 1996). The limiting factor of production was previously human-made capital while natural capital was once super-abundant. The imbalance now appears to have been reversed and, as such, an increase in GS despite a decline in natural resource assets represents an erroneous investment strategy on the part of contemporary policy-makers.

4. Biophysical indicators

4.1. Progress on indicators

Many advocates of the strong sustainability position on capital maintenance—in particular, ecological economists—have called for the development of biophysical indicators to determine the impact of economic activity on the stock of natural capital. At the bureaucratic level, this has led to the establishment of stock and flow accounts for various environmental assets. These accounts enable the casual observer to ascertain if specific resource assets have been increasing or are in decline. Most national statistical bureaus have also begun the difficult task of measuring biodiversity, the invasiveness of exotic plant and animal species, air quality (including greenhouse emissions and levels of airborne particulate matter), water quality, material waste levels, and native vegetation cover as a percentage of total land mass (e.g., ABS, 2004).

At an academic level, various biophysical indicators have been developed, some of which are now being taken up by governments (see EPA Victoria, 2005). The most publicised biophysical indicator is the Ecological Footprint

(EF) (Wackernagel et al., 1999). A country's EF is the equivalent area of land *required* to both generate the renewable resources and absorb the high entropy wastes needed to sustain economic activity at the current level (Wackernagel and Rees, 1996). To determine whether a nation is depleting its natural capital, the EF is compared with its biocapacity. Biocapacity refers to the amount of *available* land a nation has to both generate an on-going supply of renewable resources and absorb its own and other nation's spillover wastes. Unsustainability occurs if a nation's ecological footprint exceeds its biocapacity.

Table 2 reveals that most of the world's nations have an ecological footprint in excess of their biocapacity (i.e., have an ecological deficit). This is of great concern because it suggests that most national economies have exceeded their maximum sustainable scale. Although trade has been mooted as a possible means of enabling surplus countries to export ecological capacity to deficit countries, Table 2 indicates that the world, as a whole, is in ecological deficit to the tune of –0.7 hectares per person (average global footprint of 2.8 hectares/person compared to the average global biocapacity of 2.1 hectares per person).

Another more recent biophysical indicator initiative has involved the identification of specific components of the natural environment that perform critical and irreplaceable functions—what might be called "critical" natural capital (de Groot et al., 2006).[12] By defining critical natural capital as a set of environmental resources that performs vital environmental functions for which no substitutes currently exist, de Groot et al. have recently developed a "critical natural capital index".[13] The index is now being applied to forests, seas, rivers, and wetlands across the European Union. Since the results of these preliminary studies are still emerging, it is too early to comment on the value of the index as a sustainability indicator.

4.2. The shortcomings of biophysical indicators

The most obvious weakness of biophysical indicators is their accuracy, or lack of it. The natural environment is a complex system that has exceedingly more value than the aggregated value contained in its constituent ecosystems and individual resource assets. Because of this complexity, humankind's ignorance regarding the minimum level of biodiversity, etc., to guarantee sustainability is

Table 2. Ecological footprint of 52 nations as at 1997 (35 nations in ecological deficit).

	Ecological footprint (hectare/capita)	Available biocapacity (hectare/capita)	Ecological surplus (+) or deficit (-)
Argentina	3.9	4.6	0.7
Australia	9.0	14.0	5.0
Austria	4.1	3.1	−1.0
Bangladesh	0.5	0.3	−0.2
Belgium	5.0	1.2	−3.8
Brazil	3.1	6.7	3.6
Canada	7.7	9.6	1.9
Chile	2.5	3.2	0.7
China	1.2	0.8	−0.4
Colombia	2.0	4.1	2.1
Costa Rica	2.5	2.5	0.0
Czech Republic	4.5	4.0	−0.5
Denmark	5.9	5.2	−0.7
Egypt	1.2	0.2	−1.0
Ethiopia	0.8	0.5	−0.3
Finland	6.0	8.6	2.6
France	4.1	4.2	0.1
Germany	5.3	1.9	−3.4
Greece	4.1	1.5	−2.6
Honk Kong	5.1	0.0	−5.1
Hungary	3.1	2.1	−1.0
Iceland	7.4	21.7	14.3
India	0.8	0.5	−0.3
Indonesia	1.4	2.6	1.2
Ireland	5.9	6.5	0.6
Israel	3.4	0.3	−3.1
Italy	4.2	1.3	−2.9
Japan	4.3	0.9	−3.4
Jordan	1.9	0.1	−1.8
Korean Republic	3.4	0.5	−2.9
Malaysia	3.3	3.7	0.4
Mexico	2.6	1.4	−1.2
Netherlands	5.3	1.7	−3.6
New Zealand	7.6	20.4	12.8
Nigeria	1.5	0.6	−0.9
Norway	6.2	6.3	0.1
Pakistan	0.8	0.5	−0.3
Peru	1.6	7.7	6.1
Philippines	1.5	0.9	−0.6
Poland	4.1	2.0	−2.1
Portugal	3.8	2.9	−0.9
Russian Federation	6.0	3.7	−2.3
Singapore	6.9	0.1	−6.8
South Africa	3.2	1.3	−1.9
Spain	3.8	2.2	−1.6
Sweden	5.9	7.0	1.1
Switzerland	5.0	1.8	−3.2
Thailand	2.8	1.2	−1.6
Turkey	2.1	1.3	−0.8
United Kingdom	5.2	1.7	−3.5
United States of America	10.3	6.7	−3.6
Venezuela	3.8	2.7	−1.1
World	2.8	2.1	−0.7
	2.8 ÷ 2.1 = 1.3 Earths		

Note: Hectares per capita expressed in terms of world average yield in 1993.

Source: Wackernagel et al. (1999), pp. 386–387.

ultimately irreducible (Faber et al., 1992). It stands to reason, therefore, that any biophysical indicator designed to measure sustainability cannot possibly be entirely accurate.[14]

As for the EF concept itself, it has been widely criticised by practitioners from a variety of disciplines. The most common criticism is levelled at the EF methodology which appears to overlook the limiting impact of certain critical resources. For example, in Australia, water is often a critical limiting factor in terms of biophysical productivity. Thus, despite Australia's ecological surplus of 5.0 hectares per person (see Table 2), it is highly probable that Australia's limited water resources, particularly in inland areas, would greatly reduce its capacity to exploit such a surplus. If so, the ecological surplus is potentially misleading.

There is one last weakness of biophysical indicators that requires mentioning. It also applies to measures of GS. While stock-based indicators reveal something about the sustainability or otherwise of national economies, they fail to tell us what is happening to human well-being. Despite the logical desirability of a constant or rising stock of income-generating capital, one is still left asking: Is the total quality of life improving?.

5. Indicators of sustainable economic welfare
5.1. Sustainable economic welfare and Fisher's distinction between income and capital
The final green national accounting initiative I wish to talk about concerns a range of indicators designed to measure sustainable economic welfare. Arising from Fisher's (1906) distinction between income and capital, a number of economists have long argued that the ultimate aim of economic activity is the maximisation of economic welfare, not the rate of production. Economic welfare is essentially the difference between the benefits and costs of economic activity. Hence, the establishment of an appropriate macro indicator of economic welfare must involve the identification, measurement, and separation of the major benefits and costs affecting a nation's well-being. Unfortunately, GDP and SNDP fail in this regard. Not only does SNDP count some benefits as costs, it ignores some benefits altogether (e.g., non-paid household and vol-

unteer work), while it wrongly measures the timing of many consumption-related benefits.

In the case of this last point, SNDP counts all current expenditure on consumer durables as a benefit, yet overlooks the benefits provided by the existing stock of consumer durables. In the Fisherian tradition, all current expenditure on consumer durables should be classed as an addition to household capital, not income. Only as the services flow from consumer durables as they depreciate through use should a portion of the value of consumer durables appear as income for a particular year (i.e., income contribution of consumer durables = value of existing stock of consumer durables × annual depreciation rate).

As for the investment in producer goods (plant, machinery, and equipment), it effectively amounts to deprived or sacrificed consumption that is undertaken to provide the means required to generate future consumption. In this sense, current consumption and current net capital investment are the antithesis of each other. The first involves a form of conduct that generates welfare in the present; the second involves a deliberative action in the present that is designed to generate future welfare. To count current net capital investment as welfare-enhancing in the present is logically erroneous.

Does this mean that net capital investment will be overlooked in a measure of sustainable economic welfare? No, because, to a large extent, the benefit of net capital investment will be experienced in future years in terms of future consumption-related welfare. So long as the indicator used to measure sustainable economic welfare for a particular financial year accounts for the expenditure on non-durable consumption goods during that year, past net capital investment—that is, past sacrificed consumption—will be predominantly captured by the indicator. Better still, it will be captured during the period in which the consumption-related welfare is experienced.

Fisher's distinction between income and capital has one further implication. By keeping the two magnitudes separate, it forces one to recognise that since the stock of human-made capital wears out through use, its continual maintenance is a cost not a benefit. It constitutes a cost because the maintenance of human-made capital requires the production of new goods that can only occur if there is an ongoing throughput of matter-energy (the input of low entropy resources and the output of high entropy wastes). This, of course, results in the inevitable loss of some of the source, sink, and life-support services provided by natural capital—the ultimate cost of economic activity (Daly, 1979; Perrings, 1986).[15] As equation (1) showed, the calculation of SNDP requires the cost of natural capital depletion to be subtracted. Nevertheless, because Fisher's distinction between income and capital treats the production of replacement goods as the cost of keeping human-made capital intact, SNDP effectively stands as an index of sustainable cost (Boulding, 1966). While an index of sustainable cost is preferable to an index of unsustainable cost, it scarcely serves as a quality of life indicator.

Given the definition of economic welfare and Fisher's distinction between income and capital, all the indicators of sustainable economic welfare so far established begin, not with GDP as their foundation item, but with private consumption expenditure. In most cases, the value for consumption expenditure is then weighted according to changes in the distribution of income over time. This is due to the fact that the marginal utility of an additional dollar of consumption for a high-income individual is likely to be much less than it is for a low-income person (Robinson, 1962). A more equal distribution of income weights the welfare contribution of private consumption upwards, while a widening gap between rich and poor results in a downward weighting.

Unlike measures of Hicksian national income, and for reasons given above, net investment in human-made capital is excluded from measures of sustainable economic welfare. In addition, the depreciation of existing consumer durables is added to reflect the service provided as they wear out through use. In both cases, the cost of natural capital depletion is subtracted. In all, the difference between Hicksian income and measures of sustainable economic welfare (Fisherian income) can be represented by the following simple identities:[16]

Hicksian income = CON + HCI – PGD – NCD　　　　　　(7)

Fisherian income = CON + CDD – NCD　　　　　　　　(8)

where:
- CON = weighted private consumption + public consumption expenditure

- HCI = investment in human-made capital (producer goods)
- PGD = producer goods depreciation
- NCD = natural capital depletion
- CDD = consumer durables depreciation

5.2. Past studies involving the calculation of sustainable economic welfare

5.2.1. Nordhaus and Tobin's Measure of Economic Welfare (MEW)

The first major calculation of sustainable economic welfare was conducted by Nordhaus and Tobin (1972), which they referred to as a Measure of Economic Welfare (MEW). Based on a study of the USA for the period 1929–1965, Nordhaus and Tobin showed that the MEW rose at a slower rate than GNP and NNP over the same period. In fact, per capita MEW increased at an average annual rate of just 1.0% over the study period and by only 0.4% between the post-WWII years of 1947 and 1965 (1.6% per annum between 1929 and 1947). Per capita NNP, on the other hand, grew at an average annual rate of 1.7%. Believing that the difference in growth rates of NNP and MEW was not too significant, Nordhaus and Tobin concluded that standard macro-economic indicators correlate sufficiently well with economic welfare to make unnecessary the permanent establishment of MEW or any alternative indicator.

It should be said, however, that the study conducted by Nordhaus and Tobin did not include an adjustment for the change in the distribution of income, nor a deduction for the cost of natural capital depletion. Environmental disamenities were confined to the cost of increasing urbanisation which, in comparison to most of the items used to calculate MEW, was quite small. Had the cost of natural capital depletion been included, it is possible that per capita MEW could have been much lower, if not negative, for a number of the years between 1929 and 1965. If so, this may have resulted in Nordhaus and Tobin concluding very differently about their MEW results.

5.2.2. Daly and Cobb's Index of Sustainable Economic Welfare (ISEW)

The next major welfare study was conducted by Daly and Cobb (1989) on the USA for the period 1951–1986.[17] Not entirely satisfied with the methods used by Nordhaus and Tobin or their resulting conclusions, Daly and Cobb sought to calculate a more comprehensive measure of sustainable economic welfare. In so doing, they referred to their revised indicator as an Index of Sustainable Economic Welfare (ISEW).

The ISEW calculated by Daly and Cobb incorporated a number additional items overlooked by Nordhaus and Tobin. They included an adjustment for the welfare effect of a change in the distribution of income, the addition of volunteer work services, the exclusion of non-welfare-increasing defensive expenditures, and deductions for a range of social and environmental costs.

The results of Daly and Cobb's study are summarised in Table 3. The table shows that the average annual increase in per capita ISEW over the entire study period was 0.53% compared to 1.90% for per capita GDP. However, the most startling aspect of these results is the decline in per capita ISEW in both the 1970s (–0.14% p.a.) and for the period 1980–1986 (–1.26% p.a.). Even when the costs of resource depletion and long-term environmental damage are excluded, per capita ISEW* fell in the period 1980–86 at an average annual rate of –0.84%. And while per capita ISEW* increased in the 1970s, the rise is considerably less than the growth rate of per capita GDP (0.66% compared to 2.04%).

Table 3. Annual percentage growth of per capita GDP and per capita ISEW.

Years	Per capita GDP	Per capita ISEW	Per capita ISEW*
1951–1986	1.90	0.53	0.84
1951–1960	0.97	0.84	0.92
1960–1970	2.64	2.01	1.97
1970–1980	2.04	–0.14	0.66
1980–1986	1.84	–1.26	-0.84

* denotes ISEW less costs of resource depletion and long-term environmental damage
Source: Daly and Cobb (1980)

Daly and Cobb concluded that the decline in the America's sustainable economic welfare from about 1970 onwards was due principally to growing income inequality, the exhaustion of key resources, and the failure to invest adequately in the capital assets necessary to sustain the economy into the future. Interestingly, these factors were excluded from Nordhaus and Tobin's (1972) initial exercise.

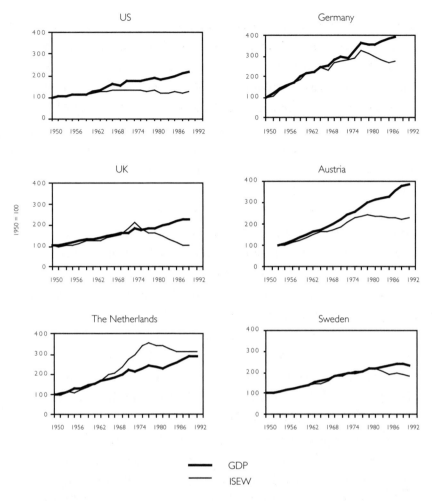

Figure 4. *Comparison of GDP and ISEW for the US, Germany, UK, Austria, The Netherlands, and Sweden (Source: Jackson, T. and Stymne, S. (1996)).*

The work of Daly and Cobb has resulted in a flood of ISEW studies (see, for instance, Diefenbacher, 1994; Moffatt and Wilson, 1994; Rosenberg and Oegema, 1995; Jackson and Stymne, 1996; Jackson et al., 1997; Guenno and Tiezzi, 1998; Castaneda, 1999; and Hamilton, 1999). As ISEW results emerged, it was clearly noticeable that a decline in sustainable economic welfare was a standard feature of all the ISEW studies undertaken of developed nations (see Figure 4). This prompted Max-Neef (1995) to put forward the theory that sustainable economic welfare might naturally cease to rise once real GDP reaches a particular level—what Max-Neef coined as a "threshold hypothesis".

Ecological economists have long argued that the growth in GDP may become undesirable as the additional costs of a growing economy (largely social and environmental in nature) eventually exceed the additional benefits (largely economic in nature). This group of economists now believe that the ISEW studies provide empirical support for their position. They are instead calling for a focus on qualitative improvement (development) and a reduced emphasis on quantitative expansion (growth).

In recent times, the ISEW has been labelled a Genuine Progress Indicator (GPI) (Redefining Progress, 1995). In principle, the GPI differs little to the ISEW. Indeed, the name change was merely brought about by a belief that it would increase its public appeal. More recently, the ISEW has been labelled a Sustainable Net Benefit Index or SNBI to reflect its theoretical underpinnings (Lawn and Sanders, 1999; and Lawn, 2003b).

5.2.3. Lawn and Clarke's GPI study of Australia and Victoria

While many ISEW and GPI studies have been conducted at the national level, few have been undertaken at the state or provincial level.[18] In a recent study by Clarke and Lawn (forthcoming (a) and (b)), the GPI was calculated for Australia, Victoria, and the Rest-of-Australia (Australia minus Victoria). The study period for Clarke and Lawn's GPI exercise was the period 1986–2003.

Because of recently emerging criticisms of the GPI, Lawn and Clarke revised the methodological approach used in many previous GPI exercises and introduced a number of novel techniques to value some of the items used to calculate the GPI. While the items and valuation methods are summarised in Table 4, the GPI for both Victoria and the Rest-of-Australia are revealed in Figure 5.

Figure 5 shows that the sustainable economic welfare of the average Victorian was consistently higher than that of the average person living elsewhere in Australia. Beginning with a difference in per capita GPI of $2,105 per person in 1986, the disparity between Victoria and the Rest-of-Australia increased to $4,331 per person by 2003. In addition, while the percentage rise in per capita GPI over the study period for Victoria was 21.8%, it was only

Table 4. Items and the valuation methods used to calculate the GPI

Item	Welfare contribution	Method of valuation
Consumption expenditure (CON) • CON(1) • CON(2) • CON(3)	+	CON = private + public consumption expenditure • No change to CON • Changes to CON as per Table 1 in Clarke and Lawn (forthcoming (b)) • Changes to CON as per CON(2) plus others described in Table 1 in Clarke and Lawn (forthcoming (b))
Expenditure on consumer durables (ECD)	−	ECD equals the sum of private expenditure on clothing, footwear, furnishings, household equipment, and vehicle purchases
Service from consumer durables (SCD)	+	Service equals the depreciation value of existing consumer durables (depreciation rate of stock assumed to be 10% per annum) • SCD = 0.1 × value of consumer durables
Adjusted consumption • Adjusted CON(1) • Adjusted CON(2) • Adjusted CON(3)		Timing adjustment of consumption benefits • CON(1) - ECD + SCD • CON(2) - ECD + SCD • CON(3) - ECD + SCD
Distribution Index (DI)	±	DI based on the change in income distribution over the study period (1986 = 100.0)
Adjusted consumption (weighted) (**) • Adjusted CON(1) (weighted) • Adjusted CON(2) (weighted) • Adjusted CON(3) (weighted)		Adjusted CON(1), CON(2), and CON(3) weighted by the DI • Adjusted CON(1) ÷ DI × 100 • Adjusted CON(2) ÷ DI × 100 • Adjusted CON(3) ÷ DI × 100
Welfare generated by publicly-provided service capital (**)	+	Welfare assumed to equal 75% of public sector consumption of fixed capital
Value of non-paid household labour (**)	+	Non-paid household labour is valued using the net opportunity cost method
Value of volunteer labour (**)	+	Volunteer labour is valued using the net opportunity cost method
Cost of unemployment, underemployment, and labour underutilisation (**)	−	Calculated by multiplying the CU8 number of under-utilised labour by the estimated cost per unemployed person
Cost of crime (**)	−	Calculated by multiplying various crime indexes by the estimated cost of each crime category
Cost of family breakdown (**)	−	Calculated by multiplying the approximate number of dysfunctional families (based on divorce numbers) by the estimated cost per family breakdown
Change in foreign debt position (**)	±	Annual cost equal to the change in net foreign liabilities from one financial year to the next
Cost of non-renewable resource depletion (*)	−	Calculated by using the El Serafy (1989) 'user cost' formula to determine the amount to set aside to sustain a flow of income equal to that generated by the exhausted resource

Table 4. continued: Items and the valuation methods used to calculate the GPI

Item	Welfare contribution	Method of valuation
Cost of lost agricultural land (*)	–	Calculated to reflect the amount required to compensate citizens for the cumulative impact of past and present agricultural practices
Cost of irrigation water use (*)	–	Calculated to reflect the amount required to compensate citizens for the cumulative impact of excessive irrigation water use
Cost of timber depletion (*)	–	Calculated by using the El Serafy (1989) formula to determine the cost in circumstances where the rate of timber extraction exceeds the rate of timber regeneration and plantation establishment
Cost of air pollution (*)	–	Calculated by weighting the estimated 1992 cost of air pollution by an air pollution index
Cost of urban waster-water pollution (*)	–	Calculated by weighting the estimated 1994 cost of urban waster-water pollution by a waste-water pollution technology index
Cost of long-term environmental damage (*)	–	Calculated to reflect the amount required to compensate citizens for the long-term environmental impact of energy consumption
Lost natural capital services (LNCS)		Sum of (*) items. The LNCS sub-total reflects the cost of sacrificing some of the source, sink, and life-support services provided by natural capital
Ecosystem Health Index (EHI)	±	EHI based on the change in remnant vegetation over the study period
Weighted LNCS (**)		Lost natural capital services (LNCS) weighted by the EHI • LNCS ÷ 100 × EHI
Genuine Progress Indicator (GPI) • GPI(1) • GPI(2) • GPI(3)		Sum of (**) items • Beginning with Adjusted CON(1) (weighted) • Beginning with Adjusted CON(2) (weighted) • Beginning with Adjusted CON(3) (weighted)
Population		Population of study region
Per capita GPI • Per capita GPI(1) • Per capita GPI(2) • Per capita GPI(3)		GPI ÷ population • GPI(1) ÷ population • GPI(2) ÷ population • GPI(3) ÷ population

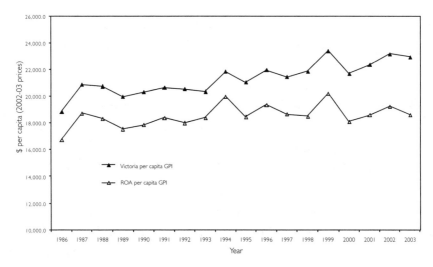

Figure 5. *Per capita GPI of Victoria versus per capita GPI of the Rest of Australia (ROA) (Australia minus Victoria), 1986–2003.*

11.3% for the Rest-of-Australia (an average annual increase of 1.2% compared to 0.6%).

The similar relationship between per capita GPI and the prevailing growth rate of the Victorian and Rest-of-Australian economies raises the possibility that sustainable economic welfare might have been higher in 2003 if the policy emphasis in Victoria and Australia over the last twenty years had been directed more towards distributional equity, resource use efficiency, and natural capital maintenance.

5.3. The shortcomings of indicators of sustainable economic welfare
Like any indicator, the ISEW and GPI are not without their shortcomings. The greatest criticism relates to the valuation methods used in their calculation—in particular, the methods employed to weight personal consumption expenditure, to estimate the cost of defensive and rehabilitative expenditures, and to calculate the cost of resource depletion (see Maler, 1991; Atkinson, 1995; Hamilton, 1994; and Neumayer, 1999 and 2000b). Since an assessment of the contentious valuation methods requires each to be thoroughly examined, I invite people to read Lawn (2005). Having said this, I would like to raise a number of aspects regarding the ISEW, GPI, and related measures that must be addressed if they are to gain broader acceptability.

First, the list of items used to calculate the GPI is not exhaustive—there are many welfare-related factors unaccounted for (e.g., the disutility of certain forms of work and the existence values of natural capital). Quite obviously, it is impossible to incorporate all welfare-related factors into a single index. Nevertheless, it may be beneficial to replace some of the lesser items currently included in the calculation of the GPI with items that can be clearly identified as having greater welfare significance.

Second, as Neumayer (1999) has pointed out, some items dominate others such that it is possible for a small variation in dominant items to overwhelm large variations in the remainder. Overcoming this problem may require decomposition of the dominant items into a number of smaller items.

Third, while the GPI conveys useful information about the current manifestations and immediate effects of past and present activities, it reveals much less about the future impact of current activities. This weakens the policy-guiding relevance of these alternative indexes. It might, therefore, be expedient to accompany the GPI with a second index that incorporates the probable future benefits and costs of current actions (i.e., attributes future benefits and costs to the present calculation of the GPI).

Finally, there is little doubt that some of the valuation methods employed to calculate the GPI are extremely crude and often involve the use of very heroic assumptions. Hence, the values of some items are likely to be, at best, distant approximations of their correct value. Clearly, the advocates of the GPI must continue to strive for more robust valuation methods. There is also a genuine need for a standardised set of items and valuation techniques to allow for a more meaningful welfare comparison of different nations.

6. Concluding comments

Green national accounting is undoubtedly an important development designed to provide a more accurate picture of how national economies are performing on both the economic and environmental fronts. Despite drastic reporting improvements over the years, it is clear that no single indicator will ever be able to convey a complete picture of a nation's sustainable development performance. A suite of indicators is therefore required of which I believe all the major indicators outlined and discussed in this paper are worthy of consideration.

Looking at the indicators individually, green GDP or SNDP is valuable because it indicates the output level available for consumption if a nation takes the steps necessary to move the economy onto a sustainable pathway. But SNDP must be premised on a sound theoretical foundation, such as the Hicksian concept of income, and deductions for resource depletion costs should follow the strong sustainability stance to capital maintenance in view of the growing complementarity between natural and human-made capital. What's more, the changing resource value method should be abandoned in favour of the El Serafy user cost approach.

The failure of SNDP to indicate something about the long-run sustainability of a national economy demands the further development and refinement of capital stock measures—both of the economic and biophysical kind. Being economic-based, GS is a very useful indicator but, like SNDP, requires its calculation to be based on the strong sustainability position. It, too, has its weaknesses, since it doesn't properly inform us of what is happening to the stock of natural capital. A measure of GS must therefore be complemented by biophysical indicators such as the EF and measures of critical natural capital. Having said this, biophysical indicators should never be incorporated directly into national income accounts since they serve as indicators of ecological sustainability, not of economic performance.

Finally, the inability of SNDP and capital stock measures to reveal the impact of a growing economy on a nation's well-being provides a strong case for indicators of sustainable economic welfare, such as the ISEW and the GPI. Since these macro welfare indicators are still in the embryonic stage of development, they will require considerable refinement before achieving policy-guiding status amongst the majority of green national accountants.

One last thought I would like to leave you with. If the progress being made with regard to green national accounting continues at its present rate, we should be well placed to make a judgment about the sustainable performance of nations very soon. Unfortunately, as time goes on, I fear that the emergent picture will be a lot uglier than the rosy picture presented by conventional national accounting aggregates.

References

Akita, T. and Nakamura, Y. (2000), *Green GDP Estimates in China, Indonesia, and Japan: An Aaplication of the UN Environmental and Economic Accounting System*, UNU/IAS.

Anielski, M. (2001), *The Alberta GPI Blueprint: The Genuine Progress Indicator (GPI) Sustainable Well-Being Accounting System*, Pembina Institute for Appropriate Development.

Asheim, G. (1994), "Net national product as an indicator of sustainability", *Scandinavian Journal of Economics* 96, pp. 257–265.

Asheim, G. (2000), "Green national accounting: why and how?", *Environment and Development Economics* 5, pp. 25–48.

Atkinson, G., (1995), *Measuring Sustainable Economic Welfare: A Critique of the UK ISEW*, Working Paper GEC 95-08. Centre for Social and Economic Research on the Global Environment, Norwich and London.

Australian Bureau of Statistics (ABS) (1995), *National Balance Sheets for Australia: Issues and Experimental Estimates, 1989 to 1992*, Occasional Paper, Catalogue No. 5241.0, AGPS, Canberra.

Australian Bureau of Statistics (ABS) (2002), "Accounting for the environment in the national acounts", Feature article in *National Income, Expenditure, and Product: National Accounts*, Catalogue No. 5206.0, AGPS, Canberra.

Australian Bureau of Statistics (ABS) (2004), *Measures of Australia's Progress, 2004*, Catalogue No. 1370.0, AGPS, Canberra.

Boulding, K. (1966), "The economics of the coming spaceship Earth", in H. Jarrett (ed.), *Environmental Quality in a Growing Economy*, John Hopkins University Press, Baltimore, pp. 3–14.

Cairns, R. (2000), "Sustainability accounting and green accounting", *Environment and Development Economics* 5, pp. 49–54.

Cairns, R. (2002), "Green accounting using imperfect, current prices", *Environment and Development Economics* 7, pp. 207–214.

Castaneda, B. (1999), "An index of sustainable economic welfare (ISEW) for Chile", *Ecological Economics* 28, pp. 231–244.

Cobb, C. and Cobb, J. (1994), *The Green National Product*, University Press of America, New York.

Common, M. (1990), *Natural Resource Accounting and Sustainability*, Centre For Resource and Environmental Studies Conference Paper, Australian National University.

Costanza, R. (1992), "Toward an operational definition of ecosystem health", in R. Costanza, B. Norton and B. Haskell (eds.) *Ecosystem Health: New Goals for Environmental Management*, Island Press, Washington DC, pp. 239–256.

Costanza, R., Erickson, J., Fligger, K., Adams, A., Adams, C., Altschuler, B., balter, S., Fisher, B., Hike, J., Kelly, J., Kerr, T., McCauley, M., Montone, K., Rauch, M., Schmiedeskamp, K., Saxton, D., Sparacino, L., Tusinski, W. and Williams, L. (2004), "Estimates of the Genuine Progress Indicator (GPI) for Vermont, Chittendon County, and Burlington from 1950 to 2000", *Ecological Economics* 51, pp. 139–155.

Daly, H. (1979), "Entropy, growth, and the political economy of scarcity", in V. K. Smith (ed.), *Scarcity and Growth Reconsidered*, John Hopkins University Press, Baltimore, pp. 67–94.

Daly, H. (1996), *Beyond Growth: The Economics of Sustainable Development*, Beacon Press, Boston.

Daly, H. and Cobb, J. (1989), *For the Common Good: Redirecting the Economy Toward Community, the Environment*, and a Sustainable Future, Beacon Press, Boston.

Dasgupta, P. and Maler, K-G. (2000), "Green accounting using imperfect, current prices", *Environment and Development Economics* 5, pp. 69–94.

de Groot, R., Hein, L, Kroeze, C., Leemans, R. and Niemeijer, D. (2006), "Indicators and measures of critical natural capital", in P. Lawn (ed.), *Sustainable Development Indicators in Ecological Economics*, Edward Elgar, Cheltenham, UK.

Diefenbacher, H. (1994), "The index of sustainable economic welfare in Germany", in C. Cobb and J. Cobb (eds.), *The Green National Product*, University Press of America, New York.

Dietz, S. and Neumayer, E. (2006), "A critcal appraisal of Genuine Savings as an indicator of sustainability", in P. Lawn (ed.), *Sustainable Development Indicators in Ecological Economics*, Edward Elgar, Cheltenham, UK.

Directorate General of Budget, Accounting, and Statistics (DGBAS) (2002), *Taiwan Area Green GDP Trial Compilation Report*, DGBAS, Taipei.

El Serafy, S. (1989), "The proper calculation of income from depletable natural resources", in Y. Ahmad, S. El Serafy, and E. Lutz (eds.), *Environmental Accounting for Sustainable Development*, World Bank, Washington DC, pp. 10–18.

El Serafy, S. (1993), *Country Macroeconomic Work and Natural Resources*, Environment Working Paper No. 58, World Bank, Washington DC.

El Serafy, S. (1996a), "Weak and strong sustainability: natural resources and national accounting—Part I", *Environmental Taxation and Accounting* 1 (1), pp. 27–48.

El Serafy, S. (1996b), "Natural resources and national accounting: impact on macroeconomic policy—Part II", *Environmental Taxation and Accounting* 1 (2), pp. 38–59.

El Serafy, S. (2006), "The economic rationale for green accounting", in P. Lawn (ed.), *Sustainable Development Indicators in Ecological Economics*, Edward Elgar, Cheltenham, UK.

England, R. and Harris, J. (1998), "Alternatives to gross national product: a critical survey", in F. Ackerman, D. Kiron, N. Goodwin, J. Harris, and K. Gallagher (eds.), *Human Wellbeing and Economic Goals*, Island Press, Washington DC.

EPA Victoria (2005), "Victoria's ecological footprint", *EPA Victoria Information Bulletin*, Publication 975.

Faber, M., Manstetten, R. and Proops, J. (1992), "Toward an open future: ignorance, novelty, and evolution", in R. Costanza, B. Norton and B. Haskell (eds.), *Ecosystem Health: New Goals for Environmental Management*, Island Press, Washington DC, pp. 72–96.

Fisher, I. (1906), *Nature of Capital and Income*, A. M. Kelly, New York.

Guenno, G. and Tiezzi, S. (1998), *An Index of Sustainable Economic Welfare for Italy*, Working Paper 5/98, Fondazione Eni Enrico Mattei, Milan.

Hamilton, C. (1999), "The genuine progress indicator: methodological developments and results from Australia", *Ecological Economics* 30, pp. 13–28.

Hamilton, C. and Denniss, R. (2000), *Tracking Well-being in Australia: The Genuine Progress Indicator 2000*, Australia Institute Discussion Paper Number 35, December 2000.

Hamilton, K. (1994), "Green adjustments to GDP", *Resources Policy* 20 (3), 155–168.

Hamilton, K. (2003), "Sustaining economic welfare: estimating changes in total and per capita wealth", *Environment, Development, and Sustainability* 5, pp. 419–436.

Hamilton, K., Pearce, D., Atkinson, G., Gomez-Lobo, A. and Young, C. (1993), *The Policy Implications of Natural Resource and Environmental Accounting*, Centre for Social and Economic Research on the Global Environment, London.

Hamilton, K. and Clemens, M. (1999), "Genuine savings rates in developing countries", *World Bank Economic Review* 13, pp. 333–356.

Hartwick, J. (1977), "Intergenerational equity and the investing of rents from exhaustible resources", *American Economic Review* 66, pp. 972–974.

Hartwick, J. (1996), "Constant consumption as interest on capital", *Scandinavian Journal of Economics* 98 (3), pp. 439–443.

Hartwick, J. (2000), *National Accounting and Capital*, Edward Elgar, Cheltenham, UK.

Hartwick, J. and Olewiler, N. (1998), *The Economics of Natural Resource Use*, Second Edition, Addison-Wesley, Reading, MA.

Hicks, J, (1946), *Value and Capital*, Second Edition, Clarendon, London.

Hill, P. and Hill, R. (1999), *A New Conceptual Approach to the Measurement of Capital Gains, Depletion, and Net National Product*, Discussion Paper 99/9, School of Economics, University of New South Wales.

Jackson, T. and Stymne, S. (1996), *Sustainable Economic Welfare in Sweden: A Pilot Index 1950–1992*, Stockholm Environment Institute, Stockholm.

Jackson, T., Laing, F., MacGillivray, A. Marks, N., Ralls, J. and Styme, S. (1997), *An Index of Sustainable Economic Welfare for the UK, 1950–1996*, University of Surrey Centre for Environmental Strategy, Guildford.

Keynes, J. M. (1936), *The General Theory of Employment, Interest, and Money*, Harcourt Brace, New York.

Kunte, A. Hamilton, K., Dixon, J. and Clemens, M. (1998), *Estimating National Wealth: Methodology and Results*, World bank, Washington DC.

Lawn, P. (1999), "On Georgescu-Roegen's contribution to ecological economics", *Ecological Economics* 29 (1), pp. 5–8.

Lawn, P. (2003a), "How important is natural capital in terms of sustaining real output? Revisiting the natural capital/human-made capital substitutability debate", *International Journal of Global Environmental Issues* 3 (4), pp. 418–435.

Lawn, P. (2003b), "A theoretical foundation to support the Index of Sustainable Economic Welfare (ISEW), Genuine Progress Indicator (GPI), and other related measures", *Ecological Economics* 44, pp. 105–118.

Lawn. P. (2004), "Response to William J. Mates' paper: Income, investment, and sustainability", *Ecological Economics* 48, pp. 5–7.

Lawn, P. (2005), "An assessment of the valuation methods used to calculate the Index of Sustainable Economic Welfare (ISEW), Genuine Progress Indicator (GPI), and Sustainable Net Benefit Index (SNBI)", *Environment, Development, and Sustainability* 7, pp. 185–208.

Lawn, P. (ed.) (2006), *Sustainable Development Indicators in Ecological Economics*, Edward Elgar, Cheltenham, UK.

Lawn, P. and Sanders, R. (1999), "Has Australia surpassed its optimal macroeconomic scale? Finding out with the aid of benefit and cost accounts and a sustainable net benefit index", *Ecological Economics* 28 (2), pp. 213–229.

Lawn, P. and Clarke, M. (forthcoming (a)), "Measuring Victoria's genuine progress: a Genuine Progress Indicator (GPI) for Victoria", *Economic Papers*.

Lawn, P. and Clarke, M. (forthcoming (b)), "Comparing Australia's genuine progress to its economic growth performance", *International Journal of Green Economics*.

Maler, K. (1991), "National accounts and environmental resources", *Environmental and Resource Economics* 1, pp. 1–15.

Mates, W. (2004), "Income, investment, and sustainability", *Ecological Economics* 48, pp. 3–5.

Max-Neef, M. (1995), "Economic growth and quality of life", *Ecological Economics* 15 (2), pp. 115–118.

Moffat, I. and Wilson, M. (1994), "An index of sustainable economic welfare for Scotland, 1980–1991", *International Journal of Sustainable Development and World Ecology* 1, pp. 264–291.

Neumayer, E. (1999), "The ISEW—not an index of sustainable economic welfare", *Social Indicators Research* 48, pp. 77–101.

Neumayer, E. (2000a), "Resource accounting in measures of unsustainability: challenging the World Bank's conclusions", *Environmental and Resource Economics* 15, pp. 257–278.

Neumayer, E. (2000b), "On the methodology of the ISEW, GPI, and related measures: some constructive suggestions and some doubt on the threshold hypothesis", *Ecological Economics* 34, pp. 347–361.

Neumayer, E. (2003), *Weak Versus Strong Sustainability: Exploring the Limits of Two Opposing Paradigms*, Second Revised Edition, Edward Elgar, Cheltenham, UK.

Nordhaus, W. and Tobin, J. (1972), "Is economic growth obsolete?", in *Economic Growth*, The National Bureau of Economic Research, Fiftieth Anniversary Colloquium, Columbia University Press, New York.

Pearce, D. and Atkinson, G. (1993), "Capital theory and the measurement of of sustainable development: an indicator of weak sustainability", *Ecological Economics* 8, pp. 103–108.

Pearce, D., Hamilton, K. and Atkinson, G. (1996), "Measuring sustainable development: progress on indicators", *Environment and Development Economics* 1 (1), pp. 85–101.

Perrings, C. (1986), "Conservation of mass and instability in a dynamic economy-environment system", *Journal of Environmental Economics and Management* 13, pp. 199–211.

Pezzey, J. and Withagen, C. (1995), "The rise, fall, and sustainability of capital-resource economies", *Scandinavian Journal of Economics* 100, pp. 513–527.

Redefining Progress (1995), "Gross production vs genuine progress", excerpt from *The Genuine Progress Indicator: Summary of Data and Methodology*, San Francisco.

Robinson, J. (1962), *Economic Philosophy*, C.A.Watts & Co., London.

Rosenberg, K. and Oegema, T. (1995), *A Pilot ISEW for The Netherlands 1950–1992*, Instituut Voor Milieu—En Systeemanalyse, Amsterdam.

Rymes, T. (1992), "Some theoretical problems in accounting for sustainable consumption", *Carleton Economic Papers*, 92-02.

Skanberg, K. (2001), *Constructing a Partially Environmentally Adjusted Net Domestic Product For Sweden, 1993 and 1997*, Konjunktur Institute Working paper 76.

Solow, R. (1986), "On the intergenerational allocation of natural resources", *Scandinavian Journal of Economics* 88 (1), pp. 141–149.

Sorensen, K. (2000), *Environmental Accounts in Norway*, Paper prepared for the 26th General Conference of the International Association for Research in Income and Wealth, Cracow, Poland, August 27–September 2, 2000.

United Nations (UN) (1993), *Integrated Environmental and Economic Accounting*, Series F, No. 61, New York.

Van Tongeren, J., Schweinfest, S., Lutz, E., Gomez Luna, M. and Martin, G. (1993), "Integrated economic and environmental accounting: a case study for Mexico", in E. Lutz (ed.), *Toward Improved Accounting for the Environment*, World Bank, Washington DC, pp. 85–107.

Victor, P. (1991), "Indicators of sustainable development: some lessons from capital theory", *Ecological Economics* 4, pp. 191–213.

Vitousek, P. Mooney, M., Lubchenco, J. and Melillo, J. (1997), "Human domination of Earth's ecosystems", *Science* 277, pp. 494–499.

Wackernagel, M. and Rees, W. (1996), *Our Ecological Footprint: Reducing Human Impact on the Earth*, New Society Publishers, Gabriola Island.

Wackernagel, M., Onisto, L., Bello, P., Callejas Linares, A., Susana Lopez Falfan, S., Mendez Garcia, J., Suarez Guerrero, A. I., and Suarez Guerrero, Ma. G. (1999) "National natural capital accounting with the ecological footprint concept", *Ecological Economics* 29, 375–390.

Weitzman, M. (1976), "On the welfare significance of national product in a dynamic economy", *Quarterly Journal of Economics* 90, pp. 156–162.

World Bank (2004), *Adjusted Net Savings Data*, World Bank, Washington DC (http://lnwb18.worldbank.org/ESSD/essdext.nsf/44ByDocName/GreenAccountingWealthEstimates)

Young, M. (1990), "Natural resource accounting" in M. Common and S. Dovers (eds.), *Moving Toward Global Sustainability: Policies and Implications for Australia*, Centre for Continuing Education, Australian National University, Canberra.

Zolotas, X. (1981), *Economic Growth and Declining Social Welfare*, New York University Press, New York.

Notes

1 Weitzman's original approach has been further developed by Solow (1986) and Hartwick (1996, 1998, 2000).

2 It should be noted that the category of defensive and rehabilitative expenditures exceeds what is required simply to maintain a nation's productive capacity. Many such expenditures protect a nation's welfare without necessarily impacting on productive capacity (e.g., crime prevention measures, private vehicle accident repairs, and cosmetic medical and dental procedures). In the calculation of SNDP, these expenditures should not be deducted from NDP.

3 Economists are all too aware that micro rationality need not equate to rationality at the macro level with the so-called "fallacy of composition".

4 The change in the value of oil reserves was adjusted for inflation only, meaning that the aggregate value of Indonesia's oil reserves appreciated massively in 1974.

5 For example, retailers earn a profit by providing a location—namely, a shop—to promote and sell the goods produced by manufacturers. While retailers do not produce anything tangible, the service they provide for both producers and consumers can be considered a value-adding activity. They are rewarded accordingly.

6 To understand what is meant by low and high entropy matter-energy, the importance of the first and second laws of thermodynamics must be revealed. The first law of thermodynamics is the *law of conservation of energy and matter*. It declares that energy and matter can never be created or destroyed. The second law is the *Entropy Law*. It declares that whenever energy is used in physical transformation processes, the amount of usable or "available" energy always declines. While the first law ensures the maintenance of a given quantity of energy and matter, the Entropy Law determines that which is usable. This is critical since, from a physical viewpoint, it is not the total quantity of matter-energy that is of primary concern, but the amount that exists in a readily available form.

   The best way to illustrate the relevance of these two laws is to provide a simple example. Consider a piece of coal. When it is burned, the matter-energy embodied within the coal is transformed into heat and ash. While the first law ensures the total amount of matter-energy in the heat and ashes equals that previously embodied in the piece of coal, the second law ensures the usable quantity of matter-energy does not. In other words, the dispersed heat and ashes can no longer be used in a way similar to the original piece of coal. To make matters worse, any attempt to reconcentrate the dispersed matter-energy, which requires the input of additional energy, results in more usable energy being expended than that reconcentrated. Hence, all physical transformation processes involve an irrevocable loss of available energy or what is sometimes referred to as a "net entropy deficit". This enables one to understand the use of the term *low entropy* and to distinguish it from *high entropy*. Low entropy refers to a highly ordered physical structure embodying energy and matter in a readily available form, such as a piece of coal. Conversely, high entropy refers to a highly disordered and degraded physical structure embodying energy and matter that is, by itself, in an unusable or unavailable from, such as heat and ash. By definition, the matter-energy used in economic processes can be considered a low entropy resource whereas unusable by-products can be considered high entropy wastes.

7   There are also the resources required to power the machinery and to extract and transport the logs to the factory. Even the labour employed to operate the machinery must be adequately nourished, housed, and clothed via the exploitation of various natural resources.

8   Thanks to the Entropy Law, the recycling of energy is not possible at all.

9   Indeed, because of this restriction, it has been shown by Lawn (2003) that the elasticity of substitution between natural and human-made capital is always less than one. A value of one or more is required to demonstrate substitutability between the two forms of capital.

10 This is likely to be the case even if SNDP continues to increase over a lengthy period since it is possible, for some time at least, for positive output additions to exceed subtractions made for natural capital depletion.

11 This is due largely to the fact that the GS equation exists in a purely additive/subtractive form. The GS equation therefore implies potential substitutability of one element in the equation for another. The equation requires a "subject to" which, in the strong sustainability case, is the need for a non-negative change in natural capital.

12 See the special section on "Identifying critical natural capital" in Volume 44 (2–3) of *Ecological Economics* (2003).

13 Based on a definition of critical natural capital outlined by Ekins et al. (2003).

14 This doesn't mean that sustainability indicators are of no value. It simply means it is sensible to operate economies somewhere short of the estimated maximum scale.

15 The lost source, sink, and life-support services provided by natural capital are regarded as the ultimate cost of the economic process because natural capital is the original source of all economic activity. If one traces the economic process from its final conclusion back to its original source—namely, natural capital—all transactions cancel out (i.e., the seller receives what the buyer pays). What one is left with is the price paid to have low entropy resources extracted from the natural

environment. Should this price reflect all sacrificed natural capital services, it would be equivalent to the uncancelled or ultimate cost of economic activity.

16 These identities appear in Lawn (2004) and are variation on equations first presented by Mates (2004).

17 A lesser known study was conducted on the USA for the period 1950–1977 by Zolotas (1981).

18 Exceptions include Costanza et al. (2004) for the US state of Vermont and Anielski (2001) for the Canadian province of Alberta.

6

Wagner's Law and the Theory of Public Goods

D. Leonard, J. McMillan and R. Manning*

Abstract

Wagner's Law asserts that, as a nation grows, public expenditure will rise not only in absolute terms but also relative to national income. This note examines the relationship between this century-old empirical hypothesis and the theory of public goods.

1. Introduction

Wagner's Law, formulated over a century ago, asserts that, as a nation grows, public expenditure will rise not only in absolute terms but also relative to national income. In its modern version it states that the share of national income devoted to public expenditure rises as per capita income rises.[1]

Several attempts have been made to test empirically the validity of Wagner's Law,[2] with some tests appearing to confirm and others to contradict the hypothesis. (This inconsistency is partly the result of confusion over what should be measured.[3]) Alesina and Wacziarg (1998) study the effect of both country size and openness on the size of government. Their model is a special case of ours.

A number of explanations for Wagner's Law have been offered: the increasing need for government intervention as industrialization proceeds, because of greater division of labour, increasing urbanization and increasing scale of investment (Wagner, summarized in Bird (1971, pp. 2–3)); the occurrence of technical progress at a faster rate in the private than in the public sector (Spann, 1977); and the tendency for bureaucracies to grow of their own accord (Buchanan and Tullock, 1977). This paper considers a further possible justification for Wagner's Law: the collective-consumption nature of public expenditure.

Wagner believed that the main function of the state was the provision of non-material goods and services which could not, by their very nature, be individually sold (Wagner, 1958, p.4). This note examines to what extent Wagner's empirical hypothesis is consistent with the pure theory of public expenditure (as formulated by Samuelson, 1954). The empirical studies seek to answer the positive question of whether or not public expenditure actually grows in accord with Wagner's Law. This paper looks at the normative question of under what circumstances such public sector growth is optimal.

2. The Model

Among the justifications offered by Wagner for his law were that (i) most public services are luxury goods, and (ii) the state will naturally take over new economic activities with increasing returns (Bird, 1971, p.2). If these statements were true, Wagner's Law would clearly follow. However, our analysis abstracts from them, and we assume (a) consumers have homothetic preferences (which rules out luxury goods), and (b) the function defining production possibilities is homogeneous (thus a proportional increase in private and public goods does not change their relative prices, and there is no built-in bias for or against Wagner's Law). In addition, the following simplifying assumptions are made: (c) only two goods are produced, one a private good in total amount X and one a (Samuelsonian) public good in amount Z; (d) there is a single factor of production, say capital;[4] and (e) there are m identical consumers, each with a strictly concave homogeneous, twice differentiable utility function $U(x, Z)$, where each individual's private good consumption is $x = X/m$. Production is constrained by a resource use function $F(X, Z) \leq km$, where F is monotonic increasing, strictly convex, and twice differentiable. k is *per capita* endowment. (The model used by Alesina and Wacziarg (1998) to analyse the effect of country size on the size of government is a special case of ours, with a CES utility function and a linear production constraint.)

The efficiency conditions are

$$F(X, Z) = km \qquad (1)$$

$$mr = t \qquad (2)$$

where $r = U_Z/U_x$ is the marginal rate of substitution for any individual and $t = F_Z/F_X$ is the marginal rate of transformation (so that equation (2) is the Samuelson (1954) summation condition). Because F and U are homogeneous, t and r are univariate functions of Z/X and Z/x respectively, with $t' > 0$ and $r' < 0$ almost everywhere, because of strict concavity of U and strict convexity of F.

By Euler's Theorem,

$$XF_X + ZF_Z = \alpha mk \qquad (3)$$

where α (a positive constant) is the degree of homogeneity of F. If the prices of the private and public good are, respectively, F_X and F_Z then per capita income is αk.

Totally differentiating the efficiency conditions (1) and (2) yields respectively

$$F_X \, dX + F_Z \, dZ = kdm + mdk \qquad (4)$$

$$\left(r + mr'\frac{Z}{X}\right)dm + \left(\frac{m^2 r' - t'}{X}\right)dZ - \left(\frac{m^2 r' - t'}{X}\right)\frac{Z}{X}dX = 0 \qquad (5)$$

Equations (4) and (5) show how the optimal production of public good Z and private good X behave as the economy expands.[5] In this model the economy can grow either because of increases in per capita endowment or because of population increase. Sections 3 and 4 examine these cases in turn.

3. Changes in Per Capita Income

Suppose the population m is constant. Setting $dm = 0$, equation (5) yields

$$\frac{dZ}{Z} = \frac{dX}{X} \qquad (6)$$

Substituting in (4) and using (3) we obtain

$$\frac{dX}{d(k\alpha)} = \frac{X}{k\alpha^2} > 0 \qquad (7)$$

$$\frac{dZ}{d(k\alpha)} = \frac{Z}{k\alpha^2} > 0 \qquad (8)$$

Thus, as per capita income rises private and public goods outputs rise in the same proportion. Therefore

$$\frac{d}{d(k\alpha)} \left(\frac{Z}{X}\right) = 0 \tag{9}$$

so that

$$\frac{dt}{d(k\alpha)} = 0 \tag{10}$$

and

$$\frac{dr}{d(k\alpha)} = 0 \tag{11}$$

Then also

$$\frac{d}{d(k\alpha)} \left(\frac{ZF_Z}{XF_X}\right) = 0 \tag{12}$$

Therefore the ratio of private to public goods, as well as their prices, and the ratio of private to public good expenditures all remain constant as per capita income increases.

According to Michas (1975), the relevant elasticity concept for examining Wagner's Law is the elasticity of per capita public expenditure with respect to per capita GNP. In this model, this is

$$\eta = \frac{d}{d(k\alpha)} \frac{ZF_Z}{m} \frac{k\alpha}{ZF_Z/m} \tag{13}$$

Using (7) and (8) we get

$$\frac{dZF_Z}{d(k\alpha)} = \frac{1}{k\alpha^2} (ZF_Z + Z^2F_{ZZ} + ZXF_{XZ}) = \frac{ZF_X}{k\alpha} \tag{14}$$

by (A4) of the Appendix. Thus

$$\eta = 1 \tag{15}$$

That is, public expenditure remains a constant proportion of income as per capita income grows.

The public good character of state expenditure alone does not imply Wagner's Law if population is constant while per capita income grows.

4. Changes in Population

Suppose that as m increases the economy is replicated in such a way that per capita wealth remains constant. Putting dk = 0 in equations (4) and (5) and re-arranging,

$$\frac{dZ}{dm} = \frac{X^2 rm - m^2 r' \, Z^2 t + t' \, ZX^2 + t'X^2 + Z^2}{(X + Zt)\,(t' - m^2 r')m} \geq 0 \qquad (16)$$

The absolute level of public good supply rises with a rise in population. To look at the effect of rising m on relative public good supply, totally differentiate equation (2) with m and Z/X as the arguments:

$$dm \cdot r + m \cdot r\left(\left(\frac{Z}{X}\right) dm + md\left(\frac{Z}{X}\right)\right) = t'd\left(\frac{Z}{X}\right) \qquad (17)$$

Hence

$$\frac{d}{dm}\left(\frac{Z}{X}\right) = \frac{r + mr'\left(\frac{Z}{X}\right)}{t' - m^2 r} \qquad (18)$$

The denominator of (18) is positive. Relative public good supply rises with rising population provided

$$r + mr'\left(\frac{Z}{X}\right) \geq 0 \qquad (19)$$

Define ζ to be a consumer's elasticity of substitution

$$\zeta = \frac{d(x/Z)}{d(U_Z/U_X)} \cdot \frac{U_Z/U_X}{x/Z} = \frac{-rX}{r'mZ} \qquad (20)$$

(18), (19) and (20) imply that

$$\frac{d}{dm}\left(\frac{Z}{X}\right) \gtreqless 0 \quad \text{as} \quad \zeta \gtreqless 1 \qquad (21)$$

The ratio of provisions of public to private good increases when population grows provided $\zeta > 1$.

(This result was independently obtained by Alesina and Wacziarg (1998) in a special case of our model, with a CES utility function.)

Consider now how the ratio of the price of the public good to the price of the private good alters when population rises.

$$\frac{d}{dm}\left(\frac{F_Z}{F_X}\right) = \frac{d}{dm}(t) = \frac{r + mr'\left(\frac{Z}{X}\right)t'}{t' + m^2 r'} \tag{22}$$

(from totally differentiating (1) and (2) and using (16)). Thus

$$\frac{dt}{dm} \gtreqless 0 \quad \text{as} \quad \zeta \gtreqless 1 \tag{23}$$

Now

$$\frac{d}{dm}\left(\frac{ZF_Z}{XF_X}\right) = t\frac{d}{dm}\left(\frac{Z}{X}\right) + \frac{Z}{X}\frac{dt}{dm} = \frac{r(1 - 1/\zeta)}{t' - m^2 r'}\left(t + t'\left(\frac{Z}{X}\right)\right) \tag{24}$$

It follows that

$$\frac{d}{dm}\frac{ZF_Z}{XF_X} \gtreqless 0 \quad \text{as} \quad \zeta \gtreqless 1 \tag{25}$$

The ratio of public to private expenditure (and hence the ratio of public expenditure to national income) rises as population increases provided the consumer's elasticity of substitution exceeds one. To see this, consider the adjustment to a population increase (from an initially optimal allocation). Outputs of private and public goods can be increased keeping their ratio constant. Then the output price ratio is unchanged, but for each consumer the price of the public good relative to the price of the private good falls in proportion to the population increase. Furthermore, for each consumer the ratio of private to public good consumption falls in proportion to the population increase. Therefore the proposed adjustment will maintain the share of each consumer's budget spent on the public good.

This is optimal if and only if $\zeta = 1$.

If $\zeta > 1$ the adjustment is sub-optimal, and the ratio of public good to private good output should be increased (so that public goods have a higher relative price and a bigger share of consumers' budgets is spent on them). If $\zeta < 1$ the opposite holds.

5. Conclusion

Under neutral assumptions on preferences and technology this note examined a theoretical justification of Wagner's Law: the assumed collective-consumption nature of public expenditure.[6]

A change in wealth but not in population does not affect the optimal ratio of outputs of public to private goods, or the ratio of their values.

An increase in population but not in per capita income increases (decreases) the optimal ratio of outputs of public to private goods and the ratio of their values if and only if the typical consumer's elasticity of substitution exceeds (is less than) one.

Even though it may seem impossible in reality to distinguish the effects of increases in population and per capita income, this analysis shows that the latter has no influence on the GNP share of public goods.

Notes

*   Leonard: Flinders Business School, Flinders University, Adelaide; McMillan†, Manning†.

1   Wagner stated this law in Wagner (1883); parts of this work are available in English translation as Wagner (1958). For a detailed history of the controversy surrounding Wagner's hypothesis, see Pryor (1968, pp. 451–454); and for modern reformulations and critiques see Peacock and Wiseman (1967) and Bird (1971).

2   See for example Gupta (1967, 1968), Goffman and Mahar (1968), Lall (1969), Musgrave (1969), Bird (1970), Gandhi (1971), Tussing and Henning (1974), Chester (1977), Wagner and Weber (1977) and Alesina and Wacziarg (1998).

3   See Goffman (1965) and Michas (1975).

4   The analysis can be interpreted as permitting many factors of production, provided that growth does not alter their ratios.

5   Although Wagner's Law is normally expressed as a description of the effect of economic growth on public expenditure, it is essentially a comparative static (rather than a dynamic) proposition, comparing public expenditures at different levels of national income. On the dynamic interactions of public goods supply and economic growth, see McMillan (1978) and McMillan and Manning (1979).

6   While it is clearly not the case that all public expenditure produces public goods (or, indeed, that all public goods are produced by the government) it is true that much public expenditure is on goods which have externalities associated with them; that is, goods near the public-good end of the commodity spectrum. (See Bird [1971, p.5] for a classification of government expenditures in terms of their degree of "publicness".)

References

Alesina, A and R Wacziarg (1998), "Openness, Country Size and Government" *Journal of Public Economics* 69: 305–321.

Bird, R.M. (1970), *The Growth of Government Spending in Canada*, Toronto, Canadian Tax Foundation.

Bird, R.M. (1971), "Wagner's 'Law' of Expanding State Activity", *Public Finance* 26: 1–26.

Buchanan, J.M. and G. Tullock (1977), "The Expanding Public Sector: Wagner Squared", *Public Choice* 31: 147–150.

Chester, e. (1977), "Some Social and Economic Determinants of Non-Military Public Spending", *Public Finance* 2: 176–185.

Gandhi, V. P. (1971), "Wagner's Law of Public Expenditure: Do Recent Cross-Section Studies Confirm It?" *Public Finance* 26: 44–56.

Goffman, I.J. (1965), "On the Empirical Testing of Wagner's Law: A Technical Note", *Public Finance* 23: 359–366.

Goffman, I.J. and D.J. Mahar (1968), "The Growth of Public Expenditures in Selected Developing Nations: Six Caribbean Countries 1940–65", *Public Finance* 26: 57–74.

Gupta, S.B. (1967), "Public Expenditure and Economic Growth: A Time Series Analysis", *Public Finance* 22: 423–461.

Gupta, S.B. (1968), "Public Expenditure and Economic Development—A Cross-Section Analysis", *Finanzarchiv*, N.F., Bard 27: 26–41.

Lall, S. (1969), "A Note on Government Expenditures in Developing Countries", *Economic Journal* 79: 413–417.

Leonard, D., J. McMillan and R. Manning (1978), "Wagner's law and the theory of Public goods" Working Paper, UNSW, Kensington.

McMillan, J. (1978), "A Dynamic Analysis of Public Intermediate Goods Supply in an Open Economy", *International Economic Review* 19: 433–446.

McMillan, J. and R. Manning (1979), "Public Goods in Optimal Economic Growth", *Zeitschrift fur Nationalekonomie* 39, 332–342.

Michas, N.A. (1975), "Wagner's Law of Public Expenditures: What is the Appropriate Measurement for a Valid Test?" *Public Finance* 30: 77–83.

Musgrave, R.A. (1969), *Fiscal Systems*, New Haven, Yale University Press.

Peacock, A.T. and J. Wiseman (1967), *The Growth of Public Expenditure in the United Kingdom*, 2nd ed., London, George Allen and Unwin.

Pryor, F.L. (1968), *Public Expenditures in Communist and Capitalist Nations*, London, George Allen and Unwin.

Samuelson, P.A. (1954), "The Pure Theory of Public Expenditure", *Review of Economics and Statistics* 36: 387–389.

Spann, R.M. (1977), "The Macroeconomics of Unbalanced Growth and the Expanding Public Sector", *Journal of Public Economics* 8: 397–404.

Tussing, A.D. and J.A. Henning (1974), "Long-Run Growth of Nondefense Government Expenditure in the United States", *Public Finance Quarterly* 2: 202–222.

Wagner, A. (1883), *Finanzwissenschaft*, 3rd ed., Leipzig.

Wagner, A. (1958), "Three Extracts on Public Finance", in R.A. Musgrave and A.T. Peacock (eds.), *Classics in the Theory of Public Finance*, London, Macmillan, pp. 1–15.

Wagner, R.E. and W.E. Weber (1977), "Wagner's Law, Fiscal Institutions, and the Growth of Government", *National Tax Journal* 30: 59–68.

Appendix

Consider any twice differentiable function $F(X_1, \cdots, X_n)$, homogeneous of degree α. Euler's Theorem states that

$$X_1F_1 + \cdots + X_nF_n = \alpha F \tag{A1}$$

Differentiate (A1) with respect to $X_1, \cdots, X_n$:

$$F_i + X_1F_{1i} + \cdots + X_n F_{ni} = \alpha F_i, \qquad i = 1, \cdots, n \tag{A2}$$

Thus

$$X_1F_{1i} + \cdots X_nF_{ni} = (\alpha - 1) F_i, \qquad i = 1, \cdots n \tag{A3}$$

$$X_iX_1F_{1i} + \cdots + X_i^2F_{ii} + \cdots + X_iX_nF_{ni} = (\alpha - 1) X_iF_i, \quad i = 1 \cdots, n \tag{A4}$$

Summing (A4) over i:

$$(X_1, \cdots, X_n) \, \mathbf{H} \begin{pmatrix} X_1 \\ \cdot \\ \cdot \\ X_n \end{pmatrix} \; = \; (\alpha - 1) \sum_{i=1}^{n} X_iF_i = \alpha(\alpha - 1)F \tag{A5}$$

where $\mathbf{H}$ is the Hessian matrix of F.

7

Are Public Private Partnerships a Viable Method of Providing Infrastructure?

M.K. Lewis

University of South Australia

Abstract

South Australia's decision to investigate some private sector involvement in delivering the state's infrastructure needs is bound to be controversial. There are many in academia and in public policy who remain implacably opposed to the idea of the private sector being involved in designing, building and operating public facilities. This paper argues that it is not such a new idea, and that there is now overwhelming international evidence that public private partnerships (PPPs) work. It then suggests some economic factors for this performance that the critics of PPPs may have overlooked.

PPPs in South Australia

South Australia's recently developed Strategic Infrastructure Plan *Building South Australia* (www.infrastructure.sa.gov.au) released in April 2005 identifies strategic priorities for infrastructure investment over five and ten year time horizons as well as actions to improve the performance and management of the State's existing infrastructure assets. As part of the plan, developed by the Office for Infrastructure Development, the government aims to identify strategic priorities for new infrastructure investment. Once priority projects have been identified, developed and assessed, all funding options will be considered, including alternative private sector delivery options such as public private partnerships (PPPs).

PPPs describe the provision of public assets and services through the participation of government, the private sector and consumers. There is no single definition of a PPP. Depending on the particular location, the term can cover a variety of transactions where the private sector is given the right to operate, for an extended period, a service traditionally the responsibility of the public sector alone, ranging from relatively short term management contracts (with little or no capital expenditure), through concession contracts (which may encompass the design and build of substantial capital assets along with the provision of a range of services and the financing of the entire construction and operation), to joint ventures where there is a sharing of ownership between the public and private sectors. Generally speaking, PPPs fill a space between traditionally procured government projects and full privatisation.

PPPs are not new to South Australia. Indeed, it could be argued that the South Australian Company was a form of PPP.[1] In more recent times, a PPP of sorts involved the $20 million contract for the integration and rationalization of prisoner movement and in-court management services that was let to the market and began in December 1996. The project can be seen as an example of what might be called "strategic outsourcing" in that it used many features of a partnership framework to deliver ancillary services (Boswell, 2003). The South Australian Government is in the process of procuring six new regional police stations and four new regional courthouses through a PPP. The capital value of the project is more than $30 million with some facilities expected to be completed later this year and others completed early in 2006. Under the agreement the buildings will be financed, designed, built, operated and maintained by private sector organizations. The Government will lease the facilities for 25 years for police and court operations.

Like most other jurisdictions in Australia, the South Australian government has developed guidelines for PPPs.[2] The over-riding consideration is that private sector involvement must deliver value for money for the Government. In broad terms, value for money is defined as the private sector delivering the project at a lower whole-of-life cost than equivalent public sector procurement (Conlon, 2005).

Do PPPs deliver value for money? In their current forms PPPs may be relatively new in South Australia, but they have been around in the UK and other places, including other states in Australia, for well over ten years. In

France and some other countries, PPP-type arrangements have been in use for over one hundred years. They are a well-developed and extensively researched form of infrastructure procurement. What does this evidence tell us about the performance of PPPs?

Do PPPs deliver value for money?

This section examines the available research on PPP performance. The first thing to be noted is that PPPs can hardly be said to be taking over the market for public procurement.[3] Despite the attention given to, and concerns raised about, PPPs in the academic literature[4] and in public discussion, they are in reality the smaller part of the public infrastructure market. PPP/PFI[5] accounts for between only 10–14 per cent of public sector investment in the UK and PPPs for about 10 per cent in Victoria, the leading market in Australia. Most public infrastructure projects are still traditionally procured, because they are too small or unsuitable for PPP contracting. As a consequence, in the most commonly used test for value for money, a potential PPP application is pitted against the benchmark cost of providing the specified service using conventional public procurement methods (the Public Sector Comparator or PSC). While there is no simple pass or fail test with this comparison, there is the expectation that the private sector bid must deliver better value for money (VFM) if it is to proceed (Grimsey and Lewis, 2005b).

The second thing to be noted is what one group of writers call "a calamitous history of cost overrun" in infrastructure projects (Flyvbjerg, *et al*, 2003). This history is well documented in the case of transport projects, but the cost overruns are by no means confined to this sector and apply to public works in general (Flyvbjerg *et al*, 2005). One of the appeals of PPPs (especially to those in charge of allocating public sector resources) is because they offer one way of resolving the large cost overruns and delays in traditional public procurement methods for infrastructure—phenomena known as "optimism bias".

Traditional procurement

Two studies of optimism bias were published in 2002. In the Danish study by Flyvbjerg *et al* (2002), 258 large transport infrastructure projects were examined covering 20 countries, the overwhelming majority of which were developed

Table 1. Differences between actual and estimated costs in large public works transport projects.

Project type	All regions		Europe		North America	
	Number of projects	Average cost escalation (%)*	Number of projects	Average cost escalation (%)*	Number of projects	Average cost escalation (%)*
Rail	58	44.7 (30.1)	23	34.2 (25.1)	19	40.8 (36.8)
Fixed-link[1]	33	33.8 (62.4)	15	43.4 (52.0)	18	25.7 (70.5)
Road	167	20.4 (29.9)	143	22.4 (24.9)	24	8.4 (49.4)
All projects	258	27.6 (38.7)	181	25.7 (28.7)	61	23.6 (54.2)

Notes

* Figures in brackets are the standard deviation of the cost inaccuracies.

1. Fixed link projects consist of tunnels and bridges

Source: Based on data in Flyvbjerg et al (2002)

using conventional approaches to public procurement.[6] Costs were found to be underestimated in 90 per cent of the cases. For rail projects, actual costs are on average 45 per cent higher than estimated, for tunnels and bridges actual costs are on average 34 per cent higher, while for road projects, actual costs averaged 20 per cent higher than estimated. Table 1 summarizes the overall results from their study.

In the other major study conducted in 2002, the UK Treasury commissioned Mott MacDonald (2002) to review the outcome of 50 large public procurement projects in the UK over the last 20 years. A wide range of infrastructure projects was covered, including offices, hospitals, prisons, airport terminals, major refurbishments, roads, rail, IT facilities, tunnels. Table 2 summarizes the results for projects procured by conventional (ie traditional) methods. There is substantial evidence of optimism bias—the estimated difference between the business case and the final outcome for each category of project (HM Treasury, 2003a). For all projects, time overruns exceed the estimated duration by 17 per cent. In the case of capital expenditure, actual costs exceeded those estimated by 47 per cent on average. For operating expenditure, actual exceeded estimated by an average of 41 per cent (although the sample was much smaller than that for capital expenditure).

Table 2. Estimates of average "optimism bias" for conventional public procurement in the UK, by type of projects.

Project Type	Works Duration[1]	CAPEX[2]	OPEX[3]	Benefits Shortfall[4]
Standard Civil Engineering	34	44	No info	No info
Non-standard Civil Engineering	15	66	No info	5
Standard Buildings	4	24	No info	No info
Non-standard Buildings	39	51	No info	1
Equipment Development	54	214	No info	No info
Outsourcing	N/A	N/A	41	No info
All projects	17	47	41	2

Notes

1 The percentage by which the time taken for the actual works programme exceeds the estimate for time allowed in the business case.

2 The percentage by which the actual capital expenditure exceeds the expenditure expected in the business case.

3 The percentage by which the actual operating expenditure exceeds the expenditure anticipated in the business case.

4 The percentage by which the delivered benefits fall short of the benefits expected in the business case.

Source: Data from Mott MacDonald (2002)

The PPP record in the UK

The authors of the Danish study consider that there are as yet insufficient data to decide whether private projects perform better or worse than public ones. By contrast, 11 of the 50 projects examined by Mott MacDonald are undertaken under the UK PPP/PFI models. The results are striking. On average, the PPP/PFI projects came in under-time (compared to 17 per cent over-time for those under conventional methods), and capital expenditure resulted in a 1 per cent cost overrun on average for PPP/PFI projects (relative to an average cost overrun of 47 per cent for traditional procurement projects). These results are attributed in the report to the better risk allocation in PPP/PFI projects, and the high level of diligence demanded to establish the business case.

Since then, further evidence has been published on the performance of PPPs. In its July 2003 review of PFIs, HM Treasury (2003b) presented the results of its research into 61 PFI projects covering a wide range of service areas (prisons, police stations, roads, bridges, trains, hospitals, schools, defence accommodation and defence equipment). The key findings were as follows:

- Overall 89 per cent of projects were delivered on time or early.
- All PFI projects in the HM Treasury sample were delivered within public sector budgets. No PFI project was found where the unitary charge had changed following contract signature—other than where user requirements changed.
- Three-quarters of public sector managers stated that their project was meeting their initial expectations.

To these results we can add the findings of the UK National Audit Office (2003) of PFI construction performance. An earlier NAO study had found that only 30 per cent of non-PFI major construction projects were delivered on time and that only 27 per cent were within budget. By contrast, its investigation into PFI construction outcomes showed that in comparison to traditionally procured projects, the PFI projects were largely being delivered on time or early (76 per cent versus 30 per cent) and on budget (78 per cent versus 27 per cent). The results are shown in Table 3. Significantly, in no case did the public sector bear the cost of construction overruns, a major change from previous non-PFI experience where the financial costs of projects that ran into difficulties were absorbed into government budgets. The significance of this point was revealed in a report commissioned by HM Treasury in 2004 which found that the outturn costs of conventional procurement projects were 2 to 24 per cent higher than the estimate in the business case (Leahy, 2005).

Striking though this evidence is, the figures relate only to construction cost and time overruns. Value for money tests based on the PPP-PSC comparisons enable us to put some numbers on the expected overall gains from PPPs. In the UK a review, commissioned by the Treasury Taskforce (now Partnerships UK) and published jointly by the London School of Economics

Table 3. Construction performance of PFI and conventional projects

Projects	Conventional Procurement 2001 Survey 2003	PFI Projects NAO census
Per cent		
– on time	30	76
– on budget	27	78

Source: National Audit Office (2005)

and Arthur Andersen in January 2000, analysed 29 public sector projects that used the PFI and it was calculated that on average the predicted savings from using the PFI, compared with conventional procurement, was 17 per cent (Arthur Andersen, 2000). In its own separate analysis, the National Audit Office produced value for money reports on 15 projects, 7 of which were evaluated for value for money against a public sector comparator for traditional public procurement. Overall, the total cost savings of these projects was 20 per cent (NAO, 2001).

Studies for some particular sectors in the UK report broadly consistent results. Parker and Hartley (2003) record claims that PPP contracts for UK defence services have resulted in cost savings between 5 per cent and 40 per cent compared with conventional public procurement, although the authors are concerned as to whether these apparent cost savings will be realized over the projects' whole-of-life due to the inherent uncertainties of long-term contracting. In the case of roads, an earlier study (NAO, 1998) of the first four DBFO (design-build-finance-operate) road contracts found that the four contracts appear likely to generate net quantifiable financial savings of around 100 million pounds (13 per cent). Hodgson (1995), reviewing the switch from conventional procurement methods to DBFO arrangements for roads, notes that for traditional procurement involving the award of design and construct contracts "the public sector's record in the design and construction of capital schemes is poor. Time and cost overruns are common. Part of the reason lies in the attitudes and culture of the public sector. In the construction sector this often results in conservative or over-engineered designs" (p. 68).

Other evidence on PPPs

Directly comparable evidence for other countries is sparse, in part because French-style concessions are widely used and a public sector comparator is not employed as a systematic test of VFM. Instead, a competitive bidding market amongst private sector contractors is relied upon to generate value for money for these concession arrangements. Nevertheless there is some evidence for other countries. In the Netherlands, the Wastewater Treatment Delfland PPP, closed in 2003, achieved an expected saving of around 15 per cent compared with the PSC. In Australia, a review in 2004 of the Partnerships Victoria policy found evidence of net benefits of PPPs, and that for the eight PPP projects examined by the review the weighted average savings was 9 per cent across all projects (Fitzgerald, 2004).

The most recent evidence from outside of the UK comes from a review undertaken of EIB-financed projects and from a pilot PPP programme in Germany. The European Investment Bank study (Thomson, 2005) is based on an in-depth evaluation of ten PPP projects financed by the Bank, which were then compared with the rest of the Bank's portfolio of infrastructure projects. The results confirm the UK findings that PPPs are more likely to be on budget and on time. There was only one case where a PPP appeared to have higher costs than the public procurement alternative, and that seemed to be attributable to the lack of competition in the bidding market. Three out of the ten PPP projects exhibited time delays and cost overruns. However, in all cases, the additional costs were carried by the promoter not by the public sector bodies. By way of comparison, there were a total of 50 public infrastructure projects identified that had used conventional public procurement. It was found that 60 per cent of these projects were more than one year late, a performance that was adjudged to be "poor" in comparison to the PPP projects (p. 119).

In Germany, a pilot PPP programme has been underway in the Lander since 2004 supported by a federal competence centre installed that year. Under the PPP guidelines established, a value for money test involving a PPP-PSC comparison is required to be applied in three steps during the course of the project development. The first step is when selecting the right project for PPP treatment. The second is to assess possible VFM gains prior to tender, when the PPP-PSC is calculated in a range to represent different risk scenarios. The third is after tender when the PPP-PSC is calculated with data from negotiations with the preferred bidder. In the initial PPP pilot project, no quantitative PSC calculation was prepared prior to tender and consequently no measurable VFM test was made. For the other projects developed to date, PSC calculations were made, and the results of the VFM test are shown in Table 4. VFM gains were achieved with all assessed projects varying from 6 to 15 per cent(Sachs et al, 2005).

Finally, Grimsey and Lewis (2004, 2005a) provide case study evidence in the form of eight case studies of PPP projects in the United States, Australia,

Table 4. Value for money tests for PPP pilot projects in Germany.

Projects (date contract signed)		VFM gains prior to tender (per cent)	VFM gains for preferred bid (per cent)
13 schools	(2004)	15–22	15.2
School	(2004)	3–12	10.4
2 schools	(2004)	5–25	9.3
Admin building	(2004)	1–7	6.2
Town hall	(2004)	1–11	13.5
15 schools	(2005)	2–15	n.a

Source: Sachs et al (2005)

United Kingdom and Pakistan covering waste water treatment projects, two hospitals, two prisons, light rail and a road project. In three of the cases, no PSC calculation was made and value for money was sought by means of the competitive bidding process. In two of the cases, the VFM gains were trivial (less than one-half of one per cent). However, in one of these projects the lowest bidder was not chosen in order to widen the market for PPP contractors, while in the other case, the PPP was preferred on the basis of lower risk to the public purse. In the case of the other three projects, VFM was clearly established, with the VFM gains ranging between 9 and 16 per cent.

These clear cut findings on PPPs raise the question of why. What aspects of a PPP might bring about this marked difference in performance? The next section seeks to provide some answers.

Why the differences in performance?

The reasons for time and cost overruns in conventional procurement have been studied extensively in the literature. Mackie and Preston (1998) in their study identified no less than 21 sources of error and bias in transport projects. Mott MacDonald's study delineated and used survey evidence to rank 15 sources of optimism bias. Flyvbjerg *et al* (2003), building on studies by Pickrell (1990) and Fouracre *et al* (1990), look to the influence of project promoters who appear to think that a degree of deception and delusion is necessary to get projects started, aided and abetted by engineers with a "monument complex" and by "empire-building politicians" with access to public funds (Flyvbjerg *et al*, 2003, pp. 45–8).

Rather than go over this ground, we focus instead on the characteristics of PPPs that differentiate them from conventional procurement. It needs to be appreciated that the defining characteristic of a PPP is not private sector involvement in itself, but "bundling". Under traditional procurement, it is possible for assets to be designed and built by the private sector under separate contracts, and then the management of the facilities outsourced to private entities under another contract. With a PPP, the asset and service contracts are combined, and there is integration of all (or most of) the functions of design, building, financing, operating and maintenance of the facility in question. The emphasis then switches to the role of incentives, financial disciplines and risk transfer that can be built into such arrangements.

Incentives

Bundling is a vehicle for introducing incentive-oriented and performance-based features into the equation. When contracts are incomplete, and not every eventuality can be covered, incentives pose a particular problem and it is necessary to get them correct. For instance, there are large information difficulties surrounding construction contracts, and determining the responsibility for cost overruns is a serious source of conflict when there are design changes and other unexpected developments. However, writing the contract in terms of the flow of services from the infrastructure facility rather than the process of construction can change the incentive structure markedly. If, for example, the same entity is responsible for both construction and supplying the services, but is remunerated only for the successful provision of services of a suitable quality, the entity needs to build the correct facility, get the process of delivery right, and contain costs while not sacrificing quality. It is important to emphasize that in a PPP arrangement, the contractor is paid only when the services are delivered to an acceptable standard.

Financial disciplines

The financial side of a PPP is important too. Indeed, finance should be seen as the "glue" that binds the risk allocation in a PPP together. Financiers have incentives to make sure that services are supplied on time and to the requisite standard when the revenue stream that is generated represents the main source for repaying debt. There is also the participation of private risk capital, which brings with it with the expectation that those with equity at risk will insist on there being a harder-nosed approach to project evaluation, risk management and project implementation—effectively, at all stages of the project. Project-financing techniques have to be "engineered" to take account of the risks involved, sources of finance, accounting and tax regulations etc. Project design requires expert analysis of all of the attendant risks and then a structuring of the contractual arrangements prior to competitive tendering that allocates risk burdens appropriately. Project implementation then requires expert management of all of the component parts of the delivery of the services, such as construction, commissioning, operation and maintenance. This last stage is essential to the successful treatment of all of the attendant risks and, from the senior financier's point of view, secures control of the sole source of security against the cashflows. In effect, having the privately-provided finance at risk acts as a catalyst to inject risk management techniques into the project in a way that is not possible under government financing.[7]

Risk transfer

Focusing upon risks and their allocation is central to understanding what is special about a PPP relative to conventional procurement. Transferring the responsibility for design of both the facility and the delivery system on to the private contractor encourages it to choose designs that will work, and explore innovations that can lower whole-of-life cycle costs by improving quality and reducing maintenance and operating costs. Giving the responsibility for construction and project management to the private entity creates the incentive for it to keep the project on track and to prevent construction delays and cost over-runs. Involving the private sector in financing the project means that the financiers will look to the security and timeliness of the revenue stream, and put in place controls over the operators that will minimize the risk of project failure. Requiring the private body to operate and maintain the facility, as well as design and construct it, reduces any incentive to skimp on the quality of materials used, while encouraging decisions that maintain services to the desired level and keep costs at a minimum. It is this integration of upfront design and financial engineering to downstream management of the construction costs and revenue flow that gives the PPP its distinctive incentive compatibility characteristics—characteristics that are difficult to replicate within the public sector.

An effective transfer of risk from the public sector to the private sector is needed for this to happen, since it is the acceptance of risk that gives the private entity the incentive to price and produce efficiently. However, for this transfer to take place, a clear property right needs to be created. Within the ambit of a PPP, this suggests an allocation of responsibilities that might have the government retaining those areas where it is difficult to establish a clear contractual specification, leaving the private sector to undertake those activities for which a clear and unambiguous contract or property right can be formed. One of the merits of a step-by-step analysis of risk, central to the PPP process, is precisely to focus attention on these issues in order to determine whether these preconditions exist and whether a PPP approach could, if used, add value for money through risk transfer and the incentives that follow.

In general, the projects that are best suited for PPPs are those, first, for which there are fixed boundaries and a clear definition of project outcomes and service requirements. Second, there needs to be a competitive bidding market amongst sponsors (contractors, facilities managers and financiers) or competitive tension introduced into bidding from the public sector alternative. Third, if PPPs are to produce value for money, it is important for the service providers and financiers to carry construction and operating risks.

Concluding remarks

This paper has endeavoured to fill in some aspects missing from the academic literature and reflected in public policy discussion. One is an appreciation of the overall evidence as to the relative performance of PPPs vis-à-vis traditional procurement. On this point, the results are clear cut. About 75 per cent of major infrastructure projects in the UK were late and over budget before PPPs came into play. Under PPP/PFI arrangements, 75 per cent of projects are on time and to budget. A second thing missing from the academic literature is an understanding of the distinctive features that PPPs can bring to public procurement. For those projects that are suitable, PPPs are a way of introducing very different incentives into the procurement process. These incentives are peculiar to PPPs relative to other procurement approaches and come about as a result of the fusion of the upfront engineering of the design and the finance with the downstream management of construction and service delivery. Private risk finance using a mix of equity and debt lies at the heart of this process, and provides the "gelatine" that holds together the transaction and the risk allocation amongst the various parties. What is more, from the evidence assembled here, it would seem that the private sector does respond to these signals and gets it right more often than not.

Notes

1 Information on the role of the South Australian Company in the formation of the colony can be found in Prest *et al* (2001).

2 A comparison (along with web addresses) of the guidelines in the various jurisdictions in Australia is made by Sharp and Tinsley (2005).

3 Thus the title of Watson's (2003) article "The rise and rise of public private partnerships" somewhat overstates the position.

4 Prominent amongst critics are Broadbent, Gill and Laughlin (2003), Broadbent and Laughlin (2003), Heald (2003), and Shaoul (2004). A particular battleground is the application of PPP/PFI to the UK's National Health Service (NHS). On this specific issue, other studies critical of PPPs are those of Mayston (1999), Pollock *et al* (1997) and Pollock (2000, 2004).

5 Private Finance Initiative (PFI) is the UK programme encompassing PPP arrangements whereby a consortium of private sector partners come together to provide an asset-based public service under contract to a public body. These, along with the introduction of private sector ownership into state-owned enterprises and the sale of government services into wider markets, constitute the current Partnership UK agenda.

6 The major and notable exception is the Channel Tunnel.

7 Here we note Heald's (2003) argument that "finance providers may impose stricter *ex ante* controls on the construction stage, thus ensuring that the project is fully costed and that the contractor does not anticipate that claims for additional work will meet a soft budget constraint" (p. 366). While agreeing, the writer would add that finance providers may also impose strict controls *ex post* (following construction) over delivery to ensure that senior debt is repaid.

References

Arthur Andersen (2000), *Value for Money Drivers in the Private Finance Initiative*, Arthur Andersen and Enterprise LSE, London.

Boswell, M (2003), *Strategic Sourcing/PPP Prison Escorts*, Address given at the University of South Australia, November.

Broadbent, J, Gill, J and R Laughlin (2003), "Evaluating the Private Finance Initiative in the National Health Service", *Accounting, Auditing and Accountability Journal*, 16(3), 422–445.

Broadbent, J and R Laughlin (2003), "Public private partnerships: an introduction", *Accounting, Auditing & Accountability Journal*, 16 (3), 332–511.

Conlon, P (2005), "Development of Public Infrastructure in South Australia", *Public Infrastructure Bulletin*, 5, May, 4–6.

Fitzgerald, P (2004), *Review of Partnerships Victoria Provided Infrastructure*, Melbourne: Review of Partnerships Victoria.

Flyvbjerg, B, N Bruzelius and W Rothengatter (2003), *Megaprojects and risk: An anatomy of ambition*, Cambridge, UK: Cambridge University Press.

Flyvbjerg, B, M S Holm and S Buhl (2002), "Underestimating Costs in Public Works Projects—Error or Lie?" *Journal of the American Planning Association*, 68(3), 279–295.

Flyvbjerg, B, M S Holm and S L Buhl (2005), "How (In)accurate Are Demand Forecasts in Public Works Projects?" *Journal of the American Planning Association*, 71 (2), 131–146.

Fouracre, P R, R J Allport and J M Thomson (1990), *The performance and impact of rail mass transit in developing countries* (TRRL Research Report 278), Crowthorne, UK: Transport and Road Research Laboratory.

Grimsey, D and M K Lewis (2004), *Public Private Partnerships: the worldwide revolution in infrastructure provision and project finance*, Cheltenham, Edward Elgar.

Grimsey, D and M K Lewis (eds) (2005a), *The Economics of Public Private Partnerships*, Cheltenham, Edward Elgar.

Grimsey, D and M K Lewis (2005b), "Are Public Private Partnerships Value for Money? Evaluating Alternative Approaches and Comparing Academic and Practitioner Views", *Accounting Forum*, 29 (4), 345–378.

Heald, D (2003), "Value for money tests and accounting treatment in PFI schemes", *Accounting, Auditing and Accountability Journal*, 16 (3), 342–371.

HM Treasury (2003a), *The Green Book—Appraisal and Evaluation in Central Government*, London: TSO.

HM Treasury (2003b), *PFI: meeting the investment challenge*, Norwich: HMSO.

Hodgson, G J (1995), "Design and build—effects of contractor design on highway schemes", *Proc. Civil Engineers*, 108, May, 64–76.

Leahy, P (2005), "Lessons from the Private Finance Initiative in the United Kingdom", *EIB Papers*, 10 (2), 58–71.

Mackie, P and J Preston (1998) "Twenty-one sources of error and bias in transport project appraisal", *Transport Policy*, 5, 1–7.

Mayston, D J (1999), "The Private Finance Initiative in the National Health Service: An Unhealthy Development in New Public Management?" *Financial Accountability & Management*, 15 (3 & 4), 249–274.

Mott MacDonald (2002), *Review of Large Public Procurement in the UK*, London: HM Treasury.

National Audit Office (1998), *The Private Finance Initiative: The First Four, Design, Build, Finance and Operate Roads Contracts*, HC 476, Parliamentary Session 1997–98, London: HMSO.

National Audit Office (2001), *Managing the relationship to secure a successful partnership in PFI projects*, HC 375 Session 2001/2002, London: HMSO.

National Audit Office (2003), *PFI: Construction Performance*, Report by the Comptroller and Auditor General, London: HMSO.

Parker, D and K Hartley (2003), "Transaction Costs, Relational Contracting and Public Private Partnerships: A Case Study of UK Defence", *Journal of Purchasing and Supply Management*, 9 (3), 97–108.

Pickrell, D H (1990), *Urban rail transit projects: Forecast versus actual ridership and cost*, Washington, DCC: US Department of Transportation.

Pollock A M (2000), "PFI is bad for your health", *Public Finance*, 6 October, 30–31.

Pollock, A M (2004), *NHS plc: The Privatisation of Our Health Care*, London: Verso.

Pollock, A M, M Dunnigan, D Gaffney, A Macfarlane and F Azeem Majeed (1997), "What happens when the private sector plans hospital services for the NHS: three case studies under the private finance initiative", *British Medical Journal*, 314, 1266–71.

Prest, W, K Round and C Fort eds (2001), *The Wakefield Companion to South Australian History*, Kent Town: Wakefield Press.

Sachs, T, C Elbing, R L K Tiong and H W Alfen (2005), "Efficient Assessment of Value for Money (VFM) for Selecting Effective Public Private Partnership (PPP) Solutions—a Comparative Study of VFM Assessment for PPPs in Singapore and Germany", CACS, School for Civil and Environmental Engineering, Nanyang Technological University, Singapore.

Shaoul, J (2004), "A critical financial analysis of the Private Finance Initiative: selecting a financing method or allocating economic wealth?" *Critical Perspectives in Accounting* 16 (4), 441–471.

Sharp, L and F Tinsley (2005), "PPP Policies throughout Australia: A comparative analysis of Public Private Partnerships", *Public Infrastructure Bulletin*, 5, May, 21–34.

Thomson, C (2005), "Public-private partnerships: prerequisites for prime performance", *EIB Papers*, 10 (2), 112–129.

Watson, D (2003), "The rise and rise of public private partnerships: challenges for public accountability", *Australian Accounting Review*, 13(3): 2–14.

8

Tax Policy 900 Years Ago: How Fair Were the Tax Assessments of Domesday England?

John McDonald

Flinders University, Adelaide

Introduction

This paper examines tax policy in England under Norman rule in 1086, 20 years after the Conquest. In particular, it assesses whether the estates of the laity, church and king were assessed on an equal basis or whether one class of estate was treated more favourably. Data on individual estate tax assessments (measured in hides) are available from Domesday Book, the results of a survey commissioned by King William, about two years before his death. Further general information on the way the tax (known as the Geld) was administered can be found in contemporary sources, but the details of the assessment system have been lost in the mists of time. Nevertheless, by analysing relationships between estate assessments and characteristics, we can gain insights into the tax structure and how the Geld was levied.

An early view, held by Victorian historians, was that the assessments were "artificial". Round, for example, on the basis of fragmentary evidence, argued that the assessments were an administrative creation. He argued they were imposed on hundreds in 100-hide units and vills in five-hide units and then apportioned to estates. As a consequence, the assessments imposed on individual estates bore little relationship to the capacity of the estate to pay the tax.[1]

In the mid 1980s Graeme Snooks and I (McDonald and Snooks, 1985a, 1986, 1987a) cast doubt on this idea. We argued that, analogous with many modern tax systems, it was possible that the Domesday assessments reflected an attempt to collect taxes in a politically acceptable way. We postulated that the assessments may have been based on a capacity to pay principle modified by politically expedient concessions and could be expected to exhibit some uneven-ness resulting from the administrative process. This unevenness occurred because the assessments were revised infrequently and, consequently, the link between assessment and capacity to pay became somewhat eroded. Also assess-ments were made at different times in the various counties and the hundreds of a county, and with slightly more rigour in some administrative units than others. There is strong empirical evidence for this hypothesis. Capacity to pay can be measured by the estate's annual value or net income accruing to the lord from working the estate. Regressions of estate tax assessments on annual values indicate that capacity to pay explains around 60 to 90 per cent of varia-tion in individual estate assessment data for the counties of Buckinghamshire, Cambridgeshire, Essex and Wiltshire, and from 72 to 81 per cent for aggregate data for 29 counties (see McDonald and Snooks 1985a, 1986, 1987a, 1990a and 1990b).[2]

Capacity to pay seems to explain the greater part of the variation in tax assessments, but some variation remains. Were some tenants-in-chief and some kinds of estate more favourably treated than others? In McDonald (1998 and 2002), I explored these questions, basing the analysis on Essex lay estate data. A further, and perhaps more interesting, question is whether lay, ecclesi-astical and king's estates were similarly assessed or whether one class of estate received beneficial treatment? This unresolved question is the focus of the current study.

Historical Background

By the time of the Survey, England was firmly under William's control with some 10,000 Normans and Continentals controlling about one and a half million Britons. Rebellion and civil dissent had been harshly put down and the Anglo-Saxon aristocracy eliminated. Most of their lands passed to less than 200 Norman barons with most lands in the hands of a handful of great lords. William imposed a feudal system. All land belonged to the king and tenants-in-chief held land from the king in return for service. Tenants-in-chief might then grant land to sub-tenants in return for rent or service or work the estate themselves through a bailiff. Estates were organized according to a modified manorial system with peasants and slaves tied to the estate.

The king ruled through the Great Council which met four times a year at different centres in the kingdom. Administration in the counties was supervised by the king's agent, the sheriff, who was usually a great magnate. Royal orders could be directed and enforced through the county and hundred courts and an effective taxation collection system using the county administration was in place.

The Normans exploited the Anglo-Saxon institutions, modifying them for their own advantage. The Geld can be traced back to the danegeld introduced by Ethelred in 911 to bribe the Danes to rape, plunder and pillage elsewhere. Originally a land tax, by Norman times it was more broadly based. It accounted for about a quarter of all state revenue and was a considerable annual burden on landholders. For example, for the average Essex lay estate, the rate struck in 1083–4 of six shillings to the hide would have generated a tax payment of about 15 per cent of net income (annual value).

The Domesday Survey was carried out in about 20 months, 1085–87, being terminated on the death of William. The English counties were grouped into (probably) seven circuits, each visited by a team of commissioners. The commissioners circulated a list of questions to landholders. Their responses were reviewed in the county court by the hundred juries and then county and circuit returns were compiled. The circuit returns were sent to the Exchequer in Winchester where they were summarized, edited and compiled into Great Domesday Book. These procedures limited the opportunities for giving false or misleading evidence. Questionnaire responses were public knowledge and responses were verified, under oath, in the courts by landholders with local knowledge.

The survey manuscript was referred to by contemporaries as the "Descriptio" and only later as Domesday Book, the book of last judgement. It was so named because in land disputes there was no appeal beyond its pages— land rights could be traced back to Domesday Book but no further. The book consists of two volumes, Great (or Exchequer) Domesday and Little Domesday. Little Domesday is a detailed original survey return of circuit VII, Essex, Norfolk and Suffolk. Great Domesday is a summarized version of the other circuit returns sent to the King's Treasury in Winchester. (It is thought William died before Essex and East Anglia could be incorporated into Great

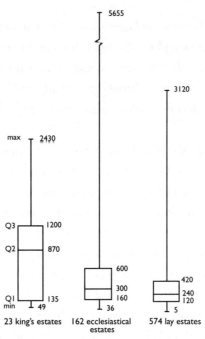

Figure 1. *Box plots of tax assessments (in fiscal acres, 120 fiscal acres to a hide), Essex estates 1086.*

Domesday). The two volumes contain information on the annual values or net incomes, tax assessments and resources of most estates in England in 1086. There is less comprehensive information for 1066 and sometimes information for an intermediate year. It is thought the information was used to revise tax assessments and document the feudal structure, "who held what, and owed what to whom".[3]

Data

Essex data are used in this study because they are more comprehensive than for most other counties and easier to interpret than the other counties of Little Domesday. By my reckoning there were 925 estates in Essex (48 king's estates, 182 ecclesiastical and 695 lay). Of these, information is incomplete for 25 king's, 20 ecclesiastical and 121 lay estates. Although a large number, these are generally very small holdings accounting for only a small proportion of the county-wide tax assessment and annual value totals (thus, they account for less than three per cent of the county annual value total). The analysis is restricted to the 759 estates for which information appears complete.[4]

Figure 1 exhibits box plots of the tax assessments of the three categories of estate. The plots display the main features of the assessment distributions (minimum and maximum values and the quartiles). They indicate that king's estates had, on average, larger assessments than ecclesiastical estates, which in turn had larger assessments than lay estates. There are two parts to my analysis. First, I assess whether, the three classes of estate, have the same average tax assessment-annual value function. Secondly, I construct a tax frontier based on all the assessments and assess whether one category of estate received favourable assessments when we allow for factors other than net income.

The Average Relationship

Using regression methods, separate tax-annual value relationships were estimated for king's, ecclesiastical and lay estates. Rather than assume the functions were linear, it was assumed they could be approximated by functions in the more general Box-Cox Extended class. Estimates of the transformation parameters were close to zero (king's -0.07, ecclesiastical, -0.03 and lay, 0.17), suggesting that log-linear relationships would be good approximations. Formal tests confirmed the log-linear hypothesis (Godfrey and Wickens, 1981, test produced p-values of 0.857, 0.245 and 0.968, in the king's, ecclesiastical and lay regressions, see McDonald and Snooks, 1986, pp. 162–167 for details of the Box-Cox method and the test).

Table 1 exhibits key statistics for the log-linear regressions. The lay and ecclesiastical functions appear quite similar and the king's function a little different.[5] The disturbance estimated standard errors take similar values, and on formal tests the hypothesis of equality is accepted at conventional significance levels.[6] A formal test of equality of corresponding intercept and slope parameters in the three log-linear functions is clearly rejected. (The maximum likelihood test p-value was less than 0.001). Equality for the ecclesiastical and lay parameters was also rejected, (p-value again less than 0.001). Figure 2 indicates that the ecclesiastical tax function lies above the lay function, indicating that, on average, at a given annual value, the ecclesiastical assessment was higher. For the annual values in the Essex sample, the king's assessments tended to be higher than the lay assessments at given annual values. For most estates, the average assessments for the king's and ecclesiastical estates were similar; for

Table 1. Average tax assessment—annual value functions for king's, ecclesiastical and lay estates, Essex 1086.

		Intercept	Log value	s	$\bar{R}^2$	n
1.	**Lay estates:**					
	Coefficients	2.41	0.71			
	Standard errors	0.11	0.02	0.661	0.561	574
	p-values	0.000	0.000			
2.	**Ecclesiastical estates:**					
	Coefficients	2.53	0.75			
	Standard errors	0.18	0.05	0.627	0.636	162
	p-values	0.000	0.000			
3.	**King's estates:**					
	Coefficients	2.97	0.63			
	Standard errors	0.22	0.04	0.529	0.797	23
	p-values	0.000	0.000			

Notes: s is the disturbance estimated standard error, $\bar{R}^2$ is the coefficient of determination adjusted for degrees of freedom and n the number of observations in the regressions.

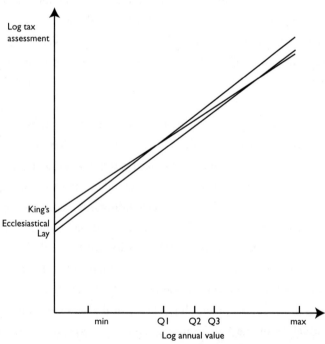

Figure 2. *Average tax assessment – annual value functions for Essex king's ecclesiastical and lay estates, 1086 (sample maximum, minimum and quartile log annual values marked on the horizontal axis).*

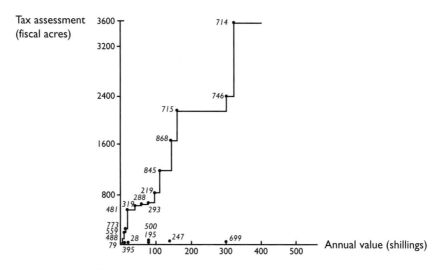

Figure 3. *Tax assessment frontier, Essex estates 1086.*

king's estates with small annual values, they tended to be higher, but for those with large annual values, they tended to be smaller.[7]

The Tax Frontier

The average tax-annual value (or tax-net income) functions appear different for king's, ecclesiastical and lay estates, but, if factors other than the net income of the estate are considered, did the lay estates still receive more favourable treatment?. To examine this issue I constructed a tax frontier for all 759 estates in the sample and calculated a beneficial tax index (BTI) value for each estate.

The index is based on the simple and attractive notion that an estate has received beneficial treatment if it has a lower tax assessment than another estate with the same or lower net income. Formally, the BTI for estate i is the ratio of the maximum tax assessment of all estates with the same or lower net income than estate i to the actual tax assessment of estate i. A BTI value of one corresponds to no favourable treatment, and a value greater than one to some favourable treatment.[8] An advantage of the frontier approach is that it is a non-parametric method that does not require the choice of a particular functional form (such as log-linear) for the tax-annual value relationship.

Figure 3 displays part of the frontier. The numbers on the frontier are the identification codes of the estates that form the frontier (and hence had a BTI

Table 2. Characteristics of estates with an unfavourable taxation index (BTI) of one, Essex estates 1086.

	Estate	BTI	Tax assessment	Frontier assessment	Annual value	Estate class / Tenant-in-chief	Tenancy	Hundred
79	Lt. Bentley	1	42.5	42.5	3	L / Count Alan	1 sub-tenant	Tendring
488	Paglesham	1	90	90	5	L / Robert son of Corbutio	1 sub-tenant	Rochford
559	East Donyland	1	188	188	7	L / Ilbodo	demesne	Lexden
773	Epping	1	255	255	15	E / Canons of Holy Cross of Waltham	demesne	Waltham
481	Leyton	1	540	540	20	L / Robert son of Corbutio	demesne	Becontree
319	Wivenhoe	1	625	625	46	L / Robert Greno	1 sub-tenant	Lexden
288	Stow Maries	1	637	637	65	L / Geoffrey de Magna Villa	1 sub-tenant	Dengie
293	Weneswic	1	640	640	80	L / Geoffrey de Magna Villa	1 sub-tenant	Dengie
219	Purleigh	1	840	840	100	L / Hugh de Montfort	demesne	Dengie
835	Ingrave	1	1200	1200	110	L / Bishop of Bayeux	1 sub-tenant	Barstable
868	South Hanningfield	1	1680	1680	142	E / Bishop of Bayeux	demesne	Chelmsford
715	Southminster	1	2173	2173	160	E / Bishop of London	several sub-tenants	Dengie
746	Tillingham	1	2416	2146	300	E / Canons of St Paul	demesne	Dengie
714	Southminster	1	3600	3600	320	E / Bishop of London	demesne	Dengie
832	Great Burstead	1	4565	4565	720	E / Bishop of Bayeux	demesne	Barstable
772	Waltham Abbey	1	5655	5655	1633	E / Bishop of Durham	denesne	Waltham

Notes: Tax assessments are measured in fiscal acres and annual values in shillings

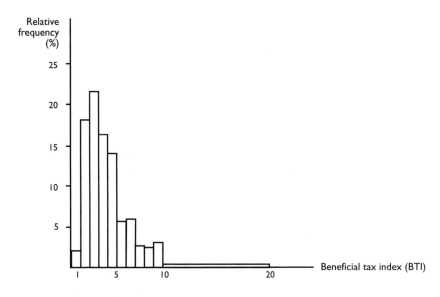

Figure 4. *Beneficial tax index (BTI) histogram, Essex estates 1086.*

= 1). Table 2 lists information about these estates. Seventy nine, for example, refers to Little Bentley, an estate of Count Alan of Brittany in the Hundred of Tendring held by a single sub-tenant. The annual value was three shillings and the tax assessment 42.5 fiscal acres. Half of the frontier estates were lay estates and half church estates. None were estates of the king. The lay estates formed the frontier for low net incomes and the ecclesiastical estates for higher incomes. Half of the frontier estates were held in demesne and half by sub-tenants. Six of the estates were located in the Dengie Hundred.

Figure 4 exhibits the BTI histogram. Two per cent of estates had a BTI = 1 and about a quarter a BTI less than two, roughly 40 per cent an index value less than three, and three quarters a value less than five. Estates not on the frontier (those with a BTI greater than 1), can be represented by points below the frontier. Some estates with very high BTIs are located in Figure 3 by a dot and their identification code. Table 3 contains information about the estates with BTIs greater than 18. They range from 395 Prested with a small annual value of only 12 shillings to a relatively large estate 699 Stisted with an annual value of 300 shillings (300 shillings exceeds the annual value of more than 90 per cent of the estates in the sample). Of the 12 estates with a BTI greater than 18, all but one were lay estates, six were sub-tenancies and six held in demesne, three estates

Table 3. Characteristics of selected estates that received favourable tax assessments, Essex estates 1086.

	Estate	BTI	Tax assessment	Frontier assessment	Annual value	Estate class / Tenant-in-chief	Tenancy	Hundred
39	Chipping Ongar	18.11	120	2173	160	L / Count Eustace	demesne	Ongar
115	How Hall	19.23	32.5	625	50	L / Richard son of C. Gilbert	I sub-tenant	Hinckford
247	Tiltey	20.00	60	1200	140	L / Henry de Ferraris	demesne	Dunmow
819	Takeley	20.00	60	1200	140	E / St Walery	demesne	Uttlesford
500	Sibil Hedingham	25.60	25	640	80	L / Roger Bigot	I sub-tenant	Hinckford
453	Stevington End	28.23	42.5	1200	115	L / Tithel the Breton	demesne	Freshwell H-H
28	Toppesfield	36.00	15	540	20	L / Count Eustace	I sub-tenart	Hinckford
207	Radwinter	36.00	15	540	30	L / Eudo dapifer	I sub-tenart	Freshwell H-H
555	Tendring	36.00	15	540	20	L / Moduin	demesne	Tendring
395	Prested	37.60	5	188	12	L / Ranulf Peverel	I sub-tenant	Lexden
699	Stisted	40.27	60	2416	300	E / Holy Trinity of Canterbury for the support of the monks	demesne	Witham
195	Broxted	71.11	9	640	80	L / Eudo dapifer	I sub-tenant	Dunmow

Notes: Tax assessments are measured in fiscal acres and annual values in shillings.

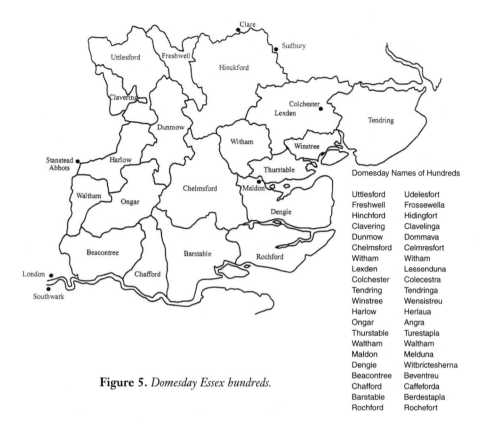

Figure 5. *Domesday Essex hundreds.*

Domesday Names of Hundreds

Uttlesford	Udelesfort
Freshwell	Frossewella
Hinchford	Hidingfort
Clavering	Clavelinga
Dunmow	Dommava
Chelmsford	Celmresfort
Witham	Witham
Lexden	Lessenduna
Colchester	Colecestra
Tendring	Tendringa
Winstree	Wensistreu
Harlow	Herlaua
Ongar	Angra
Thurstable	Turestapla
Waltham	Waltham
Maldon	Melduna
Dengie	Witbrictesherna
Beacontree	Beventreu
Chafford	Caffeforda
Barstable	Berdestapla
Rochford	Rochefort

were in Hinckford Hundred, two in Dunmow Hundred and two in Freshwell Half Hundred. In footnotes to the Victoria County History entries for Essex (VCH, 1903), Round commented that four of the 12 estates with very high BTIs (and hence low assessments) had abnormal or nominal assessments. These were 195 Broxted, 247 Tiltey, 28 Toppesfield and 500 Sibil Hedingham). He also commented on the low assessments of other estates with smaller BTIs.[9] By calculating BTIs for each estate it is possible to identify estates with low or abnormal assessments in a comprehensive fashion. Round's impressionistic approach enabled him to identify some but not all estates with very favourable assessments.

Allowing for the Hundred Effect

If we control for factors other than estate net income, did lay estates (on average) receive more favourable tax assessments? Figure 5 is a map showing

173

Table 4. Mean BTI of estates by hundred, Essex estates 1086.

Hundred	Mean BTI	Standard deviation of mean	Deviation from overall mean	Number of estates in sample
Barstable	2.52	0.15	-2.13	65
Beacontree	2.40	0.28	-2.26	17
Chafford	3.51	0.37	-1.15	32
Chelmsford	2.67	0.14	-1.98	66
Dengie	2.45	0.19	-2.21	57
Dunmow	7.29	1.30	2.64	53
Clavering hundred and half hundred	2.83	0.30	-1.82	10
Colchester	2.59	0.00	-2.06	1
Freshwell half hundred	10.77	1.83	6.12	19
Harlow	3.75	0.85	-0.91	18
Harlow half hundred	4.14	1.20	-0.51	8
Hinckford	8.16	0.58	3.50	84
Lexden	6.40	1.05	1.75	36
Ongar	5.43	0.55	0.78	46
Rochford	4.58	0.45	-0.07	45
Tendring	4.01	0.62	-0.64	58
Uttlesford	3.71	0.46	-0.94	48
Waltham hundred and half hundred	1.79	0.41	-2.87	8
Winstree	2.41	0.20	-2.24	20
Witham	6.34	1.17	1.69	34
Maldon half hundred	4.69	1.79	0.04	3
Thunreslau half hundred	4.59	1.24	-0.06	3
Thurstable	3.15	0.32	-1.50	28

the Essex hundred divisions and Table 4 gives a break-down of mean BTI by hundreds. A statistical test indicates that the BTI varied significantly with hundred location.[10] Hundreds for which estates received milder assessments included Freshwell Half-Hundred (mean BTI = 10.77), Hinckford (mean BTI = 8.16) and Dunmow (mean BTI = 7.29). Some with high mean assessments were Waltham Hundred and Half-Hundred (mean BTI = 1.73), Beacontree (mean BTI = 2.40) and Winstree (mean BTI = 2.41).

It would clearly be interesting to see if lay estates received more favourable treatment when we allow for the hundred effect. In the regressions described in Table 5, I also control for the size of the estate, the kind of agriculture under-

Table 5. Regression of BTI on estate characteristics, Essex estates 1086.

	Coefficient	Standard error	p-value
Lay estate effect	6.55	1.11	
Ecclesiastical effect	6.50	1.30	} 0.602
King's estate effect	6.00	1.17	
Size (annual value) effect	−0.001	0.001	0.080
Kind of agriculture (grazing/arable ratio) effect	−0.000	0.000	0.934
Tenure effect	−0.206	0.333	0.537
Hundred effect	−	−	0.000

Notes: The tests are heteroskedasticity-consistent tests (see White, 1980). The first p-value tests the null that the lay, ecclesiastical and king's coefficients are equal. The other p-values test that the effects have no impact in the regression equation $\bar{R}^2 = 0.169$, n = 759.

taken on the estate (the grazing/arable mix) and the tenancy arrangement.[11] The regression statistics indicate that these additional factors did not have a very significant influence on the tax assessments (p-values for the kind of agriculture and tenancy variable coefficient estimates are greater than 0.5 and the size variable p-value is 0.080), but confirm the importance of the hundred effect (p-value = 0.000). When we control for the factors, the difference (on average) between the tax treatment of king's, church and lay estates is largely eliminated. The table indicates that the estate class effects are very similar (6.55, 6.50 and 6.00 for king's, church and lay estates, respectively) and this difference is not significant at the 60 per cent level.

Conclusion

The details of the levying of the geld in 1086 are largely lost in time, but the evidence clearly indicates that the estate tax assessments varied with capacity to pay (as measured by the estate's annual value or net income), and the analysis of estate BTIs suggests that administrative factors also had an influence. There was a clear hundred tax assessment differential in Essex which could have resulted from the assessments being only infrequently revised, with revision occurring at different times and with more rigour in some hundreds than others. Although analysis of tax-net income functions suggests that lay estates were treated more favourably, if allowance is made for the hundred effect one class of estate was not (significantly) favoured above another. The leniency shown to the lay estates can be explained by their hundred location, but the direction of causation is unclear. Was the favour shown to lay estates deliberate policy and the hundred effect simply a consequence? Or was the favouritism an accidental consequence of unevenness in the administrative process across the hundreds? It would be interesting to explore this issue further and see if similar results are obtained for other counties.

Acknowledgement:

I would like to thank Eva Aker and Beverley Vickers for excellent research assistance, S. Snap and M. Muggles for their caring assistance, colleagues and seminar participants for their comments and The Australian Research Council and Flinders University for financial support.

References

Aston, T.H., (ed), (1987), *Landlords, Peasants and Politics in Medieval England*. (Cambridge: Cambridge University Press).

Ballard, A., (1906), *The Domesday Inquest*, (London: Methuen).

Britnell, R.H. and M.S. Campbell, (eds), (1995), *A Commercialising Economy: England 1086 to c. 1300*. (Manchester: Manchester University Press).

Brown, R.A., (1984), *The Normans*, (Woodbridge:Boydell Press).

Clanchy, M.T., (1983), *England and its Rulers, 1066–1272*, (Glasgow: Fontana).

Darby, H.C., (1952), *The Domesday Geography of Eastern England*, reprinted 1971, (Cambridge: Cambridge University Press).

Darby, H.C., (1977), *Domesday England*, reprinted 1979, (Cambridge: Cambridge University Press).

Darby, H.C. and I.S. Maxwell (eds), (1962), *The Domesday Geography of Northern England*, (Cambridge: Cambridge University Press).

Galbraith, V.H., (1961), *The Making of Domesday Book*, (Oxford: Clarendon Press).

Godfrey, L. G., and M. R. Wickens, (1981), "Testing linear and log-linear regressions for functional form." *Review of Economic Studies*, 48, 487–96.

Godfrey, A. and Hooper, K. (1996), "Accountability and Decision-making in Feudal England: Domesday Book Revisited," *Accounting History*, NS Vol. 1, No. 1: 35–54.

Goldfeld, S. M., and R. E. Quandt, (1965), "Some Tests for Homoscedasticity." *Journal of the American Statistical Association*, 60, 539–47.

Hallam, H.E., (1981), *Rural England 1066–1348*, (Brighton: Fontana).

Hallam, H.E., (ed), (1988), *The Agrarian History of England and Wales, II: 1042–1350*, (Cambridge: Cambridge University Press).

Harvey, S.P.J., (1983), "The Extent and Profitability of Demesne Agriculture in the Latter Eleventh Century." In *Social Relations and Ideas: Essays in Honour of R.H. Hilton*, T.H. Ashton et al. (ed) Cambridge: Cambridge University Press.

Hollister, C.W., (1965), *The Military Organisation of Norman England*, (Oxford: Clarendon Press).

Holt, J. C., (ed), (1987), *Domesday Studies*. Woodbridge: Boydell Press.

Langdon, J., (1982), The Economics of Horses and Oxen in Medieval England, *Agricultural History Review*, Vol. 30, No. 1: 31–40.

Lennard, R., (1959), *Rural England 1086–1135: A Study of Social and Agrarian Conditions*, (Oxford: Clarendon Press).

Loyn, R., (1962), *Anglo-Saxon England and the Norman Conquest*, reprinted 1981, (London: Longman).

Loyn, R., (1965), *The Norman Conquest*, (London: Hillary House).

Loyn, R., (1983), *The Governance of Anglo-Saxon England, 500–1087*, (London: Edward Arnold).

Maitland, F.W., (1897), *Domesday Book and Beyond*, reprinted 1921, (Cambridge: Cambridge University Press).

McDonald, J. (1997), "Manorial Efficiency in Domesday England", *Journal of Productivity Analysis*, Vol. 8, No. 3: 199–213.

McDonald, J., (1998), *Production Efficiency in Domesday England*, (London: Routledge).

McDonald, J. (2000), "Domesday Economy:An Analysis of the English Economy Early in the Second Millennium", *National Institute Economic Review*, Vol. 172, No. 2: 105–114.

McDonald, J. (2002), "Tax Fairness in Eleventh Century England", *The Accounting Historians Journal*, Vol. 29, 173–193.

McDonald, J. (2005), Using William the Conqueror's accounting record to assess manorial efficiency, *Accounting History*, Vol. 10, 125–145.

McDonald, J. and G.D. Snooks, (1985a), "Were the Tax Assessments of Domesday England Artificial? The Case of Essex", *Economic History Review*, Vol. 38, No. 4: 353–373.

McDonald, J. and G.D. Snooks, (1985b), "The Determinants of Manorial Income in Domesday England: Evidence from Essex", *Journal of Economic History*, Vol. 45, No. 4: 541–556.

McDonald, J. and G.D. Snooks (1985c), "Statistical Analysis of Domesday Book" (1086), *Journal of the Royal Statistical Society*, series A, Vol. 148, No. 2: 147–160.

McDonald, J. and G.D. Snooks, (1986), *Domesday Economy: A New Approach to Anglo-Norman History*, (Oxford: Clarendon Press).

McDonald, J. and G.D. Snooks, (1987a), "The Suitability of Domesday Book for Cliometric Analysis", *Economic History Review*, Vol. 40, No. 2: 252–261.

McDonald J. and G.D. Snooks, (1987b), "The Economics of Domesday England", in *Domesday Book Studies*, A. Williams (ed.), (London: Alecto Historical Editions).

McDonald J. and G.D. Snooks, (1990a), "A Case of Mistaken Identity: National Taxation and Local Authority Administration in Domesday England", School of Economics Research Paper 90: 8, (Adelaide: Flinders University).

McDonald J. and G.D. Snooks, (1990b), "The Taxation System of Domesday England", School of Economics Research Paper 90: 12, (Adelaide: Flinders University).

Miller, E., and J. Hatcher, (1978), *Medieval England: Rural Society and Economic Change 1086–1348*, (London: Longman).

Morris, J., (gen. ed.), (1975), *Domesday Book: A Survey of the Counties of England*, (Chichester: Phillimore).

Postan, M.M., (1966), "Medieval Agrarian Society in its Prime", *The Cambridge Economic History of Europe*, Vol. 1,. M.M. Postan, (ed.) (Cambridge: Cambridge University Press).

Postan, M.M., (1972), *The Medieval Economy and Society: An Economic History of Britain in the Middle Ages*, (London: Weidenfeld & Nicolson).

Raftis, J.A., (1957), *The Estates of Ramsey Abbey: A Study in Economic Growth and Organisation*, (Toronto: Pontificial Institute of Medeival Studies).

Round, J.H., (1895), *Feudal England: Historical Studies on the Eleventh and Twelfth Centuries*, reprinted 1964, (London: Allen & Unwin).

Round, J.H., (1903), Essex Survey, in VCH Essex, Vol. 1, reprinted 1977, (London: Dawson).

Stenton, F. M. (1943)*Anglo-Saxon England*, reprinted 1975, (Oxford: Clarendon Press).

Stenton, D.M., (1951), *English Society in the Early Middle Ages*, reprinted 1983, (Harmondsworth: Penguin).

Victoria County History, (1900), (London: Oxford University Press).

White, H. (1980) A Heteroskedasticity-consistent covarience matrix estimator and a direct test for heteroskedasticity, *Econometrica*, Vol. 48, No. 5: 817–838.

Williams, A., (ed)., (1987), *Domesday Book Studies*, (London: Alecto Historical Editions).

Notes

1   As Graeme and I indicated in (1986, p. 54), "After visual examination of only two hundreds (containing 12 observations) in *Inquisitio*, Round (1895, 48–49) asked rhetorically:

> What is the meaning of it? Simply that ASSESSMENT BORE NO RATIO TO AREA OR TO VALUE in a Vill, and still less in a Manor.

Assessment was not objective, but subjective; it was not fixed relatively to area or to value, but to the five-hide unit. The aim of the assessors was clearly to arrange the assessment in sums of five hides, ten hides, etc."

   In the following pages (pp. 54–58) we summarized the views of Maitland and more recent work of Domesday scholars.

2   In (1990a) and (1990b), we argued that the vill five-hide and hundred 100-hide regularity that occurred in many counties may have been the result of vill and hundred administrative boundaries being set so that assessments of estates contained within summed to these round totals. That is, we hypothesised that tax was assessed for estates and the assessments were then instrumental in determining the vill and hundred boundaries. This would explain both the five and 100-hide regularity (and the geographical irregularity of hundred and vill boundaries), why estate assessments bore a close relationship to an estates capacity to pay and why Domesday Book lists tax assessments for estates but not vills and hundreds.

3   Background information on Domesday England is contained in McDonald and Snooks (1986, Ch. 1 and 2; 1985a, 1985b, 1987a and 1987b) and McDonald (1998). For more comprehensive accounts of the history of the period see Brown (1984), Clanchy (1983), Loyn (1962), (1965), (1983), Stenton (1943), and Stenton (1951). Other useful references include Ballard (1906), Darby (1952), (1977), Galbraith (1961), Hollister (1965), Lennard (1959), Maitland (1897), Miller and Hatcher (1978), Postan (1966), (1972), Round (1895), (1903), the articles in Williams (1987) and references cited in McDonald and Snooks (1986). The Survey is discussed in McDonald and Snooks (1986, sec. 2.2), the references cited there, and the articles in Williams (1987). The Domesday and modern surveys are compared in McDonald and Snooks (1985c).

    Reconstruction of the Domesday economy is described in McDonald and Snooks (1986). Part 1 contains information on the basic tax and production relationships and Part 2 describes the methods used to estimate the relationships. Tax and production frontier analysis and efficiency comparisons are described in McDonald (1998). The book also explains the frontier methodology. A series of articles describe features of the research to different audiences: McDonald and Snooks (1985a, 1985b, 1987a, 1987b), economic historians; McDonald (2000), economists; McDonald (1997), management scientists; McDonald (2002), (2005) accounting historians (who recognize that Domesday Book possesses many attributes of an accounting record); and McDonald and Snooks (1985c), statisticians. Others who have made important contributions to our understanding of the Domesday economy include Miller and Hatcher (1978), Harvey (1983) and the contributors to the volumes edited by Aston (1987), Holt (1987), Hallam (1988) and Britnell and Campbell (1995).

4   The king's entries are usually longer, more complex and involve more holdings than the ecclesiastical and lay entries. Often there is one main estate and several satellite smallholdings. Many of the latter were held by Harold in 1066, and by 1086 had passed to lay or ecclesiastical lords. An example is the Lawford entry, which contains information on one large estate still held by the king in 1086 and six or more smaller holdings no longer in the king's hands in 1086, (Victoria History of Essex, pp. 434–5). Some of the larger ecclesiastical entries also involve several holdings, with the land held in both 1066 and 1086. The data file was compiled directly from Domesday Book entries in the Victoria County History of

Essex which were checked against a facsimile of the Latin transcript and an English translation in the Phillimore edition, (Morris, 1975). For a few estates, the value is not recorded (three king's estates, two ecclesiastical and 12 lay) and, for others, it is unclear how production was carried out because no labour is listed (although in some cases it could have been provided by the tenant) or, alternatively, no ploughteams and no livestock listed (21 king's, 18 ecclesiastical and 98 lay estates). A further five lay estate entries appear implausible, two more could not be located geographically and four other lay and one king's estate had no tax assessment.

5   The lay and ecclesiastical functions are very similar, but not the same, as those reported in McDonald and Snooks (1986) pages 63 and 69. The discrepancies result from differences in the samples. In this study, only estates for which there is comprehensive information are included in the sample. In the earlier study, all estates for which there is assessment and annual value information are in the sample.

6   A battery of tests indicates no heteroskedasticity in the disturbances. The test that the disturbance variances in the ecclesiastical and lay functions were equal is the Goldfeld-Quandt test, Goldfeld and Quandt (1965). When testing that disturbance variances in the king's and ecclesiastical equations were equal, the p-value was 0.358; for king's and lay it was 0.221 and for ecclesiastical and lay, 0.428.

7   For estates with annual values equal to the sample mean (of 30 shillings), the sample first quartile mean tax assessments for lay, church and king's estates were 124, 161 and 166 fiscal acres, respectively (that is, 30 per cent less for lay than church estates and 34 per cent less for lay than king's estates). For estates with annual values equal to the sample mean (80 shillings), the mean assessments were 250, 335 and 308 fiscal acres, respectively (34 per cent less for lay than church estates and 23 per cent less for lay than king's estates) and for estates with annual values equal to the sample third quartile (140 shillings), the mean assessments were 371, 510 and 438 fiscal acres, respectively (37 per cent less for lay than church estates and 18 per cent less for lay than king's estates).

8   In McDonald (1998, ch. 6.4) and (2002, pp. 178–182), there are extended discussions of this and other possible tax frontiers and BTI definitions, and the question of whether the "true" frontier can be determined empirically. The major conclusion to the latter question is that it is not possible to determine the "true" frontier empirically, but, if there is a reasonable number of observations, well-distributed over the net income values, the alternative plausible functions will be similar and the index numbers similar.

9   Examples are the assessments of 273 High Easter (BTI = 6.08) described as "a very low hidation" (VCH,1903, footnote 4, p. 509), 241 Stambourne and Toppesfield (BTI = 12.78) referred to as "an almost nominal amount" (footnote 4, p. 502), 374 Fairsted (BTI = 15.27), described as "strangely low" (VCH, 1903, footnote 4, p. 527) and 571 Gestingthorp (BTI = 14.48) also referred to as "strangely low" (footnote 9, p. 564).

10 The test was carried out by regressing estate BTIs on hundred dummy variables taking the value 1, if the estate was in the hundred; 0, otherwise. Since the regression diagnostics indicated heteroskedasticity in the disturbances, White's (1980) heteroskedasticity-consistent test was used. The test p-value was zero.

11 The hundred location was indicated by 22 dummy variables, size was measured by the single best indicator of the economic size of an estate, the estate's annual value. An index of whether production was mainly arable or grazing is given by the grazing/arable ratio, defined as livestock less cattle and beasts (which were required for ploughing) divided by the number of ploughteams on the estate. (Livestock less cattle and beasts is a weighted average of swine, sheep and goats with prices as weights. Five estates had no ploughteams. For them, the ratio was set at 2000, the largest ratio value for estates with some ploughteams being 1376). Finally, tenure was measured by dummy variable taking the value 1, if the estate was held in demesne; 0, otherwise. Test statistics are heteroskedasticity-consistent tests statistics obtained by White's (1980) method.

9

Rural Transformation and the Plight of the Displaced in Industrializing Britain

Eric Richards

Flinders University, Adelaide

Abstract

Modern economic development almost always causes large-scale displacement of agrarian peoples. The British case was dramatic and attracted the attention of contemporary continental European observers, one of whom, Sismondi, placed the problem at the centre of his precocious critique of the newly industrializing economy of Britain. The agrarian part of his indictment drew heavily on the special example of rural transformation in the Scottish Highlands and this also flowed into his influence on other thinkers, notably Hugh Miller and Karl Marx. But none of them had answers to the problem of what to do about the displaced rural populations; nor did their contemporaries have anything much better to offer. So what actually happened to the displaced? Their plight was part of the great adjustments in the British economy which occupied many decades of the 19th century. The social costs were greatest in places where alternative employment was either distant or slow to develop.

I

In the 1960s, at Flinders as elsewhere, the study of economic development and economic history were closely entwined. Two issues dominated their landscapes. One was the genesis and maintenance of economic growth which drew a new and exciting literature. The second concerned the consequences of rapid economic change, and this caused some bracing controversies, more among historians than economists. For both questions there existed a backlog of ideas from the history of political economy and this intellectual legacy gave the debates interesting, but often dubious, foundations.

One aspect of these questions is my present concern: namely the problems of population displacement generated by rapid agrarian change under conditions of modernization. The question is: what do societies do with the people dislocated by rural transformation? This is a generic problem that recurs in most cases of recent economic development but it also reaches back to the earliest examples we can document in economic history. The problem was expressed in classic form during the industrialization of the British economy, identifiable as early as the 1780s, but persisting as a political and economic dilemma for the best part of the following century.

The first stages in the passage of the British economy towards industrialization compare closely with later societies undergoing structural change.[1] The British case was associated with two crucial and widespread conditions. The first was population growth after 1780 on an unprecedented scale and velocity. The second was a rapid and momentous acceleration in the growth of agricultural productivity (which had been building for several decades). Population growth was in many places at a rate which expanded the resulting rural labour force much faster than the agricultural sector was able to absorb or employ.[2] Concurrently new agricultural techniques made gains in productivity in every dimension, including labour inputs. Consequently there was an implacable problem concerning the displacement of people from the land. It was a problem much accentuated by the fact that agricultural improvement required a radical reconfiguration of the entire rural sector. This, in practice, usually took the form of the consolidation of land holdings, the rationalization of land use and tenures, the redeployment of resources and tenantries, economies of scale and a much more rigorous quality control of all aspects of production. It all added up to the doom of the old rural economy, sometimes at breakneck speed. It was a process of change at the heart of British history in the late 18th century. The displacement of the rural population, in its many different variants, became the hallmark of the wider progress of agriculture: dislocation was the *sine qua non* of adjustment in this sector of the British economy—which was, of course, the biggest sector until 1851, in terms of employment.

The British case was *sui generis*, but was repeated in endless versions across the globe during the following decades of modern history. The pressure to induce rapid rural change has been widespread, almost universal. Often the change takes on cataclysmic proportions. Sometimes the transformation is forced through by State *fiat*, or by the concentrated powers of the landowning class. Inevitably there is a turbulent dislocation of traditional rural systems— and often there is a negative reaction among the people dislocated, sometimes erupting into overt or subterranean resistance. Wherever such changes occur— in, for example, Scotland, the Philippines, Ireland, Zimbabwe, Spain, Poland, Cuba and Russia, at different times—the consequences have been fundamental in the restructuring of the rural community.

The questions posed here are: What becomes of these people displaced in the early phases of economic change? What are they supposed to do? More particularly we can ask what generally were the solutions advocated in the British case? What did the political economists have to say? In this paper I pursue the thinking of a relatively neglected theorist of the time, and then refer to some of the contemporary efforts to grapple with a problem which was, as I have already claimed, an inescapable hurdle along the pathways of all modern economic development.

II

In the British case the problem was sometimes referred to as "the severance of the peasant from the soil". It was not a new phenomenon in the history of the British economies: it was indeed a central political question in Tudor and Stuart times—in "Tawney's Century", when wool production and enclosures shifted large parts of the rural population of England. In Ireland the invasion of Scots and English plantation settlers caused massive disruption, and the political consequences have reverberated down to the present. In the 18th century the accelerated progression of enclosures generated a literature of protest and melancholy, most elegantly registered in Oliver Goldsmith's "Deserted Village" of 1770. The drive and urgency of agricultural improvement created widespread dislodgment but, in the early phases, many of the people ousted were mopped-up in the new agriculture which continued to absorb some of the net increase in labour until the 1840s.

In the history of political economy this generic problem seems to have been first fully-focussed in the writings of certain foreign observers who witnessed British industrialization at first hand in the early and most momentous decades of the great change. There was, indeed, a succession of continental commentators whose representations of the vast structural change were somewhat out of harmony with the "eternal verities" of the Smithian School. Among these discrepant observers from Europe were Jean Baptiste Say, J.C.L. Simonde de Sismondi, Léone de Lavergne, and J.A. Blanqui; even Hegel was much persuaded, and the tradition, of course, was later carried to Marx and Engels.[3] Most of them, instead of admiring the achievements of the revolution in the British economy, reached decidedly negative judgments about its consequences.

Among these continental observers, Sismondi (1773–1842) was one of the earliest and most troubled and his place in the history of economic thought is perhaps the least secure. His personal background was exotic: he was born in Geneva of Swiss-Italian roots and into an affluent family. They were caught up in the French Revolution and fled to London in 1793–4 where they stayed for 18 months, later returning to Geneva and then settling on a farm in Italy. Sismondi led a peripatetic life. He married an Englishwoman with good literary connections in England and Scotland, but they mainly lived in Geneva. He visited England in 1818, 1819, 1820, 1826, 1828, 1832 and 1840, and he knew the country well. His literary output was prodigious—he wrote with ceaseless energy, including dozens of volumes on historical subjects, as well as many works on political economy. It is the trajectory of his economic ideas that attracts my attention here. Sismondi began as an admiring disciple of Adam Smith, keenly aware of the benefits of trade and of the extending division of labour. Indeed Sismondi introduced such ideas to French-speaking audiences and prepared several of his early works and texts in a grand effort to spread the Smithian gospel.

Sismondi was, however, seriously disconcerted by his direct observations of the social and economic condition of Britain during his visits. The timing of his excursions may have been crucial since Sismondi visited the cradle of industrialization at particularly severe moments in its headlong expansion—that is, during the post-Napoleonic War years when the economy experienced extremely unstable conditions, recurrent mass urban unemployment and rural upheaval, not to mention the political context which seemed to veer towards revolution. Whatever the immediate circumstances, Sismondi underwent a decided alteration in his understanding and appreciation of the new industrial economy. By the middle of the second decade of the new century he began a series of criticisms which emerged into a substantial critique of the free liberal economy and its home-grown ideologues. He was one of the earliest analysts to question the benefits of industrialization. In the process he delivered some of the first propositions to question the key tenets of classical political economy— and consequently he has always occupied a significant niche in the evolution of critical economic ideas. Malthus and Ricardo were both engaged by his writings; later it is clear that Marx was also influenced by Sismondi, even if somewhat irritably and reluctantly. But Sismondi's ideas were evidently derived from his first-hand exposure to the realities of industrialization during his visits to Britain.

His conversion was the work of ten years. In 1805 his economic writing was a perfectly conventional version of Adam Smith. Within a decade, in an article for Dr Brewster's *Edinburgh Encyclopaedia*, he performed a personal turnabout and was now eloquently critical of free trade, *laissez faire* and industrial capitalism. He declared, for instance, that "the progress of its [the nation's] wealth is illusory, when obtained at the price of general wretchedness and mortality".[4] Now, according to Blaug, Sismondi was "Convinced that the new industrial system was doomed to suffer recurrent depressions and a chronic tendency towards under-consumption; he was particularly struck by the labour-saving bias of technical progress to which he saw no answer except government intervention of a far-reaching kind, including a guaranteed minimum wage in and out of work, a ceiling on hours of work, a floor and ceiling on the age of work, and the introduction of profit-sharing schemes."[5]

Beyond these ideas was the even more fundamental notion that seized Sismondi's mind in the Depression that followed the Napoleonic Wars— namely the evidence of over-production (or under-consumption) which he deduced from his direct observation of the extreme unemployment, hunger and poverty after Waterloo. The idea of "over-production" led to the notion of recurrent and inevitable gluts occurring in the new economy. It was a position which put Sismondi in doctrinal opposition to the prevailing ideas of Say in particular, and he was generally condemned by everyone except Malthus. There is indeed a line of thought which credits Sismondi as a precursor of basic ideas about aggregate demand analysis which may be traced through Malthus and then towards Keynes. In his *Nouveaux principes d'économie politique* (1819) Sismondi argued that current economic science had concentrated its entire attention on the means of increasing wealth but only at the expense of the ways in which wealth was to be used to increase human happiness. The new economic system, he declared, did not behave in a benign fashion and produced disastrous and worsening fluctuations of economic activity: "Let us beware the dangerous theory of equilibrium which is supposed to be automatically established. A certain kind of equilibrium, it is true, is re-established in the long-run, but it is after a frightful amount of suffering."[6] Sismondi was also, in the process, identifying the problem of transition in the changing economy, the transition which caused dislocation and deprivation among groups deprived of protection since they possessed minimal market power.

Sismondi had been one of the first observers to say openly that the prevailing doctrines of political economy had failed to recognised the inherent contradictions and negative consequences of unfettered competition in the market economy. As Halévy points out, Sismondi was able to "go further than Jean-Baptiste Say and to note the insufficiency of the remedies proposed by classical political economy and the theoretical weakness of that political economy."[7] He diagnosed the internal conflict in the rise of industrial society: in Sismondi's words, "basing all political economy on the principle of unlimited competition is to justify the efforts of every man against society and to sacrifice the interest of humanity to the simultaneous action of all forms of industrial greed."[8]

As Blaug insists, Sismondi was less a theorist than a man who appealed to the "facts", to his response to realities about him, and his observations were essentially about the mass suffering of the working people in the new industrial Britain. According to Halévy, Sismondi, after he had visited England in 1818, "returned to the continent shocked by the spectacle that had met his eyes. He had come across nothing but incoherence and anarchy, excess of industrial activity and excessive poverty." He had witnessed "badly paid workmen [who] were dying of hunger in the face of this pile of wealth. As against these realities he found in possession of public opinion a supposed economic science which suggested no other remedy for the crisis than the abstention of the government."[9] Most of all, Sismondi identified the working people as "the victims par excellence of the factory system"—and declared that the "workers and owners ... [are] locked in a perpetual class struggle". This indeed was his coinage, and his diagnosis appealed greatly to Marx and his school.[10] Consequently Sismondi is regarded as among the forerunners of both Marx and Keynes, and as "the first critic of industrial capitalism." As Eric Roll pointed out, Sismondi was "one of the earliest economists to speak of the existence of two social classes, the rich and the poor, the capitalists and the workers, whose interest he regarded as ... in constant conflict with one another" and the rich were, therefore, the actual enemies of the poor.[11] Competition, the division of labour, the proliferation of machines and the resulting competition, he argued, brought about "the concentration of wealth in the hands of a smaller and smaller number of individuals and the concentration of business in larger and larger firms."[12] Most of all, "He denied the liberal theory of automatic harmony between private interests and the general interest." It is not difficult to see the attraction of Sismondi to subsequent radical critics of capitalism.[13]

Sismondi made the case that the great advance of economic production in Britain had produced the "most alarming disturbance in the relations and conditions of the members of society". It had polarised society between the capitalists and the wage-earner; in the process the small proprietors, small farmers, small businesses had been eliminated in the new industrial system.[14] This was his theory of the "progressive proletarianization of the masses."[15]

As his biographer, De Salis, says, Sismondi was a critic of "unbridled economic freedom". He was "profoundly shocked by the often tragic consequences of the industrial revolution". This, however, was combined with an admiration for England and its progressive ways and throughout Sismondi's critique there is an air of ambivalence and intellectual perplexity which put him off side with the Marxists and the liberals. He would not sanction socialism but wanted some vague degree of government intervention. Marx and Engels regarded him as "at once reactionary and utopian". De Salis describes Sismondi as "a wanderer between two ages, who wanted progress and at the same time feared its consequences" and was "the admirer of English constitutionalism."[16]

Sismondi was, therefore, a precocious critic not only of industrialism but also of its attendant philosophy in the form of classical political economy. Yet he generally failed his more doctrinaire successors in the tradition of radical theory. The trouble with Sismondi was that he was authentically perplexed about what could be done. His prescriptions were modest and essentially gradualist or backward-looking. McCulloch dismissed Sismondi as "too much a sentimentalist to make a good political economist".[17] As a social reformer Sismondi held off from root and branch prescriptions—he was in all this no revolutionary. This brought him damnation in the pantheon of socialist thinkers. Sismondi was regarded by Marxists as a "petty-bourgeois critic of capitalism". For Marx he was an interesting but seriously limited theorist.[18]

In 1845 Peel referred to the criticism of "Italian [sic] economists that their English colleagues concentrated on wealth and overlooked welfare" and Peel was probably alluding to Sismondi.[19] Joseph Schumpeter remarks that Sismondi's fame rose steadily until "with social reformers and opponents of *laissez-faire* in general, he was eventually raised to one of those positions to which it becomes etiquette to pay respect".[20] For the radical critics the problem with Sismondi was his continuing attachment to liberalism and the sheer modesty of his recommendations and his apparent reluctance to advocate revolutionary action.

III

From this broad critique of industrial capitalism we may extract the strand which applied specifically to the travails of the rural economy under the pressures and incentives of modernization. The ferocious tendencies identified by Sismondi were not confined to the new regime of industrial capitalism. They were equally rampant in rural society. I want to examine the roots of Sismondi's exposition and their adoption by later writers—which became part of a powerful interpretation of the British and, particularly, the Scottish experience. After that I want to consider, in the briefest manner, the way in which some contemporaries actually wrestled with the problem of rural displacement.

In terms of agricultural performance the British had, for decades, been filled with self-congratulation: they "preened" themselves on their superiority over other countries in terms of agricultural improvement and technical advancement. But European observers—not least Sismondi himself—were much less impressed by the economic efficiency of British agriculture; they reacted much more to the "the dire social effects of landlordism and especially the concentration of landownership". Both Say and Sismondi believed that "the hallmarks of the English system were the creation of a mass of impoverished landless labourers as a result of enclosure, and a rural poverty aggravated rather than relieved by the operation of the unreformed poor laws".[21] It was an indictment parallel to the case relating to the factories—agriculture itself had been industrialized into great commercial farms which culminated in "the displacement of artisans and peasants by a swelling class of day labourers", i.e. a proletariat. And it was all built on the foundation of unconstrained internal competition and a growing polarity between "rich and poor guided by economists whose constant refrain was *laissez faire et laissez passer*".[22]

Sismondi claimed that the English peasantry had been hastened to its destruction in contrast to their preservation in France. He remarked, "we must shudder at the idea that the law, as it is interpreted in England, permits the expulsion of a whole nation from its hearthstones, without providing in any way for its subsistence and its future fate."[23] He saw the conversion of land into great commercial farms as causing the destruction of the cottagers, and with it the end to all "the charm of property" as he put it.[24] He harked back to the lost paternalism of the countryside before industrialism.

Sismondi had no particular remedies for these perceived consequences except a vague invocation of some kind of protective state framework of regulation of the rights of property—a sort of buffer against the gale of change "to replace feudal protectors in the countryside." His thinking was an echo of the kind of "rural nostalgia" which is mainly associated with Coleridge and Cobbett.[25] This may have carried virtually no theoretical clout, but it was a potent strain in political thinking for much of the following century—that is to say, the notion that many economic and social problems of the new age could be diminished by a return to pre-industrial forms. It was, in effect, "the philosophy of the smallholder". This did not appeal to the Marxist/Leninist school, but it was influential in many parts of the British Isles and the source of inspiration to many social idealists and utopians across the "Anglo World" in the 19th century.

Sismondi derived much of his diagnosis from a particularly extreme case of rural transformation in the classic years of the industrial revolution, a case which reverberated in the subsequent literature, even down to the present. This was in northern Scotland and was later called the "Highland Clearances"— which entailed the widespread removal of a large portion of the so-called indigenous population out of their traditional inland communities to make way for the much more lucrative and newly commercialized sheep farming. Highly capitalized, sheep farming used the land intensively and extensively, and required large-scale entrepreneurial risk-takers (many of them men from outwith the region). Sheep-grazing possessed very weak backward- and forward-linkages to other employment-generating activities within the Highlands. Most of all, the new sector of the economy had little use for labour in any quantity. This combination of characteristics, therefore, created an intense crisis for the existing labour supply: the people of the region were rendered redundant at a time when their own numbers were rising at a spectacular rate. This was a severe variant of technological displacement, a great structural disturbance in a remote corner of the British Isles. The Highland Clearances caused widespread distress and were accompanied in many instances by episodes of cruelty and rough handling by estate officials, police and even the militia, all working at the behest of the landlords. Inevitably the story became a prime example of class conflict, the alleged betrayal of the people by their traditional protectors, the lairds, and the destruction of a Gaelic culture. There were even allegations of genocide. (Parallels with the current "History Wars" in Australia spring to mind.) The Highland Clearances remains a subject which raises temperatures even now—witness the ongoing proceeding in the new Scottish Parliament designed to correct the iniquities of the past in the Highlands.[26]

In the Highland example, the consequences of this sudden, sometimes cataclysmic, rural displacement were greatly exacerbated by the rapid growth of the local population which continued to the mid 19th century. This was a demographic increase loaded upon a society which had, since time immemorial, been vulnerable to seasonal and recurrent harvest shortfall, to conditions repeatedly close to famine, and these recurred later than elsewhere in mainland Britain.

The Highland Clearances were brought to public attention by Sismondi himself, especially in his essay on "Landed Property," published in February 1834, which trained a spotlight on the evictions in the extreme northern Highlands taking place since the 1810s.[27] Sismondi employed his considerable powers of rhetoric not only to denounce the landlords but also to expose the consequences of what he saw as the industrialization of agriculture. In effect the small producers had become the victims of the process and his only answer was to urge the State to intervene to ameliorate the damage on their behalf. He employed the Highlands as his central example of the impact of capitalist transformation and the concentration of production in the old rural world.

Sismondi's rendition of the Highland case later entered several branches of economic literature giving the story a far wider currency over many decades. Within Scotland Sismondi's analysis helped the case against the lairds and his authority was assimilated into the campaigns of rural protest—most especially in the hands of the eloquent and fiery journalist and Presbyterian/Free Church spokesman, Hugh Miller (1802–1856). Miller in 1841 produced a devastating denunciation which employed electrifying language and metaphor to undermine the landlords—but his intellectual inspiration clearly derived from Sismondi (who had probably never been anywhere near the Highlands). Miller's indictment of the clearing landlords was first and foremost a moral argument directed against the alleged greed, insensitivity and cruelty of the landlords.[28] But Miller also asserted a pragmatic intellectual case: it was based on the notion that the great changes in the Highlands were unnecessary and had culminated in economic and social disaster for all parties. The people were dispossessed, degraded and impoverished; the landlords themselves gained little in the long run and the nation as a whole benefited very little. It had been "a disastrous change".[29] He believed that the Clearances simply made no sense. Miller's case was a blanket denial of the need for any kind of change in the Highlands—the past was better than the new context of the modernizing Highlands.

Even greater influence from Sismondi flowed into the Marxist tradition. Drawing directly on Sismondi, Marx himself used the Highland example as the clearest instance of capitalist expropriation of the lands of the people, and the conversion of peasantries into the labour fodder for the hungry jaws of industry.

Marx drew on Sismondi's *Études sociales* in his writings denouncing one of the great landowners, the duchess of Sutherland; this subsequently became the key example of "aristocratic expropriation" in *Das Capital*.[30] Marx spoke of the "systematic robbery of the communal lands" of the people, and the creation of the large farming industry which ejected the agricultural population for the uses of modern manufacturing industry. It was the prime version of the "expropriation of the agricultural population from the soil".[31]

Two points may be made regarding the status of this line of thinking about the displacement of the Highland peasantry as used in Sismondi, Miller and Marx. The first involves the original source of the analysis invoked by all three, and by their successors. Almost all the details of the case in the Highlands were, oddly enough, derived from an elaborate defence of the landlords published in 1816 and 1820.[32] Sismondi read the material and manipulated it into his critique of the entire system of agricultural improvement. In effect he assimilated the landlord's own rationale of the argument for radical change and then denounced it on the grounds that the consequences were too damaging for the communities caught up in the process.

The second point is more central to the gravamen of this paper. The powerful critiques expounded by Sismondi and Miller seemed to terminate in despair. They certainly excoriated the landlords and their system which sanctioned the great rural transformations, and their social consequences. But they had no remedy except to exhort the landlord to behave in a more humane fashion and for the government to intervene to curb their policies. Their prescriptions were essentially conservative and backward-looking, entailing a return to the pre-industrial world which was evidently being lost.[33] Moreover they were both averse to radical resistance and both recoiled from the idea of revolutionary change in society. Sismondi, in particular, suffered a particular fate—he offered no ammunition to the radicals and was, as we have seen, finally denounced by the Marxists a mere *petit bourgeois*, described by Lenin as an "economic romantic".

Sismondi wept over the costs which industrialization imposed upon the proletarians but had no other remedy than a return to the simple life of the long-gone rural economy of tradition.[34] At the end of his life Sismondi despaired that he had been ignored, declaring in 1835 that no one showed any interest in his ideas. He believed that "the gospel of greed and opulence" had prevailed and that commercialism and the immiseration of the working class had continued unabated. One of his last diary entries declared:

> I cry, take care, you are bruising, you are crushing miserable persons who do not even see from whence comes the evil which they experience, but who remain languishing and mutilated on the road which you have passed over. I cry out, and not one hears me: I cry out and the car of the Juggernaut continues to roll on, making new victims.[35]

In the outcome, despite the eloquence and seriousness of their critiques of industrialism and the landlords, neither Sismondi nor Miller offered any answer to the question of rural displacement. And as for Marx, his answer—revolutionary upheaval—proved difficult to achieve and, everyone seems to agree, disastrous in practice (for example, in Russia under Stalin), with consequences which make the British case look like one of history's tea-parties.

IV

The displacement of people by radical agricultural change was, as I have suggested, a general phenomenon in the course of economic development. The difficulties faced by armchair theorists as they struggled with the question seem relatively slight when compared with those confronting the real world at large—landlords, governments, farmers, philanthropists, poor law administrators and, of course, the people themselves (who were rarely consulted in the process). The plight of the displaced threw up a large array of solutions, many still-born, and most of which were, at best, only partially effective. This section offers a few contemporary examples, set in the general context, and again with a somewhat Scottish flavouring.

In Scotland, from at least 1750, there was a widespread and identified problem of coping with the dislodged and redundant population, and this was by no means confined to the Highlands. Population growth and agricultural dislocation—usually termed "Improvement"—caused rising problems of relocation and alternative provision for the people affected. The Scottish solution was distinctive—across the country there was a concerted movement to develop new villages, specifically to accommodate the people displaced out of the farming sector.

Scotland was small country, with a population of about 1.26 million in 1750, but during little more than a century about 400 new villages were created. They almost always catered for people from within a few miles of their former places of residence; few had to move more that 20 miles. The villages provided houses, new lines of employment, some intensified arable cultivation, and investment in what now looks like proto-industrial infrastructure.[36] Mostly they were the initiatives of the landlords, partly motivated by paternalistic considerations, partly by the belief that the re-accommodated people would stay on their estates and contribute to further rent increases. Not least, the proprietors were inspired by the mercantilist doctrine which sought to retain as large a population as possible. (This notion was weakened substantially by 1800–10 when the fear of overpopulation began to grip many districts.) As one commentator puts it, "landowners built planned villages to re-house some of the excess labour, subsidized local textile industries, and built new harbours to provide employment for tradesmen and fishermen." Some of the villages were spontaneous developments responding to new market potential but the majority seem to have been planned as part of an articulated policy of modernization and absorbing the off-loaded population out of agriculture. The scale and substantial success of many of them seem to have helped Scottish rural society to cope with the revolution in demography and employment.[37] Part of their function was to retain enough seasonal labour for the newly commercial agricultural sector—some of them were likened to "holding centres" in this context.[38]

Some of these villages were sustained but many faded away and eventually—by the mid-19th century—the aggregate labour force in rural Scotland, both Lowland and Highland, was falling. In the Highlands the village solution was attempted, in some cases with immensely ambitious investment plans, but conditions for labour retention were much more difficult and were almost universally ineffective, merely palliatives to the growing problem of a displaced and impoverished people. Indeed in the Highlands where, as we have seen, the reputation of the landlords was among the lowest in the British Isles, there was a spectrum of landlord responses to the problem. They ranged from, at one end, instant eviction and ejection from the soil, often with tragic consequences. At the other extreme, there were elaborate efforts to provide expansive alternative accommodation, usually associated with "the village model". In the end, most of the Highland villages failed and few now exist as ongoing communities.

What else could have been done with the displaced rural populations in Britain? It was obviously one of the most alarming and threatening questions that gripped the age of Malthus and his contemporaries—namely how to deal with the surplus of people manifested, once and for all, in the early census returns and, more palpably, in the congestion of population in the west of Ireland and the instant slums of English and Scottish cities. Malthus himself announced that the population growth would be inevitably checked, one way or another, and should not be encouraged beyond its own natural propensity to exceed its capacity to sustain itself. In rural areas the possibility of emigration might, he conceded, provide some temporary alleviation—but only if the cottages of those departing were immediately destroyed to prevent their re-occupation (which would then lead to further demographic resurgence).[39] And many rural people did take to the roads and to the emigrant ships in the early 19th century. As David Fitzpatrick remarks, "Many Irish migrants to Britain were typical of that vast force of surplus labourers from many parts of the British Isles, which roamed about the industrial centres hoping for casual employment. These migratory habits were already commonplace among the Irish of the east long before the Famine."[40] Irish emigration indeed was rising rapidly and well before the much anticipated famine of the 1840s.

But emigration was never enough and was opposed in many places as any kind of solution to the problem of oversupplied labour in agriculture, even in the Irish case. Irish nationalist opinion, which had its analogue in Scotland and in parts of England too, deplored the loss of Irish bone and sinew, and advocated the coordinated internal colonization of Ireland: there was an influential idea to reclaim waste land and the Bog Commissioners in Ireland reported (1810–1814) that there were huge acreages of potentially reclaimable land available and that intensive cultivation could provide sustenance for the masses of the people.[41] In retrospect these schemes seem extraordinarily improbable, and most historians now accept the proposition that the acceleration of emigration from Ireland in the decades before the Famine operated therapeutically to diminish the subsequent catastrophe of the Potato Famine.

The idea of encouraging the small-scale producers in the rural sector to modernize their methods and their mentalities—in effect, to compete with the new commercial agriculture—was recurrently advocated throughout the 19th century. There were ideas for co-operative enterprise, for small peasant farms, for crofting and for new rural industries on the handicraft basis. Others advocated breaking up the great estates into small farms; and there was a parallel movement to promote "the allotment system", partly to re-engage the working class with the land, even if only in a marginal fashion.[42]

The results were, of course, very limited and had little real bearing on the vast mass of people disengaged from the rural world. Yet the history of these solutions is integral to the story. They often owed much to the romantic "ruralist nostalgia" for the age of the small producer (in Raymond Williams' phrase), to the "philosophy of the smallholder".[43] There subsisted also the equally fanciful notion that the peasant life typical of so much of continental Europe, was preferable to the proletarianized form of British rural life, whatever its efficiency. Some British landlords, especially those troubled by the plight of their population, attempted to revive and modernize small-scale production, specifically as an alternative to mass displacement and emigration. There is an older literature extolling the virtues of peasant life—and William Cobbett can be counted as one of its English exponents. Back in the Scottish Highlands there were examples of landlords—humanitarians—who tried with great sincerity to resurrect the smallholder economy, to rescue it from its squalor and inefficiency. There was, for instance, a well-meaning attempt to replicate the Belgian peasant system in Gairloch in the west Highlands—but it ended in depression and a sense of hopelessness, the landlord, typically, descending towards bankruptcy.[44] The counterpart of this sort of response was the attitude of the people facing displacement: this, almost invariably, was to resist change and dispossession in a thousand different ways.

V

What then were the consequences of rural displacement? What became of the millions of British people no longer attached to the soil? We should not understate this point—the sheer scale of the question was masked for many decades by the fact that the new agriculture absorbed a substantial proportion of the swollen rural population—indeed in many places the agricultural labour force, in total numbers, rose cumulatively until the census of 1851—after which it declined continuously to the present day. But this is not the real point—the rural sector was unable to absorb or employ the great accumulating increments of population increase in the long succession of decades after 1750. In every rural region of the British Isles the population went into absolute decline after 1850 as rural productivity continued to rise throughout the decades of industrialization. On top of this was the astonishing growth of population which doubled twice between 1800 and 1900.[45] This, of course, massively increased the problem of absorbing the increase, most tragically in Ireland in the 1840s, but also creating practical and profound problems across the British Isles.

If Sismondi, Malthus, Marx and Miller and their contemporaries had no operational solutions to the problem, what then did become of the displaced? They were ultimately, of course, absorbed into the wider economy which, again over the very long run, not only accommodated the greatly increased population but also supported a higher and more secure living standard. This skates over the vast achievement entailed in the transformation; it also discounts the heavy costs of the transition, most of which were carried by the most vulnerable elements in the economy. But the process was complicated and drawn out, entailing countless millions of small and large adjustments across the industrializing economy. These adjustments can best be seen in individual lives or in small communities, following their actual careers longitudinally over several decades. Such detailed studies in certain districts of Yorkshire, for instance, are able to trace the lives of people who were "surplus to local employment requirements" in the early decades of the 19th century, in parts of Wensleydale. As a visitor in 1805 reported, "many of the poor families in this dale are very numerous ... [and] the country is not able to find support for all the inhabitants, insomuch that a great part of the youth when old enough are compelled to migrate." Over the following six decades Wensleydale lost most of its natural population increase to short-distance migration, and this was indeed the local solution: after 1831 the population fell absolutely in Wensleydale. There was little apparent cohesion in the movements, nor was much of it in the form of emigration (not at least directly to the emigrant ports). Traced in individual detail, it seems that the Wensleydale "migrants moved relatively short distances and, wherever possible, followed occupations with which they were familiar". Emigration was certainly talked about widely but affected only a few, some to the United States, a few with capital leaving for Australia in the 1830s.[46] The most interesting element in the process was its incremental and repeated character—it was a series of adjustments over short distances, internal movements much more significant than external migration. Yet the effect of these short movements was to shift the entire population and a massive realignment of people out of the rural sector over a relatively short historical time period.

Scotland's most incisive modern historian, T.C. Smout, once wrote about the manner in which European societies chose different ways to avoid "a subsistence Armageddon"—that is, the threatened outcome of the "over rapid demographic growth that sabotages so many modern countries in their attempt to make gains in per capita income." He notes the way in which the poorer members of rural communities "have wished to leave the land for the towns for their own good and sufficient reasons." He cites examples in Norway, Aberdeenshire, northern Sweden, the Scottish Highlands and Finland. He asks, "Are we to weep about these things too? And by what right?" The solution to prolonged structural poverty in such places as the Scottish Highlands and Ireland, says Smout, was out-migration.[47] This, naturally, was a solution only if there was somewhere better to which to migrate—for the British Isles this overwhelmingly meant the towns and cities of the new industrial economy which, astonishingly, absorbed the concurrent revolutionary demographic growth and the human consequences of massive rural displacement.

Sismondi, seeing the transformation at close quarters in its most strained moments (in 1818, for instance), completely misread the long-term effects of economic change and perceived only the immediate social costs. He was not alone.

Notes

1 The problem of displacement is not, of course, confined to passages of agrarian development. Comparable consequences evidently occur in wartime; similarly the termination of slavery and re-organization of the old plantations created large problems regarding the re-settlement and re-accommodation of former slaves. On the latter in the Caribbean context, see, for instance, Douglas Hall, "The Flight from the Estates Reconsidered: the British West Indies, 1838–42", *Journal of Caribbean History*, 10/11 (1978), pp. 7–24, for which reference I thank Professor Barry Higman.

2 See for instance references in Eric Richards, "Agriculture and Veterinary Science in the Enlightenment", in Alan Charles Kors (ed.), *Encyclopaedia of the Enlightenment* (New York, 2003) vol. 1, pp.32–38.

3 See Gareth Stedman Jones, "National bankruptcy and social revolution: European observers in Britain, 1813–1844," in D. Winch and P.K. O'Brien (eds), *The Political Economy of British Historical Experience, 1688–1914* (Oxford, 2002), pp. 61–92, and W.A. Armstrong, "Labour", in G.E. Mingay (ed.), *The Agrarian History of England and Wales* VI (Cambridge, 1989), p.641f.

4 Article "Political economy", *Edinburgh Encyclopaedia* (Edinburgh, 1815), p. 50.

5 Mark Blaug (ed.), *Henry Thornton, Jeremy Bentham, James Lauderdale, Simonde de Sismondi* (Aldershot, 1991), p. xiii.

6 Sismondi, *Nouveaux principes d'économie politique* (Paris, 1819) I, pp. 21–2. [*New Principles of Political Economy*, English translation by Richard Hyse (New Brunswick, N.J., 1991).]

7 Elie Halévy, "Sismondi" [1933], in *The Era of Tyrannies* (New York, 1966), p.6.

8 Ibid. p. 7, quoting Sismondi.

9 See Elie Halévy, *The Growth of Philosophic Radicalism* (London, 1928, ed. 1972), p. 318.

10 See on these connections and issues Ronald L. Meek (ed.), *Marx and Engels on Malthus* (London, 1953), passim.

11 Cited in J.K. Galbraith, *A History of Economics* (London, 1987), p. 97. My thanks go to Dr Robin Haines for this reference.

12 See especially Elie Halévy, "Sismondi" [1933], in *The Era of Tyrannies* (New York, 1966), pp. 11 and 1–20.

13 J.R. De Salis, *Switzerland and Europe: Essays and Reflections* edited by Christopher Hughes (London, 1971), p. 247. Marx indeed remarked that "Sismondi has a deeply-rooted presentiment that capitalist production is in contradiction with itself; that on the one hand its forms, its relations of production, stimulate an unbridled development of the productive forces and of wealth; that on the other hand these relations of production are subject to certain conditions; that their contradictions—between use value and exchange value, commodity and money, purchase and sale, production and consumption, capital and wage labour, etc.— are increasingly accentuated with the development of the productive forces." In other words Sismondi had divined the essential contradiction of the capitalist system and its inevitable conflicts. R.L. Meek, *Marx and Engels*, pp. 161–62.

14 Sismondi, *Political Economy and the Philosophy of Government* (London, 1847), p.152.

15 J.-R. De Salis, *Switzerland and Europe: Essays and Reflections*, edited by Christopher Hughes (London, 1971), p. 248.

16 Ibid., especially pp. 245–6, 250, 252. The major biography is J-R. De Salis, *Sismondi 1773–1842: la vie et l'oeuvre d'un cosmopolite philosophique* (Paris, 1932).

17 M. Blaug, *Henry Thornton*, p. 204, fn. 32, quoting McCulloch to Ricardo, 18 April 1819, in Piero Sraffa (ed.), *The Works and Correspondence of David Ricardo* vol. 8 (Cambridge, 1962), pp. 24–5.

18 See Karl Marx, "The Duchess of Sutherland and Slavery", *New York Daily Tribune* No. 3687, 8 February 1853, reprinted in *Collected Works* vol. 11 (Moscow, 1979), pp.486–94. See also Mao-Lan Tuan, *Simonde De Sismondi as an Economist* (AMS Press, New York, 1927), reprint, 1968). The extent of Malthus' reliance on Sismondi regarding the theory of gluts is treated sceptically by Joseph Schumpeter, *History of Economic Analysis*, (London, 1954), p. 481, fn 2. See also J.E. King, "Non-Marxian Socialism", in J.E. Biddle, W.J. Samuels, and J.B. Davis (eds), *A Companion to the History of Economic Thought* (Malden, Mass. 2003), pp. 185–6.

19 See G.M. Young, *Victorian England: Portrait of an Age* (Oxford, 1949), p.54, fn 1.

20 Schumpeter, *History*, p. 493. Sismondi was an early advocate of employers guaranteeing their workmen security against unemployment, sickness and destitution in old age; he also propounded a crude under-consumptionist theory of economic crises—in effect arguing that economies, at least in the short run, are not self-equilibrating and self-correcting. He thus emphasized the "terrible sufferings" resulting from severe upheavals in the economy which most economists dealt within a cavalier fashion. As Schumpeter puts it, Sismondi pointed out that "the economic process is chained to certain sequences that will exclude certain forms of adaptation and enforce others ... the economic process is a system of periodicities and lags and, by virtue of this alone, harbors a world of problems that simply do not exist for Ricardian economics or any economics of the time." Schumpeter, *History*, p.495. It is not difficult to see how these doctrines appealed to social reformers and Hugh Miller in particular. In terms of the chronology, Sismondi had written an article in 1815 for the *Edinburgh Encyclopaedia* (published in 1816) which contained the essentials of the doctrine in *Nouveaux Principes d' économie politique* which was widely known from 1819. They were further amplified and disseminated in 1837–8 in his *Etudes sur l' économie politique*, p. 493.

21 F.M.L. Thompson, "Land Tenure in Britain, 1750–1914," in Winch and O'Brien (eds), *Political Economy*, p. 127.

22 G. Stedman Jones, "National bankruptcy", p. 74.

23 J.C.L. de Sismondi, *Political Economy and the Philosophy of Government* (London, 1847; reprint New York, 1966), p. 185.

24 Sismondi, *Political Economy* (the article "Political economy", taken from Brewster's *Edinburgh Encyclopedia*, 1815; reprint New York, 1966), p. 50.

25 See for instance, Stefan Collini, "The Literary Critic and the Village Labourer: 'Culture' in Twentieth-Century Britain", *Transactions of the Royal Historical Society*, 6th series, XIV (2004), pp. 93–118.

26 For a recent summary see Eric Richards, *The Highland Clearances: People, Landlords and Rural Turmoil* (Edinburgh, Birlinn Books, 2000, new ed. 2002).

27 Sismondi derived his findings primarily from the well known *Account of the Improvements on the Estates of the Marquis of Stafford* (1816, 1820) by James Loch (1820). See J.C.L. De Sismondi, *Political Economy and the Philosophy of Government* (London, 1847), pp. 151–193.

28 Miller believed that the Highlander needed more education and material prosperity; the Lowlander more virtue and attention to things of the spirit. M. Shortland, *Hugh Miller's Memoir: From Stonemason to Geologist* (Edinburgh, 1995), p. 54.

29 Miller, *Sutherland As it Was*, p. 17.

30 See Karl Marx, "The Duchess of Sutherland and Slavery", *The People's Paper*, March 1853, reprinted in Karl Marx and Frederick Engels, *Articles on Britain*, (Moscow, 1971) pp. 142–48. See also Mao-Lan Tuan, *Simonde De Sismondi*.

31 Eric Richards, *A History of the Highland Clearances: Agrarian Transformation and the Evictions 1746–1886* (London, 1982), pp. 24, 11 (citing G.E. Mingay).

32 James Loch, *Improvements on the Estates*.

33 See Eric Richards, "Hugh Miller and Resistance to the Highland Clearances", in Lester Borley (ed), *Celebrating the Life and Times of Hugh Miller: Scotland in the Early 19th Century*, (Cromarty Arts Trust, 2003), pp. 48–63

34 See Mark Blaug, *Henry Thornton*, p. xii.

35 Mark A. Lutz, *Economics for the Common Good* (London, 1998), p. 50.

36 Take for instance the case of two villages in the 1780s at Kirkmichael and Tomintoul—here "the village was intended to retain a large and industrious population on the estate, thus providing a local market for agriculture, boosting the rental and avoiding the moral degradation associated with urban settlement," D.G. Lockhart, "Patterns of Migration and Movement of Labour to the Planned Villages of North-east Scotland", *Scottish Geographical Magazine* 98 (1982), pp.35–47; D. Turnock, "Stages of agricultural improvement in the uplands of Scotland's Grampian Region", *Journal of Historical Geography* 3 (1977).

37 Some of the motivation was that of deterring emigration: an example was that of the considerable Enlightenment figure, Lord Kames, who sought to persuade footloosened families to settle on his estate at Blair Drummond. He was involved also with associated bodies such as the Board of Trustees for Fisheries, Manufacture, and Improvements in Scotland whose purpose was to develop employment and subsistence levels across the country. See Ian Simpson Ross, *Lord Kames and the Scotland of this Day* (Oxford, 1972), pp. 322–3.

38 This point is made by P. Aitchison and A. Casssell, *The Lowland Clearances*, p.8.

39 See Eric Richards, *Britannia's Children: Emigration from England, Scotland, Wales and Ireland since 1600* (London and New York: Hambledon and London, 2004), p. 145.

40 David Fitzpatrick, "Irish emigration in the later nineteenth century", *Irish Historical Studies*, XXII no. 86 (1980), p. 130.

41 See Joanna Innes, "The distinctiveness of the English poor laws, 1750–1850", in Winch and O'Brien (eds), *Political Economy*, pp. 381–407.

42 See Jeremy Burchardt, *The Allotment Movement in England, 1793–1873*, Royal Historical Society studies in history. New series (Suffolk, UK : Boydell Press, Boydell & Brewer Inc., 2002).

43 On the long tradition of the philosophy of the smallholder, see F.M.L. Thompson, "Land tenure".

44 See John Mackenzie, *Pigeon holes of Memory: The Life and Times of Dr John Mackenzie (1803–1886)*, edited by Christina Byam Shaw (London, 1988).

45 As Donald Winch remarks, "One way of bringing this home to present day readers is to ask them to consider the likely effect on the current political agenda if the British population had doubled during the period between 1950 and 2000." See Winch, "Introduction", Winch and O'Brien, *Political Economy*, p.7, fn 8.

46 This paragraph draws on Christine S. Hallas, "Migration in Nineteenth-Century Wensleydale and Swaledale", *Northern History* XXVII (1991), pp. 141–157; and Christine Hallas, *Rural Responses to Industrialization: The North Pennines, 1790–1914* (Bern, 1999).

47 T.C. Smout, review of Ian Carter, *Farm Life in Northeast Scotland*, in *Social History*, vol. 5, (1980), pp. 4842–5, and a review of S. Akerman et al, *Chance and Change*, in *Social History* 5 (1980), pp. 147–8. See also T.C. Smout "Scotland and England", in *Review* 3 (1980), p. 627 where he argues that some societies were able to control their population by self-restraint, e.g. Sweden, 1750-1850.

48 I am grateful to Dr Robert Fitzsimons for his assistance with references.

10

The Use and Misuse of Economic Theory in the Reform of Medicare

Jeff Richardson

Monash University

1 Introduction

There is widespread agreement that the performance of the health sector is problematical and represents a major challenge for policy makers. However there is less agreement about what the problems are and what should be done about them. In this paper it will be argued that recent policy has not focused upon the very significant inefficiencies and inequities in Medicare. Policies may have been adopted because of (legitimate) political objectives. However they have been justified using economic arguments to suggest that the reforms are technically necessary to sustain the short and long run viability of the public health scheme. The economic arguments are not correct and may well have been used to rationalise a (possibly intentional and certainly covert) redistribution of income. What is less speculative is that recent policies have created and reinforced financial incentives which are inimical to the achievement of allocative efficiency within and between sub-sectors of the health system.

Before turning to these policies the article commences in Section 2 below with a discussion of health-sector related social objectives. These are more complex and controversial than objectives in other industries as the health sector has been the scene of an ongoing ideological struggle between two (legitimate) "world views". Recent policies are better understood as a means for promoting one of these views rather than as policies for achieving economic efficiency. The "flagship" of these policies—the preservation of private health insurance (PHI)—is discussed in Section 3 along with two other recent policy issues.

It is beyond the scope of the paper to consider long term policy options. However five general observations are made with respect to the constraints and prerequisites for an optimal health scheme.

It is concluded that recent health policy has been not only disappointing but has failed in its duty of care: policy has not fulfilled a fundamental role of government, namely, the protection of its citizens against the risk of injury and death. It has not responded to the need to achieve efficiency and equity. Rather, the policy agenda has been dominated by ideological concerns. It is suggested that part of the reason for this is that universities and research bodies have not responded to the need to train an adequate number of students to analyse and influence the complex motives and behaviours in the health sector.

2 Social Objectives and the Health Sector

The objectives and the health sector are clearly complex and the nexus between objectives, policies and the optimal health system is problematical. Nevertheless it is clear that different "world views" or "social philosophies" imply different social policies.

Table 1 describes two broad social philosophies which, it is suggested, broadly correspond with the values which dominate the health policy debate. The first, labelled liberal/libertarianism is well known and particularly by economists. It emphasises individualism and individual rights. It describes the almost universal values which pervade private markets. Individuals are driven by self-interest and seek to maximise utility. With this world view the social welfare function is usually perceived as being a function of individual utilities. Following Sen (1979) this theory of value is referred to in the literature as "welfarism" (Hurley 2000). Welfarist social values are more readily accommodated in a private market where a multitude of products may be custom-made for particular individuals who have differing revealed preferences because of differing willingness or abilities to pay. With this social philosophy, concern for others is generally met by the provision of a safety net—targeted welfare payments to the very poor and very sick.

The contrasting social philosophy is less well articulated (at least in English speaking countries). It focuses upon the community and what is or should be entailed by membership of that community. Concern about others does not

Table 1. Two archetypal social philosophies.

	Liberal/Libertarianism	Communitarianism
Focus of concern	individual rights	community relationships
Funding	private premiums	taxation
Benefits	function of private premium	egalitarian
Criterion for service	willingness to pay	need
Maximand	utility (welfarism)	health (extra welfarism)
Distributive goal	safety net	redistribution
Ideal scheme	**private**	**public**

take the form of a safety net. Rather there is a desire to "remove health and health care from the economic reward system" in the same way as citizens are, in principle, given equal protection by the law, and have access to public parks without payment. This is not because payment is impractical or that parks are a form of charity but because there is a desire to live in a community which shares certain benefits and pays for them collectively. In the context of a health scheme this social philosophy was clearly articulated in a review of the Canadian health system, Medicare, as follows:

> "Canadian Medicare is far more than just an administrative mechanism for paying medical bills. It is widely regarded as an important symbol of community, a concrete representation of mutual support and concern ... it expresses the fundamental equality of Canadian citizens in the face of death and disease."
>
> Quoted by Evans R and Law M (1995)

In many European countries this motivation is described by the term "solidarity". As there is no commonly used word which precisely corresponds with this notion in English speaking countries ("Communitarianism" is closest) articulation of social values is often ambiguous. The same terms—"fairness, equity, and 'social Justice'"—are used to describe both value systems. Without widely recognised labels discussion of social philosophies can, and has, become confused as the same words may refer to different concepts.

With this second philosophy fairness refers to an egalitarian access to health services and their financing through taxation. This latter characteristic implies a significant redistribution of resources to the poorer members of the community.

In principle it is possible that the object of collective concern with this world view could be utility. However there is a wealth of evidence to suggest that people believe the purpose of a national health scheme is to ensure access to, and the use of, health services as a means of achieving better health. There is little doubt that the community would reject a proposal to spend some part of an individual's entitlement to health dollars on a family holiday because the latter was a source of greater utility. While liberal values suggest the superiority of a private scheme, Communitarianism suggests the superiority of a public health system. It is easier to achieve egalitarian goals when a single authority is providing benefits and collecting revenues via taxation.

It is, of course, impossible to draw conclusions with respect to the superiority of one scheme over another without considering their impact upon costs. The limited information available suggests that publicly run schemes are somewhat cheaper than schemes that are more reliant upon private contributions (Gerdtham 2000). However the differences are too small to be of great significance. They could not be used to justify a national, in preference to a private, scheme. More generally it is reasonable—and common practice—to pay more for something that is desired even if the alternative, unwanted product, is cheaper!

Economic theory and analyses have commonly failed to recognise that the liberal/libertarian values of a normal marketplace need not be the dominant social value in the context of (some part of) the medical market. Rather, it is assumed that welfarism is the universal social philosophy. (There is something odd in this orthodox view which assumes that people have well-formed, complete and individualistic preferences for services and commodities but identical "meta preferences": that there is no difference between people's motivations and that personal utility maximisation is a universal description of people's motives.)

3 Recent Policies

Recent policy has clearly been designed to shore up the institutions and polices needed to promote the liberal/libertarian philosophy in the context of the health sector. The most important policy in this respect has been the preservation of private health insurance (PHI) as this is the vehicle for allowing the purchase of (what are believed to be) better services and shorter queues. Other policies to promote this world view include the transfer of spending responsibilities back to the public and the privatisation of hospitals.

Private Health Insurance

For almost one and a half decades the conventional wisdom in the popular press—and amongst many policy analysts—has been that private health insurance (PHI) should be supported to ensure the viability of Medicare. The supporting argument has been persuasive; viz, that *"because private health insurance is in competition with a product which is free at the point of service (Medicare) people have increasingly dropped PHI. Initially it was the healthiest members who opted out as their likelihood of benefiting from PHI was smallest and the PHI premiums high relative to their expected benefit. But as the best risk members left, and the overall risk profile deteriorated, premiums were forced to rise which drove out the next healthiest group of members. (The problem of adverse selection.) The observed decline in PHI has meant that fewer people can afford to be in a private hospital. This puts pressure on public hospitals which explains increasing public queues. Consequently it has been a policy imperative to halt and reverse the decline in private health insurance."*

The argument is logical and consistent with the two observations selectively quoted. However it is also wrong and, for some time this error has been public information.

Relevant data reveal that until 1999 a significant decline in the membership of *basic health insurance* but little decline in the membership of the auxiliary table which are necessary to cover the cost of private hospitals. As shown in Table 2 column 3, private health expenditure from 1989/90 to 2001/02 rose by 200 per cent, significantly more than the 103.7 per cent increase in public expenditures. From Table 3, in the 14 years to 1999/00 private hospital separations rose from 25.9 to 34.4 per cent of the total while bed days rose from 21.9 to 28.1 per cent of the total. These data unambiguously contradict the simple argument above. Private hospital admissions did not decline and this did not cause queuing in public hospitals.

Despite the public availability of these data this pseudo economic analysis ("pseudo" because it adopts the language of economics) was used for over a decade to justify the need for PHI. That this could happen is a lamentable

Table 2. Recurrent expenditures, source and application of funds ($ billions).

Year	Total recurrent expenditure on healthcare	Hospital expenditure by type of hospital		Expenditures funded by		
		Public	Private	Government	PHI gross*(net)	Individuals
1989–90 (a)	26.8	8.2	1.7	18.3	3.1	4.4
1997–98 (b)	44.0	12.8	3.7	30.0	4.4	7.6
2001–02 (c)	66.6	16.7	5.1	45.5	7.0 (5.1)*	12.5
Per cent change						
89/90–97/98	64.2	56.1	117.6	63.9	41.9	72.7
97/98–01/02	51.4	30.5	37.8	51.7	59.1 (15.9)	64.5
89/90–01/02	148.5	103.7	200.0	148.6	125.8 (64.5)	184.1

Source: AIHW Health Expenditure Bulletin, (a) AIHW 1994, (b) AIHW 2001, (c) AIHW 2003a
* $7.0 billion = gross revenue of which thepremium rebate paid by the Commonwealth was $1,950 million

Table 3. Private hospital services as a percentage of total public and private hospital activity.

	Separations	Bed Days
1985–86	25.9%	21.9%
1989–90	26.7%	22.0%
1995–96	30.8%	26.3%
1997–98	32.0%	26.6%
1999–00	34.3%	28.1%
Change 85/86–97/98	23.6%	21.5%
85/86–99/00	+32.4%	+28.3%

Source: Duckett 2000; AIHW 2000

comment on the press and the "intellectual market place" in Australia. Pseudo economics has presumably been used as it is more persuasive to (wrongly) argue that a policy is unavoidable for technical reasons than to argue (correctly) that it is being adopted as part of a controversial social policy.

Rather than a demand side phenomenon, trends in Tables 2 and 3 are best explained by changes on the supply side. State governments severely cut back on real hospital budgets. Between 1991/92 and 1994/95, for example, *nominal expenditure* by Victoria's public hospitals declined by 8 per cent despite a 12 per cent increase in unit costs per separation. During this time public hospital expenditures across Australia rose by only 2.4 per cent per annum which represented a decline in real expenditures (AIHW 1999). A contributory factor was almost certainly the emerging shortage of specialists (as new technologies permitted additional beneficial therapies). There are also very powerful motives for medical practitioners to treat private in preference to public patients. As illustrated below in the case of acute myocardial infarction (AMI-heart attack) it is likely that the expansion of the private sector resulted in a disproportionate growth in the services per private patient. Consequently the transfer of patients from public to private hospitals was probably accompanied by a disproportionate transfer of doctors from public to private hospitals thereby exacerbating the problem of queuing.

These unusual policies failed to achieve their stated purpose. Analysis of post implementation PHI, membership, and service use by the Melbourne Institute of Applied Economic and Social Research (Dawkins et al 2004) did not find that there had been a reduction in the pressure upon public hospital beds for public patients. Rather—and as predicted by Richardson 1999—a very large part of the subsidy benefited those who already had PHI, with wealthy households receiving a disproportionate share of the benefits.

As judged by economic theory the policies adopted to solve this misidentified problem were bizarre. In July 1997 a tax penalty was introduced for Australians who did not purchase PHI. Specifically, a 1 per cent surcharge was introduced for individuals with an annual income above $50,000 and families with combined incomes above $100,000 when these individuals and families did not purchase PHI. This means that for such families the effective net price for PHI is negative! For example, a family with a combined income of $120,000 which purchases a family policy for $800 (net of the subsidy) will have a net income which is $400 higher than a similar family which does not purchase PHI. An analogous policy would be to assist the automobile industry by levying a 1 per cent surcharge on the income tax of any citizen who failed to buy an Australian car. Undoubtedly with the resulting negative price Australian cars would increase their market-share. However negative prices do not send appropriate information signals between consumes and producers.

In September 1999 "life time community rating" was introduced. This means that a surcharge of 2 per cent per annum is now added to the premium of any individual or family which has not purchased PHI by the age of 30. This measure (which was highly successful) suggests that policy makers may have forgotten the purpose of insurance and now treat it merely as a device for raising revenue (which it does very inefficiently). It has always been possible for an uninsured person to use a private hospital or doctor. PHI simply reduces the risk to a person's income if the individual is uninsured; that is, the purpose of insurance is to reduce risk. However the lifetime tables have the opposite effect. Instead of the need to assess likely service use over a 3 to 4 year period, individuals and families must now consider the likelihood of ill health over a 30–40 year period. This clearly increases risk and uncertainty over the (now longer) decision period. That is, in order to increase PHI membership, lifetime tables increase the very thing insurance is designed to reduce, viz, risk. (An analogous policy to encourage people to purchase fire insurance would be to send a team of arsonists throughout the country to randomly burn down people's homes. The increased risk of fire would almost certainly encourage laggards to purchase fire insurance!)

The only aspect of recent PHI policy which does not seriously distort the calculation of costs and benefits is the 30 per cent subsidy on the cost of PHI introduced in 1999. PHI "competes" with a free product, Medicare. It is a legitimate policy to reduce the price of PHI if there is a long term social objective of sustaining and promoting the private sector. Perhaps perversely, it has been this policy which has attracted the greatest criticism on the grounds that a significant part of the subsidy is directed towards services which are not available under Medicare. Viewed as an incentive for the achievement of a government policy this is not a damaging criticism. The fact that PHI membership did not increase after the subsidy was introduced and, at best, slowed the decline, implies that it was not very effective with respect to this criterion (Butler 1999). It did, however, achieve an unstated but possible objective of redistributing income to those who held PHI.

Two Tier Payments

There are two other areas where the government has recently drawn upon economic arguments to help achieve its policy objectives. The first of these was the introduction in June 2004 of a two tier schedule of benefits (rebates) for GP fees, with higher benefits paid to pensioners, children and health care card holders and with more paid to GPs located in designated (rural) areas. At the same time, policy was amended to pay 80 per cent of medical expenditures beyond a defined "safety net". The measures are clearly designed to achieve the protection of vulnerable groups and to do so in an "efficient" way, namely, by targeting the most vulnerable patients and giving doctors an economic incentive to increase and improve services provided to them.

However the changes have obvious, if unintended, implications for equity and efficiency. The creation of two tier payment creates a foundation for a more extensive two tier system. The open-ended commitment to pay 80 per cent of expenditures, no matter how high, additionally increases demand and would be expected to increase fees. Consistent with this Richardson and Segal (2004), note that insurance payments above the schedule fee rose from $7 million in 1998 to $125 million in 2000/01 and $330 million in 2002/03, a clear indication of the likelihood of further inflation as demand increases.

Pharmaceuticals

The second health sub-sector where economics argument has been recently employed is the regulation and payment for drugs on the Pharmaceutical Benefits Scheme (PBS). On the demand side the ongoing policy has been to increase co-payments to reduce the overall consumption of drugs and to reduce the cost to the Medicare funded PBS. In September 2005 ordinary Australians paid the full price of a drug when this was less than $28.60. For health care card holders this figure was $4.60. Medicare payed for the remainder of the bill. After a safety net has been reached the net price now drops to $4.60 for ordinary Australians and Medicare pays the full bill for card holders.

A second tier of the pharmaceutical policy and one pioneered by Australia is the requirement (since 1983) for drugs to be subject to economic evaluation before being offered through the PBS. It is commonly argued that co-payments encourage the cost-effective use of services by patients and the economic evaluation of drugs appears to be self-evidently beneficial. Despite this, these measure do not ensure the efficiency of the sector. First it has not been established that the "problem" of uncapped drug expenditures is a significant problem which justifies the relatively draconian co-payments which have been used, increasingly, as the basis for cost control. Table 4 indicates that Australian expenditures in 2000 were modest in relation to many other countries. Even allowing for the subsequent inflation, the drug bill remains well below the level in Canada, USA, Italy and France. Recent expenditures have increased the

Table 4. Expenditure on pharmaceuticals as per cent of GDP.

	2000 (%)		2000 (%)
France	1.9	Australia	1.1
Italy	1.8	New Zealand	1.1
USA	1.6	Switzerland	1.1
Belgium	1.4	UK	1.1
Canada	1.4	Finland	1.0
Germany	1.2	Netherlands	0.9
Japan	1.2	Denmark	0.7
Sweden	1.2	Ireland	0.7
Mean	1.2		

Source: Tiffen & Gittins (2004) p. 102

pharmaceutical share of total health expenditures to 14 per cent. Nevertheless this remains well below the 22.4 per cent of health expenditures in 1960/61.

Secondly, the impact of co-payments on drug use is not well understood. One of the clearest results from the monumental Random Control Trial of co-payments in the USA (the "Rand Experiment") was that co-payments were indiscriminate in their effect (Lohr 1986, Newhouse 1993). There was no evidence that, as commonly asserted, medically unnecessary services would be dropped first and more efficacious services retained. In one of the few studies of the differential impact of co-payments on drug use Reeder and Nelson (1985) found that, perversely, patients facing a co-payment initially dropped potentially life saving medications such as cardio vascular drugs which had no immediate impact upon symptoms and continued to spend upon analgesics which gave immediate pain relief. That is, co-payments had the opposite impact to the effect predicted by its proponents.

Thirdly, pharmaceutical co-payment policy has not been informed by knowledge of the cross-price elasticity between pharmaceuticals and other medical services. Pharmaceuticals are often a relatively cheap form of therapy. If co-payments reduce the use of efficacious medicines then the result is likely to be an increased expenditure on doctors and hospital care and at a significantly higher price to Medicare. The substitution of drug for hospital care would often lower the total health bill. Arithmetically drug expenditures would, however, become a larger percentage of the total.

Turning to the PBS regulatory framework, the mandatory conduct of an economic evaluation does not ensure a lower price or the better use of drugs. At best, it ensures that under the conditions incorporated in the evaluation, benefits would exceed a particular threshold set by the PBAC. However if a drug is highly efficacious this threshold could be passed despite a significantly inflated cost. Perversely, as the pharmaceutical company is aware that the regulatory authorities are aware of the efficacy of their product, it is likely that costs will be inflated. This is easily achieved via transfer pricing of raw materials from overseas manufacturers.

Equally problematical, it is not possible to ensure that doctors administer drugs in the way described by protocols in an evaluation study. Rather, their incentive is to prescribe a drug where there is any positive benefit (or where there is no harm and the patient wants some form of medication). For this reason it is probably the capacity and motivation to negotiate low prices that determines the success with respect to cost of the regulatory system. In the pre 1993 regulatory environment direct negotiation was spectacularly successful. While sparing in its praise, the Industry Commission enquiry into the industry noted that Australian pharmaceuticals were priced at about 50 per cent of the OECD average (Industry Commission 1997). A careful consideration of economic theory in the context of negotiations between a monopsonist buyer and an effectively monopolist seller would be unlikely to conclude that economic evaluation alone would be a satisfactory policy lever for reducing prices.

4 Issues Neglected by Health Policy

The health policies discussed above have three common themes. First, they are primarily concerned with funding and the demand for health services. Second, each is concerned with the share of the health bill that will be paid for by the patient. Third, by comparison with the neglected issues below, they are relatively small scale problems. Price elasticities are sufficiently low that co-payments only have a modest effect; private health insurance provides only 7.5 per cent of total health care revenues and is more concerned with queue jumping, choice of doctor and medical incomes than with population health. In contrast, two of the three issues discussed below—and the two with greatest implication for health outcomes—are concerned with the supply side of health care.

Small Area Variation

Perhaps the most important empirical fact which must be explained by an analysis of the health sector is that the rate of service delivery varies enormously, both geographically and by patient characteristic. The variation cannot be explained by the usual economic variables of price, income and tastes or by medical need. The explanatory power of these variables is significantly less than the observed variations. This is not a recent phenomenon. Table 5 reports the rate of GP and specialist consultations per capita in three statistical divisions in the first year after the introduction of the universal insurance scheme, Medibank, and the collection of such data. For both types of services, per capita use varied by a factor of 4.6.

Figure 1 presents the variation in the use of 15 hospital procedures between statistical sub-divisions in Victoria using the complete database of public and private Victorian separations over a 2 year period. On the scale, "100" represents the standardised service use per 100,000 population predicted from the demographic structure. The observed rates in different SSDs are displayed in

Table 5. Practice Variations 1976.

| | Consultations per capita, 1976 | | |
Statistical Division	GP/(GP)	Q(Spec)	Total
Sydney	5.1	2.3	7.4
Tasmania	3.1	1.3	4.4
Darwin	1.1	0.5	1.6
Sydney/Darwin	4.6	4.6	4.6

Source: Richardson and Deeble (1982)

Table 6. (Likelihood of procedure after admission to a private hospital) ÷ (Likelihood as a public patient)

	Angiography	Revascularisation
Within 14 days		
Men	2.20	3.43
Women	2.27	3.86
Within 12 months		
Men	2.16	2.89
Women	2.22	2.84

Source: Robertson and Richardson (2000).

relation to the expected rate of 100. The central bar for each procedure represents the 25th and 75th percentiles. Dots represent the age-sex standardised rate for SSDs outside the 95 per cent confidence limit indicated by the thin unbroken line. Consistent with the earlier data, service use in each of the categories varies by at least 200 per cent. For some procedures where there is particular scope for discretion (such as coronary revascularisation) service rates vary by a factor of 10. Because some of these discrepancies might be attributable to random variation the actual variance was divided by the variance expected from random variation. The ratio to the left of the bar chart indicates that actual variance exceeded expected variance by a minimum of 70 per cent (exploratory laparotomy) and by up to 4,430 per cent (colonoscopy—where the expected variance is small).

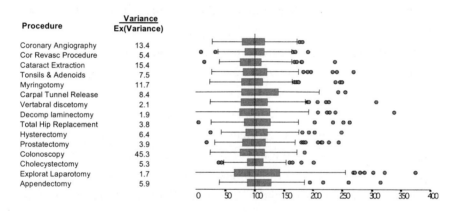

Figure 1. *Standardised rate ratios for various operations in the statistical local areas in Victoria, compared to the rate ratios for all Victoria.*
Source: Richardson (1999)

The same authors calculated the likelihood of a high tech procedure for a patient admitted to hospital following acute myocardial infarction (heart attack). The procedures studied were angiography and revascularisation (coronary artery bypass surgery, angiography or a stent to remove the blockage of a coronary artery). It was found that procedures were more common for men than women, residents of high SES residential areas, patients with private health insurance and younger patients. Table 6 compares the probability of a procedure after admission to a private hospital with the probability after admis-

217

sion as a public patient in a public hospital. The discrepancy in procedure rates is very large. Over a 12 month period men and women were (respectively) 2.16 and 2.22 times more likely to receive angiography in a private hospital than as a public patient. Within fourteen days after the admission men and women were 3.43 and 3.86 times more likely to have a revascularisation procedure in a private hospital.

The magnitude of these variations dwarfs the variation which could be attributed to price and income. While the appropriate utilisation rate cannot be determined from aggregate data it is not possible that both the upper and the lower rates of service delivery are consistent with best practice medicine or an equitable distribution of services. Patients undoubtedly live or die because of either under- or over-use of procedures. Health policy in Australia has not addressed this issue and following publication of each of these results there was little interest in them.

A second significant problem with the health sector is more widely recognised. This is the inflexibility of funding. There are an exceedingly large number of "vertical" programs which reimburse particular activities but which cannot be transferred from one type of service to another. This violates a necessary condition for allocative efficiency. Dollars flow to activities irrespective of the cost-effectiveness of the alternative treatments. Each of the States fund a plethora of specific programs. However the most intractable problems arise from the division of responsibilities between the State and the Commonwealth Governments. In addition to the direct impact upon service substitution this impinges upon the coordination of services. An example of this noted in a recent review of the Tasmanian hospital system is the problem of "bed blockers". Patients are kept in (scarce) acute hospital beds for an extended period because there is no other facility which can care for these patients. The cost of acute care falls upon the States; the cost of nursing home beds falls upon the Commonwealth. The dollars spent through the State acute care budget are not transferred to nursing home, step down facilities or a primary health care facility—there is no integrated primary health care network which draws upon State funds and Commonwealth expenditures on general practitioners.

In an attempt to address this problem the Australian Health Ministers'

Advisory Council established a series of Coordinated Care Trials in 1995. With inadequate funding for the experiment and an insufficient time for behavioural change these trials failed to show patient benefits in the form of improved health. Following this result, interest in the coordination of services appear to have diminished. An offer by the New South Wales State Government to transfer its responsibilities, revenue and expenditures to the Commonwealth Government was rejected. The recent "Richardson Report" (Tasmanian Department Health and Human Services 2004) recommended a transfer of Commonwealth responsibilities, revenues and funding to Tasmania on a trial basis. While endorsed by the State government the recommendation was rejected by the Commonwealth.

These problems indicate that the prerequisites for allocative efficiency do not exist and there appears, at present, to be little interest in this issue.

A third and the most significant problem concerns the technical efficiency of health care delivery. The problem relates to adverse events (AEs) arising from avoidable medical errors. In 1995 the "Quality in Australian Health Care Study" (QAHCS) published the results of an analysis of more than 30,000 admissions in 28 hospitals in both the public and the private sectors (Wilson et al 1995). Each admission was triaged to identify hospital episodes where the medical record suggested a possible error had occurred prior to, or during, the hospital episode. Cases were then evaluated by a panel of specialist doctors. Extrapolating from the sample the authors estimated that AEs resulted in 18,000 deaths and 50,000 cases of permanent disability in the study year. In order to meet some criticism and to make the study more consistent with a US methodology the authors revised their estimate to about 12,000 deaths annually.

The response to this horrific finding was muted. In 1999 an editorial in the Medical Journal of Australia commented that

Welcome though (various initiatives) are, the pace of change nevertheless seems slow given the stark message of the original study four years ago … 50,000 Australians suffer permanent disability and 18,000 die at least in part because of their health care.
(MJA 1999).

Six years later in September 2005 a second editorial commented that:

> Based on QAHCS outcomes 25 patients die each day in our hospitals from preventable adverse events ... We have had report after report ... yet we continue to suffer hospital scandals affecting life and limb. 10 years after QAHCS ... we still have no nationally accepted framework for clinical governance to assure the safety and quality of Australian health services ... This ongoing vacuum is an indictment of our health ministers and organised medicine.
>
> (Van Der Weydan, *MJA*, 2005, p. 284)

In 2004 tenders were called to review the governance of quality in Australia.

It is difficult to understand the sedate nature of the regulatory response unless the results were not truly believed and that the magnitude of the problem was beyond credulity. Nevertheless the accuracy of the data have not been seriously challenged and the study has not been repeated. To put the astonishing mortality rate in some perspective, Table 7 halves the initial rate and compares it with other events—events which would be likely to generate more interest than the apparent carnage in the health system. (The preventable death of at least 10,000 people each year—100,000 since the publication of the QAHCS—justifies strong language!)

Table 7. Events equivalent to avoidable AE deaths*.

- 1 in 10 customers to restaurants poisoned: annual deaths 9,000
- Jumbo jets crash every 2 weeks: 350 Australian passengers die each crash
- Bali bombing every 4 days, with 100 Australian killed per episode
- 50 per cent more deaths than annual total from AIDS + suicide + motor vehicle accidents + homicide + drownings + falls + poisonings

---

*assuming preventable deaths = 50 % QAHCS (Wilson et al 1995)

As discussed in Richardson (2005) it is not difficult to find examples where regulation could have an immediate beneficial effect. Information systems within and between hospitals and other parts of the health system could be brought to the standards achieved by other industries well before the turn of the century. The lack of an electronic patient history, the loss of undigitised radiological film, the inability to read case notes on a 19th century clipboard, the non-existence of evidence-based protocols, the non existence of electronic alerts when incompatible drugs are administered or correct drugs not administered and the widespread absence of adequate discharge planning must all exact their toll on the patient population. Remedial action could be commenced more or less immediately. In view of the QAHCS results it would appear appropriate to make the accreditation of hospitals compulsory not voluntary and for there to be minimum staffing requirements so that, following a complex operation with the potential for subsequent and serious complications, a medically qualified practitioner should be in the hospital.

Importantly, these problems are systemic and should not be viewed as a result of incompetent individuals. Mistakes are a normal occurrence and there is a systems science concerned with the minimisation of errors. One important principle is error learning. In Australia the chance of this occurring is minimised by allowing uncapped litigation against individual doctors who will then, understandably, be reluctant to admit to error. Uncontrolled litigation encourages a culture of protection of colleagues since at some future date the colleague may need to protect the protector.

Whatever the sociological explanation for the comparative lack of interest in the issues discussed above it is clear that there is a yawning gap between the motives, constraints and behaviours associated with this sector and the motives, constraints and behaviours of *homo economicus*, the well-informed, empowered and rational denizen of orthodox economic theory. The issues which have occupied the medical-economic debate appear to be distant and an order of magnitude less important than the issues which should be at the forefront of the policy agenda.

5 Australian Health Policy

While it is beyond the scope of this paper to present a comprehensive analysis of Australian policy options five general observations are made below, some of which emerge from the earlier discussion.

Sustainable Expenditure

First, it is commonly argued that the responsibility for health spending must be returned to individuals. The argument, which is supportive of the liberal/libertarian world view, has two parts. Both are wrong or at least greatly exaggerated. The first argument is that the economy will soon be unable to cope with accelerating health costs: that these costs will soon become "unsustainable". Responsibility for funding of medical services must therefore be passed back to patients as this will reduce demand and cost and encourage a more discriminating use of services.

Possibly the most important message of economics is that we have choices, and this is true in the health sector. The USA spends 14 per cent of its GDP on health care. One projection by its Health Care Financing Agency (HCFA) suggested that this might rise to more than 30 per cent. The projections were shown to be consistent with a continuing growth of non-health GDP. A similar projection is displayed in Table 8 for Australia. Despite sharply rising health costs, non-health GDP continues to rise. While the table only reports the outcome of a single scenario, the general point should be clear: low but positive GDP growth is sufficient to support a much higher growth of health services while still allowing an increase in the material standard of living. Those who argue that the rapid growth of health expenditures is economically unsustainable are misusing Economic Theory.

A similar argument—that the rising cost of Medicare places unsustainable pressure on *government budgets*—is also unambiguously wrong unless the judgment is based upon political, not economic, considerations. There is a weak but negative association between the health share of GDP and the government share of health expenditure (Gerdtham and Jonsson 2000). This does not imply the need for a greater role by government. It does, however, indicate that a larger government share is possible without increased costs. The obvious caveat is that this would imply increased taxation. However there is little association between taxation and GDP indicating that expenditures in a government health scheme are not constrained by the effect of taxation upon the standard of living.

The size of the health sector and the government share of its revenues are matters for social policy not, as implied by these arguments, technical matters

Table 8. Extrapolation of health care expenditure.

Growth GDP	...	2% pa	
Growth Drugs	...	9% pa	
Growth Health	...	4% pa	

Indices: GDP (2002/03 = 100)			
	2002/03	2022/23	2042/43
GDP	100	148.6	220.8
Health	9.0	19.7	43.2
Non Drug GDP	91	127.9	177.6

implying policy imperatives. The relevant question is whether health expenditures result in benefits that are greater than benefits elsewhere. If future medical technologies could extend life expectancy to 120 without illness but at a cost of 30 per cent of the GDP it is likely that this option would receive the enthusiastic support of the entire population.

In Australia, like most other developed countries, public health expenditures are a major vehicle for the redistribution of economic benefits and whether or not future health expenditures are privately or collectively financed depends upon Australia's social philosophy and "social generosity". By world standards (and despite their self-image) Australians are not generous. Indeed, the evidence summarised in Table 9 suggests that Australians are probably the least generous people in the western world. With each of the indices of social generosity Australia is either at the bottom or one of the three bottom countries. Contrary to widespread belief its poverty rates are the highest and social service transfers the lowest amongst the countries compared. This is not because of a crippling tax burden which in 2000 was the fourth lowest in the OECD (Tiffen and Gittins 2004).

In view of this evidence it is probably unsurprising that government finances a smaller proportion of the health bill than any other country in the OECD except the USA and Switzerland (Tiffen and Gittins 2004). Despite this, the evidence unambiguously indicates almost universal support for a health scheme which provides comprehensive health care. The policy questions only relate to the interface between the public and private sectors, their relative sizes and, in the long run, the range of services to be offered by the public scheme.

The Competitive Market

Second—and a controversial point for some economists—the evidence also indicates that simple market forces are unlikely to result in "consumer driven health care"; the medical market fails. Almost all of the characteristics of the idealised competitive market do not exist (see Rice 1995, 2002 for a comprehensive review of these failures). The uncertainties, anxieties, motivations, incentives, behaviours, expectations and the balance of power between consumers and producers—in sum, all the elements of the culture which pervades the health sector—are different from the culture envisaged in the economist's competitive model. As a consequence a policy focus upon elements of the competitive model—privatisation, co-payments, competition—may be seriously misleading and will not address the most pressing policy issues.

One of the principal failures is that the health system does not/cannot respond to the well-informed preferences of autonomous consumers. The reason cited in most health economics texts is that there is asymmetrical information between the purchaser and provider. The more plausible version of this argument is that even with technical information provided by a doctor a patient is commonly unable to make a judgement between options: there is an "asymmetrical capacity to *evaluate* and *judge*" various options[1]. As noted earlier, the RAND experiment found no relationship between services eliminated by co-payments and their importance.

In principle, this problem could be mitigated by the patient's adoption of an agent to overcome these asymmetries. With present institutions the only candidate for this role is the family GP. However there is little evidence that people search for, or can evaluate, their agent-GP or that, in the absence of any evidence about the quality of care provided by hospitals and medical specialists, the GP can fulfil the role of patient-agent. The most conclusive evidence of a patient's inability to evaluate medical services is the evidence that the medial profession cannot do this and the resulting small area variations in the provision of services noted earlier.

This problem of patient autonomy is particularly troublesome when there is a welfarist social welfare function. Consumers cannot maximise utility when they lack information and judgement. Their preferences are incomplete. The extent and consequences of this problem undoubtedly varies with the type of

Table 9. How Australia Compares*

The rank order of Australia compared with 17 other OECD** countries: selected statistics

	Year	Rank	No of countries	Australia's rank	Absolute Value		
					Australia	Highest	Lowest
Social Security transfers (%GDP)	1990–1999	1 = highest transfer	17	17	8.3	20.9	8.3
% population with income below 50% of median income	late 1990s	1 = lowest % below median	16	15	14.3	17.0	5.4
Income at 90th percentile/Income at 10th	late 1990s	1 = lowest inequality	17	13	4.3	5.5	2.6
Poorest 30% income earners share of income	Mid 1990	1 = highest	14	14	7.4	11.9	7.4
% (absolute poverty) population with income <$US11.00/day	1995	1 = lowest %	10	10	18	18	4
% elderly in poverty	late 1990'	1 = lowest %	16	16	29.4	29.4	2.7
Income of elderly (above 65) ÷ Income 18–64 (%)	mid 1990's	1 = highest income	16	16	60	92	60
% children in poverty							
—single mother	mid 1990s	1 = lowest %	15	13	46.3	49.6	6.6
—2 parents		1 = lowest %	15	13	11.9	19.6	1.5
Official Aid/GDP (US$)	2000	1 = highest	18	15	$54	$337	$29
Total tax/GDP (%)	2000	1 = highest tax	18	15	31.5	54.2	27.1

*Tiffen R and Gittins R 2004, *How Australia Compares*, Ligare Press/CUB.
** All OECD countries with a population above 3 million.

service (Segal 1998). However, for the majority of complex and costly interventions reform options must extend beyond the simple provision of information.

Managed Competition

Third, in view of these problems and constraints, the model that is most suitable for a country which wishes to integrate a public and a private health sector is, in theory, one that incorporates the principles of "Managed Competition", as described in numerous publications by Scotton (1995; 1999) and reviewed in detail by the Productivity Commission (2002). Based upon a suggestion by Enthoven (1988) Scotton envisages the creation of a small number of competitive health schemes or "fund holders" which compete for patients and provides or organises access to comprehensive contracted services. Unlike the existing PHI organisations, a fund holder would actively interfere in the market to obtain the most cost-effective package of services for its members. Public and private service providers would compete for contracts. Fund holders would receive a risk-adjusted premium from the government for each patient in exchange for the provision of a comprehensive package of health services. Premiums might or might not be topped up through additional patient payments. Individuals who did not opt into a private Fund Holding group would automatically be assigned to the public Fund Holder for the geographic location of the patient. Governments would play an important and ongoing regulatory role to ensure that fund holders did not cream skim or cost shift.

The model is attractive. Equity is achieved through tax-based funding and universal access. Undistorted price signals in the "internal market" between providers and health funds should reflect the benefits and costs of services. The creation of a single pool of funds for each individual satisfies the prerequisite for allocative efficiency. Technical efficiency should be achieved because of the capacity of the fund holder to investigate cost effectiveness of services and the quality of providers. Fund Holder size helps achieve the countervailing economic power necessary to match the enormous power of service providers. Constraints upon patient co-payments may be used to minimise cost shifting to patients although competition may satisfactorily achieve this goal. Based upon evidence from the Netherlands it is likely that competition between fund holders would lead to higher quality care (the public being suspicious of non-government health care delivery).

The model remains largely untested. Some countries, notably the Netherlands, have implemented some form of Managed Competition. Technical problems (and in particular determining appropriate risk-rated premiums) must be overcome before the model can be fully embraced. In the long term the model may also result in an inequitable run-down in the quality of the public default system if the educated and politically powerful members of society sign up with private fund holders.

Quality and Cost Effectiveness

Fourth, fund holders—public or private—must accept responsibility for the quality and cost-effectiveness of services provided to their members. The incidence and history of adverse events is so lamentable that external intervention is needed and this is most easily achieved by those purchasing services. There will be resistance from doctors who, for professional or financial reasons, have adopted an idiosyncratic approach to service delivery. But the doctors "right to clinical freedom" must be balanced against the patient's right to safe and evidence-based medical care. Protocols must be developed for which practitioners take ownership. This is best achieved by the development of guidelines by practitioners themselves in combination with the relevant colleges and the government.

Incentives:

Finally, irrespective of social values and the overall model of health care it will be necessary to ensure that on the supply side there are appropriate information systems, evidence based clinical pathways and protocols. Systems must incorporate discharge planning, electronic patient records and ongoing assessment of the cost effectiveness of services. Achieving these objectives will be difficult. In these circumstances there is a compelling case for the pervasive use of economic incentives which encourage but do not coerce practitioners to adopt evidence-based guidelines. The incentives can apply to the reimbursement of individual practitioners who do or do not adopt protocols and, similarly, accredited hospitals—those incorporating designated systems—may be rewarded with a small percentage increase in the case-based revenue they receive. As noted previously, it is not unreasonable or without precedent for society to pay more for something it wants rather than for something it does not want!

6 Conclusion

Recent health policy has probably done more harm than good when judged by the criteria of allocative and technical efficiency. The issues capturing public attention have been small in terms of their likely impact upon health and well-being. However it appears unlikely that these criteria drove policy. Rather, the policy agenda appears to have been driven by the desire to promote the liberal/libertarian world view: that individuals should take primary responsibility for their health and health care; and that, following from this, the redistributive role of Medicare (healthy wealthy to unhealthy less wealthy) should be at least partially rolled back. With this world view a multi-tier health system is an acceptable outcome as long as basic care is satisfactory and there is an adequate safety net. With these values, health and health care are appropriately part of the economic reward system.

It is a legitimate role of government to promote a particular world view. Independent evidence suggests that it is a view strongly supported in other areas of social welfare policy. However, most Australians appear to be committed to communitarian values with respect to health services and the resulting tension has dominated the health care debate. The real failure of government is not its choice of objective but its inability to reconcile this with policies that are consistent with economic principles of efficiency. Medicare continues to have serious structural problems and these are inflicting great harm on the population as compared with a health system which was allocatively and technically efficient.

As compared with the self-congratulatory satisfaction of many assessments of the health system, this article has identified a number of dismal failures—perhaps appropriate from a member of the dismal science! Government has focused upon issues which are almost trivial when compared with the fundamental problems of the health sector. As a system, and as judged by the rate of adverse event rate, it is dangerous and, at best, highly inefficient. There is little coordination of services or ongoing monitoring of effective access. Error learning is optional and information for the public about system performance and the quality of services does not exist. Inequities are widespread but they have been allowed to persist.

Irrespective of the type of health scheme there are compelling reasons for immediately implementing measures to reduce adverse events, for ending the federal-state divide, for integrating services and, in particular, revising and upgrading the coordinating role of primary health care. Data systems at all levels should be upgraded and, in particular, a patient and his/her doctor should be able to access electronically their health history.

At the political level these problems have been largely ignored or inadequately addressed and the medical profession has, by default, determined behaviour and performance. It has failed to create a satisfactory delivery system.

The health sector is replete with theoretical and applied challenges for the economist. The subject matter of health economics is probably broader than for any other economic sub-discipline. The 1,910 page *Handbook of Health Economics* contains thirty five review articles of different economic issues arising from the health sector. Research is *relatively* well-funded and most of the research is of immediate policy relevance. Despite this few universities include the subject in their course offerings. In the absence of good health economic and health services research the likelihood of system fairness and efficiency is diminished.

References

AIHW (Australian Institute of Health and Welfare), Australia's health services expenditure to 1997–98, Health Expenditure Bulletin No. 15, cat. no. HWE 13, Health and Welfare Expenditure Series No. 12, Canberra: AIHW, 1999 viewed 17 August 2004, http://www.aihw.gov

Butler JR, Health Expenditure, in *Economics and Australian health policy*, G Mooney and R Scotton (eds), Sydney: Allen & Unwin, 1999, pp. 40–71.

Chassin MR, "Achieving and sustaining improved quality: lessons from New York State and cardiac surgery", *Health Affairs*, 2002, vol. 21:4 pp. 40–51.

Dawkins P, Welster E, Hopkins S and Yong J, Recent Private Health Insurance Policies in Australia: Health resource utilisation distributive implications and policy options, Report 3, University of Melbourne, 17 March 2004.

Duckett S, *The Australian Health Care System*, Melbourne : Oxford University Press, 2000.

Enthoven AC, *Theory and Practice of Managed Competition in Health Care Financing*, North Holland: Amsterdam 1988.

Evans R, Law M, The Canadian health care system: where are we and how did we get there', Economic Development Institute of the World Bank, 1995.

Gerdtham UG and Jönsson B, "International comparisons of health expenditure", in (eds) AJ Culyer and JP Newhouse *Handbook of Health Economics*, North Holland: Elsevier, 2000.

Hurley J, "An overview of the normative economics of the health sector", in (eds) AJ Culyer and JP Newhouse *Handbook of Health Economics*, North Holland: Elsevier, 2000.

Industry Commission, Private Health Insurance, Report No 57, 28 February 1997, Canberra: Industry Commission, 1997.

Lohr KN, "Use of medical care in the Rand health insurance experiment: diagnosis and service-specific analysis in a randomized controlled trial", *Medicare Care*, 1986 (suppl) S1-87.

Newhouse JP, *Free for All? Lessons from the RAND Health Insurance Experiment*, Cambridge: Harvard University Press, 1993

Productivity Commission, Managed Competition: The Policy Context, Managed Competition in Health Care, Productivity Commission Workshop Proceedings, AusInfo: Canberra, 2002.

Reeder CE, Nelson AA, The differential impact of co-payments on drug use in a Medicaid population, *Enquiry*, 1985, vol. 22:4, pp. 396–403.

Rice T, "Can markets give us the health system we want?", *Journal of Health Politics, Policy and Law*, 1997, 22:2, 383–426.

Rice T, *The Economics of Health Reconsidered*, Chicago : Health Administration Press, 2nd ed, 2002.

Richardson J, "The health care financing debate", in *Economics and Australian Health Policy*, eds G Mooney & RB Scotton, Sydney: Allen and Unwin 1999.

Richardson J, Why economic costs may not be of interest in a national health scheme, or: costs, fairness and reverse order analysis, Working Paper 126, Centre for Health Program Evaluation, Melbourne: Monash University, 2001.

Richardson J, "Priorities of health policy: cost shifting or population health", *Australia and New Zealand Health Policy*, 2005, vol. 2 no. 1 http://www.anzhealthpolicy.com/content/2/1/1.

Richardson J, Deeble J, Statistics of Private Medical Services in Australia 1976, HRP, Canberra: ANU, 1982.

Richardson J, Segal L, Private health insurance and the Pharmaceutical Benefits Scheme: how effective has recent government policy been, *Australian Health Review*, 2004, vol. 28 no. 1 pp. 34–47.

Robertson I, Richardson J, "The effect of funding upon hospital treatment: the case of coronary angiography and coronary artery revascularisation procedures following acute myocardial infarction", *Medical Journal of Australia*, 2000, vol. 173, pp. 291–295.

Scotton RB, "Managed competition: issues for Australia", *Australian Health Review*, 1995, 18:1 82–104.

Scotton RB, "Managed competition", in: *Economics and Australian Health Policy*, eds G Mooney & RB Scotton, Sydney: Allen & Unwin; 1999, pp. 214–231.

Segal L, "The importance of patient empowerment in health system reform", *Health Policy*, 1998, vol. 44 pp. 31–44.

Sen A, "personal utilities and public judgements: or what's wrong with welfare economics", *Economic Journal* 1979, vol. 89 (September) pp. 537–58.

Tasmanian Department of Health and Human Services, Reforms for the 21st Century' Report of the Expert Advisory Group into Key Issues for Public and Private Hospital Services in Tasmania (The Richardson Report), 2004. http://www.dhhs.tas.gov.au/corporateinformation/publications/documents/2004-06-Richardson-Report-v2.pdf

Tiffen R and Gittins R 2004, *How Australia Compares*, Ligare Press/CUB, 2004.

Van Der Weydan, The Bundaberg Hospital scandal: the need for reform in Queensland and beyond', *Medical Journal of Australia*, 2005, vol. 183:6.

Wilson RM et al, The Quality in Australian Health Care Study. *Medical Journal of Australia*, 1995, vol. 163 pp. 458–471.

Note
1   As noted by Segal (1998) "Patients with a long term chronic problem may be an exception to this generalisation". Evidence of patient disempowerment is widespread and conclusive.

South Australia and Australian Economic Development

W.A. Sinclair

Monash University, Melbourne

The received economic history of the white settlement of Australia has tended to be written from the perspective of New South Wales. N.G. Butlin's pioneering estimates of Australian GDP[1] appear, on closer inspection, to bear the distinct imprint of that colony/state.[2] This paper considers Australian economic development through the eyes of one of the peripheral regions. South Australia is chosen as particularly interesting because its economic history starts as a shining example to the other colonies but later becomes an especially revealing manifestation of the problems involved in sustaining the economic development of Australia.

The paper relies heavily on the present author's estimates of the GDP's of the colonies/states of Australia for the period 1861–1976/77.[3] They can be regarded as extensions of estimates previously made for the Australian colonies up to 1860[4] amended by the present author by new estimates for Tasmania from 1804–60 and Western Australia from 1829–60. Linkage with the ABS estimates of State Gross Product beginning in 1977/78[5] provides a complete series from 1788 to the present day.

In essence, South Australia replicated the pattern of Australian economic development but with significant variations. For Australia as a whole, the economic course of white settlement can be summarized as initially a period of rapid economic expansion based on discovery and exploitation of natural resources sustained for most of the nineteenth century followed by a hiatus up to the end of the 1930s. A prolonged renewal of rapid economic expansion associated with industrial transition ensued from the Second World War until the mid-1970s with a break before a further period of economic growth dating particularly from the early 1990s. South Australia was, until the end of the 1870s, a leading player in Australian economic development. It then suffered a more prolonged and severe hang-over than in the other colonies/states but was again prominent in the rise of manufacturing from the end of the 1930s. For most of the time since the 1970s, however, it has been a muted version of Australian economic growth.

I

South Australia was a remarkably successful exercise in colonisation. There was a virtually instant "take-off" into sustained economic growth in a manner not seen in the other Australian colonies and perhaps in the rest of the world. Within three years of its foundation, South Australia appears to have been enjoying a level of GDP per head well in advance of that of Western Australia, founded seven years previously. By the mid-1840s, it had caught up with the much older settlements of New South Wales and Tasmania (see Table 1). It re-asserted its economic prominence in the 1870s when it shot clear of the other colonies to emerge as the leader by a long margin in terms of GDP per head.

Table 1. Real GDP Per Head (A$ equivalents)

	NSW	Tas	WA	SA
1841–45	55.8	79.6	52.4	75.8
1846–50	75.0	93.2	63.4	101.8
1851–55	71.8	106.0	68.4	76.2
1856–60	79.2	78.4	67.0	85.0
1861–65	91.6	81.2	67.0	86.6
1866–70	91.6	88.4	76.0	93.0
1871–75	102.4	87.6	84.6	123.4
1876–80	109.0	70.2	84.6	129.8

Source: See text

The Western Australian experience is an instructive contrast with that of South Australia. By the time South Australia was well on the way to sustained economic growth, settlers had still not been attracted to Western Australia in sufficient numbers to allow the population to attain a critical mass. For the successful foundation of a new private colony, a circular relationship between agriculture and population is crucial. On the one hand, population is attracted by the prospect of converting land to profitable agriculture and, on the other, the extent of the market for agriculture is determined by the size of the population. From this relationship there can be a flow-on to demand for locally produced goods other than food and for services, so promoting a further inflow of population. There can be other influences on the size of the population, namely, the exploitation of natural resources for export markets as well as migration decisions not connected with the pull of natural resources. In early Western Australia, however, these additional stimuli were weak. The main hope of an export sector rested on wool but pastoralists experienced great difficulty in establishing their sheep flocks in the face of the hazards of local natural conditions and the lack of transport facilities. Wool failed to establish supremacy over agriculture and sheep numbers reached a premature peak in 1848. As for other possible sources of population, the fact that Western Australia missed out on the sort of increasing injection of funds from the British Government which helped to tide New South Wales and Tasmania over their early difficulties set it apart from those attempts at colonisation. The payment for the establishment of a British official and military presence was an initial help and may have tipped the scales in favour of the initial viability of agriculture and the colony. But the inflow of public funds was a static, if welcome, contribution and not intended as the prelude to a long-term program of transportation of convicts. Nor was there any other strong governmental stimulus to population increase. The local authorities had little scope for expenditure on infrastructure which could have directly employed labour and helped to reduce the onerous costs of transport of the land-intensive industries. In these circumstances, the inter-play between agriculture and population assumed even greater significance. But the land in the vicinity of Perth, except for narrow river frontages, was of poor quality for agricultural purposes. The colony was thus trapped in a vicious circle whereby agriculture was not attracting much population and population was not adding appreciably to the market for agriculture. The resort to transportation of convicts in 1850 provided only a short-term solution to this dilemma at the cost of damaging Western Australia's image as a free colony. Until the discovery of the Kalgoorlie and Coolgardie gold fields in the 1890s, the colony remained pretty much out of sight and out of mind elsewhere in Australia.

It was probably only the expenditure of the British Government on the convicts which saved New South Wales from a similar fate. The conflict between managing a gaol and an economy bedevilled the colony for more than 30 years after the First Settlement. In the early years it was only the substantial subvention of the British Government for the maintenance of the convicts which kept the settlement afloat. Progress towards the key goal of expanding the area of land for high-yielding food production was slow. To some extent this was because of natural impediments. The land adjacent to Port Jackson was of poor quality and the first movement on to alluvial soil was dogged by frequent flooding. It was not until 1809 that agriculture began to shift to selected sites in the forest region to the west of Sydney. But a series of governmental errors exacerbated the problem. An initial attempt at public agriculture using convict labour was quickly aborted. It was not, however, followed by a serious attempt to encourage private farming. On the contrary, the larger landowners came to disdain agriculture especially after Governor King arbitrarily reduced the price offered for grain for the commissariat which was the main market. The closing years of the Napoleonic Wars, which ended in 1815, provided a window of opportunity through a greatly increased inflow of convicts transported. But Governor Macquarie chose to deploy a large part of the increased work force in public building and road construction so diverting resources which could have gone into agriculture. According to J.T. Bigge, who was officially commissioned to report on the state of the colony in 1821, the yield of wheat per acre actually fell by about 25 per cent after 1815. It was to be Bigge's report which finally recognized the appropriate way forward and set the New South Wales economy off on a path of improvement in the 1820s.

In departing so positively from the early experience of its sister colonies, South Australia had luck on its side. The infant colony was blessed with good land, well-placed to allow grain producers to take advantage of the cost savings offered by water transport. Early discovery of rich copper deposits led, in the second half of the 1840s, to the first mineral boom in Australian history. Initially wrong-footed by the loss of labour to the Victorian gold fields in the 1850s, South Australians were then presented with a spectacular enlargement of the market for wheat. The discovery of copper at Wallaroo in the 1860s was another godsend and, at the end of the decade, the passage of an act of parliament facilitating larger landholdings in new regions now open for settlement was nicely timed to benefit from the wool price boom of the 1870s. It allowed wheat growers selling into New South Wales, where the pastoral boom was centered, to join South Australian pastoralists in the fortunate turn of events. The upshot was the particularly felicitous decade of the 1870s when a strong rural upswing based on wool and wheat became enmeshed with an accelerating demand for labour associated with booming urban construction and energetic railway building. By the middle of the decade, the rapid inflow of population had triggered a major extension of the Adelaide suburbs and re-building of the Central Building District which became a magnet for further waves of immigrants. All things seemed to be working together for good.

It would probably be telling only part of the story, however, to portray South Australia's economic leadership as simply an early version of The Lucky Country. South Australia differed from Western Australia and New South Wales in the alacrity with which the early settlers solved the problem of self-generating population increase through profitable agriculture. Indeed, it took only the passage of a few years for the colony to become a regular and growing *exporter* of wheat to New South Wales, displacing Tasmania as the main source of imports of grain into New South Wales. Not only were the mistakes of governmental decision makers avoided, but the motivation of the new inhabitants of South Australia differed from those of either New South Wales or Western Australia. Whether or not it was a *paradise* of dissent,[6] South Australia might well be viewed as an interesting social experiment. The founding settlers were imbued with a theology based on individual conscience and freedom from authority. The combination of this with a set of legal institutions which they brought with them and which had provided the framework for the economic transformation of Britain, set the scene for economic progress. One of the apparent outcomes was the vigorous development of a commercial agriculture. Although one group of the dissenters, the Lutherans, opted for a self-sufficient form of land-use, others had no qualms about responding to market signals. The South Australian farmers were quick to exploit surges in the demand for food in other parts of the continent resulting from such developments as the

Victorian gold discoveries and the New South Wales pastoral boom. This continuing readiness to take up opportunities to find markets for South Australian produce is suggestive of an exceptional enterprise culture. Certainly, the growth rate of real GDP per head of 7.7 per cent per annum throughout the 1870s was impressive by any standards. Exceeded only by New South Wales, the centre of the great pastoral boom of the 1870s and 1880s, it was far in excess of that of all the other colonies. It would seem that the colonists made the most of their good fortune.

II

Up to the end of the 1870s, South Australia had enjoyed over 40 years of uninterrupted economic progress propelling it to the top of the Australian ladder of GDP per capita; nearly 60 years later, at the outbreak of the Second World War its real per capita GDP was lower than it had been in 1880. For no other colony/state was this the case. What had gone wrong?

The answer needs to be set in a nation-wide context. Perhaps the most arresting implication of N.G. Butlin's estimates of Gross Domestic Product was the revelation that Australia apparently made scarcely any advance in per capita terms between 1890 and 1939.[7] Later research may suggest some slight qualification of this finding. My estimates for separate colonies/states point to an example of the dominance of New South Wales in the Butlin estimates. They purport to show that whereas New South Wales recorded a slight per capita decline over the period concerned, all the other colonies/states showed a slight increase. It is also the case that B.D. Haig's estimates of real Australian GDP per capita,[8] which should be regarded as an alternative to Butlin rather than an updated version, suggest some over-all improvement. But none of this revision does anything to correct the impression that the surging economic growth of most of the nineteenth century had given way to a long period of near stagnation.

The depression of the 1890s had ushered in a phase in the development of the Australian economy when the more obvious opportunities to exploit the abundant natural resources which had been fuelling economic growth had been taken. With natural resources now imparting less drive to the economy, Australia was a collection of centres of population which were becoming more reliant on industries constrained by the small scale of the local market.

South Australia laboured under this joint disadvantage more than any other colony/state. It reached its natural-resource barrier earlier and with an abruptness not seen elsewhere. The end of the 1870s was the high water mark of movement on to new agricultural land and the signal for actual retreat. The colony's copper deposits had now been worked out. And it could not match New South Wales and Victoria in population. All the other smaller colonies still had untouched natural resources. Western Australia was only just beginning to discover the extent of its gold deposits which would project it on to a new growth path in the 1890s. Queensland was still in process of bringing its vast area of land into productive use and of exploiting its mineral resources and Tasmania was about to enter on a period of mineral development which would continue into the twentieth century. It was the failure to share in the general economic growth of the 1880s which explains why the colony lost touch with other colonies/states in per capita terms. During that time the South Australian real GDP per capita fell about 25 per cent. In the remaining fifty years or so up to the outbreak of the Second World War it performed about as well, or more accurately, not noticeably worse than the other colonies/states.

Even in the 1880s, there were signs of resilience in the face of adversity. In the first half of the decade, the multiplier-accelerator mechanism associated with the inter-related rural and urban booms went into reverse. The rural boom collapsed initially because of drought and then because of the realization that dry seasons were simply a warning that the wheat farmers had overstepped the boundaries set by climate for long-term occupation. One of the supports of an over-priced urban land market was thus removed. It was the sharp drop in urban construction which most reduced the level of income in the early part of the downturn. The government then reacted to the changed economic scene by sharply curtailing its expenditure on railway building as well as on other activities. The continuing decline in copper mining added to the general gloom. The economy contracted by about 30 per cent between the sharp peak of 1880 and the trough of 1886, although the effects on unemployment were somewhat ameliorated by the high demand for labour in other colonies, especially Victoria. Nevertheless, recovery was under way before the economy succumbed to the generally depressive conditions of the first half of the 1890s in Australia. GDP in real terms appears to have been a little higher in 1890 than in 1879, the year before the previous peak. Agriculture rebounded somewhat with two good harvests and manufacturing showed the benefit of reduced costs by more than doubling its value-added.

But a 60-year fall in per capita GDP is, to say the least, unusual in modern economic history and merits closer examination. The picture that emerges is not one of unrelieved decline but of a roller-coaster ride. South Australia fared worse than the other less populated colonies in the 1890s.[9] The GDP estimates suggest that the severity of the depression which was clearly in train by 1891 was largely a Victoria and New South Wales phenomenon resulting from these having been the centres of the urban and pastoral construction booms, respectively, of the preceding years. Mining development in Western Australia, Queensland and Tasmania (and even, to a lesser extent in Victoria) acted as a buffer against other depressive influences. In South Australia, the continuing natural constraint dragged the economy down for most of the 1890s. Between then and 1939, however, real GDP per head twice peaked at levels close to or slightly above that of 1880, first at the end of the opening decade of the twentieth century and again in the first half of the 1920s (see Table 2).

Table 2. Real SAGDP Per Head

	A$ equivalents	% of rest of Australia
1880	145.6	131
1890	107.2	89
1897	81.8	76
1910/11	142.2	90
1913/14	130.2	84
1925/26	153.2	101
1938/39	125.8	86

Source: See text

The earlier instance was associated with a technological breakthrough, itself conceived in South Australia, which liberated the colonial economy from the effects of low agricultural productivity. The new "Federation" strain of wheat was particularly suited to the dry climate of South Australia. It came at an especially propitious time in that about ten years earlier the technical problem of combining steam power and steel in shipbuilding had been overcome in Britain. Steel steamships quickly replaced the sailing ships which had been the main carriers of freight between Australia and the rest of the world and, with their greater reliability and speed, greatly improved the possibilities of shipping wheat to the European market. In the first decade of the twentieth century, surging productivity and cheap ocean transport generated a sharp rise in exports of South Australian wheat. On the back of this development, the South Australian economy recovered the ground lost in the preceding 20 years. It would seem that the earlier spirit of enterprise had not been lost by South Australian farmers.

In the first half of the 1920s, Australian governments resumed programmes of rural infrastructure spending interrupted by the War and financed to a large extent from overseas borrowing. South Australia shared in this development although to a lesser extent than in some other states. A broad-based expansion of both rural and urban industry carried real GDP per head to a peak just above the 1880 level in the mid-1920s, bringing it fleetingly above the average of the rest of Australia.

It was, then, a failure to maintain momentum which dogged the post-1880 South Australian economy. South Australian GDP per head fell from rough parity with that for the rest of Australia in the mid-1920s to 85 per cent at the end of the 1930s. The immediate reason for the descent from the 1924/25 summit was the severe drought of the second half of the 1920s in South Australia. But there were more continuing forces at work. One was the turbulence of the international economy after 1914 when the disruptive effects of the First World War extended into the 1920s culminating in the depression of the 1930s. South Australia was particularly vulnerable to these events because of the importance of wheat exports to its economy. In 1880, South Australian agriculture, at about 20 per cent of GDP, greatly exceeded all other colonies and wheat was an exceptionally high proportion of the net value of agriculture. This was still the case up to the outbreak of the First World War following the post-1900 resurgence of wheat growing based on increased exports of wheat at rising prices. In the inter-war period, world commodity markets were generally over-supplied but especially wheat. South Australia was now suffering from its heavy reliance on one industry, wheat growing.

Another factor contributing to the generally poor economic performance may have been Federation. Although it had many facets, the so-called

"Federation settlement" comprising, among other things, wage regulation behind a tariff wall, may be seen in one sense as a policy response to the emerging natural-resource constraint on economic growth. The depression of the 1890s, if not the death knell of the old order, ended the pastoral boom which had seemed to define Australia and was a dramatic agent of structural adjustment. For most of the nineteenth century, Australia had been a high-wage economy as a result of the labour demands from rural expansion and a very high level of construction. In this historical setting, the protection of manufacturing industry seemed an obvious way to encourage the creation of a new source of demand for labour and to meet the expectation of good wages and working conditions. The alternative would have been to allow costs to fall into line with overseas and concentrate on improvements in agricultural productivity and such other industries as could withstand overseas competition for economic progress. This could have led to a rise in per capita income in the following decades. But the implication was that Australia would have been settling for a lower rate of population increase than that to which it had become accustomed. Such an attitude would have flown in the face of the fact that population increase had been the dominant influence on Australian economic development in the nineteenth century. The rise in income per head during that period was almost incidental to the developmental process. It was the high rate of increase of aggregate GDP on the standards of the contemporary international economy which was remarkable. The emphasis was on settling an empty continent and much of the gains from natural-resource development were swallowed up by population inflow.

Not only was South Australia thus locked into a national policy of promoting population increase at the possible sacrifice of per capita GDP but it bore a disproportionate burden of the costs of the tariff. With its emphasis on agriculture, South Australia was one of the states which stood to lose from manufacturing protection. It also received less recognition in attempts to compensate for this at the federal level. Not until 1927, did it become a recipient of any of the various special grants made to the less populous states and at no time up to the outbreak of the Second World War did such grants have an significant effect on income per head. Nor did Commonwealth Government decisions to provide forms of protection for primary industries, mainly dating from the

1920s, offer much to growers of wheat, the South Australian specialty. In the period up to the end of the 1930s, then, Federation may have worked as a dampener on South Australian economic growth.

III

The rapid and sustained increase in South Australia's real GDP from 1939 to the early 1970s looks all the more impressive against the lacklustre background of the preceding 60 or so years. South Australia was an active participant in the long expansion of the Australian economy when the Second World War was the occasion for a continuation of the previously occurring recovery from the depression of the 1930s followed by about 30 years of exceptionally rapid output increase. Although Australia did not match the rate of increase of real GDP in some of the large industrial countries during the long post-war boom in the world economy, it returned to the pace it had known in the nineteenth century. In no state was the turn-around more marked than in South Australia. The colony/state which had fallen from the top to the bottom rung of the ladder of real GDP per capita between 1880 and 1939 now rose to be exceeded only by New South Wales and Victoria.

The sharpness of the change in economic fortunes was matched by the abruptness of the adoption of a new policy of economic development immediately preceding it. The advocacy of J.W. Wainwright, the former Auditor-General who was appointed as a government adviser, led to the acceptance by the State Government in the second half of the 1930s of promotion of manufacturing industry as the way forward for the state. In the context of what had been happening in Australia, governmental intervention in favour of manufacturing was not unusual. But until the later 1920s, governmental rhetoric generally throughout Australia, reiterated as late as 1934 by South Australian Premier Butler, had tended to equate economic with rural development.[10] What was remarkable was the example of the government of what had been the most agricultural state publicly declaring its acceptance that manufacturing development was the way to go for South Australia.

The apparent causal connection between the structural change in the economy and governmental policy, embodied in the term "Playfordism", invites sceptical examination. Playford, succeeding Butler as Premier in 1938, took up the baton of induced industrialization and greatly extended its post-war scope. But Playford's South Australia was not alone. Manufacturing expanded to become a larger part of the economy after 1945 in all the Australian states. The Commonwealth tariff which, together with other forms of protection from overseas competition, rose to new heights, played its role. There were also some local factors favouring South Australian manufacturing. One was the War, during which a Commonwealth Government policy of concentrating the production of defence materials in a fairly compact and less threatened corner of the Australian mainland led to the choice of Adelaide as a major site. This not only allowed for continuity with the pre-war development of an automobile industry but left a post-war legacy of capacity for that industry and of relevant skills. Secondly, South Australia, given its greater specialization than any other state in consumer durables, was favoured by the high income-elasticity of demand for these products. Thirdly, a benign climate of industrial relations, compared with some other states, and the appearance of labour costs lower than the Australian average may have been an inducement for the investment of inter-state and international capital in South Australia. Michael Stutchbury goes so far as to argue that the South Australian manufacturing profile does not look sufficiently different from other states to justify attributing significance to Playfordism.[11]

GDP estimates suggest a less clear-cut position. It does appear that the South Australian economy underwent a greater shift to manufacturing between the end of the 1930s and the later 1960s than that of any other state. In 1880, the manufacturing sector of the South Australian economy, as a proportion of its GDP, had been falling for about 20 years and was the smallest in Australia.[12] The competition for resources from primary industry and rural and urban construction imposed a level of costs on manufacturing which exposed it to inroads into its local market of imports at falling prices. The only manufacturing industries of any significance were those protected by high transport costs and proximity to local raw materials. South Australians enjoyed a benign climate of surging production and cheap manufactured goods. As a result of the retreat from agriculture and the downturn in construction in the 1880s followed by the depression of the 1890s, a new economic structure, in which manufacturing was substantially more important, emerged. But there was little change in the share of manufacturing in GDP between the outbreak of the First World War and the late 1930s, despite the rising height of the tariff wall and the establishment of some more capital-intensive forms of manufacturing, notably car assembly. The big break with the past occurred during the period of the Second World War, so much so that a slight further rise in the immediate post-War years carried the share of manufacturing to what was to prove to be very close to the highest point for the subsequent period of manufacturing expansion. In the following 20 years, that is, manufacturing did little more than hold its share in GDP. Nevertheless, South Australia was unique amongst the states in the extent to which manufacturing retained its importance in the economy. In all the other states, except Victoria, the share of manufacturing in GDP peaked in the late 1950s. South Australia, in 1967/68, was the last to do so. In fact, South Australia was the only state in which value-added in manufacturing grew at a substantially faster rate than the net product of agriculture in real terms in the period 1950-65. The transformation of Australia's most agricultural colony into an industrial state was manifest.

If it cannot safely be concluded that Playford was a minor player in South Australian industrialization, there is a further question of what this may have meant for the average South Australian. Playford's immediate aim was the increase of the population through the provision of manufacturing employment but he, of course, also had living standards in mind. Indeed, he actively promoted the latter through such measures as the provision of cheap housing and the retention of some wartime price controls. His apparent success is indicated by the unequivocal improvement in real SAGDP per head over the course of his premiership. On the other hand, inter-state comparisons cast some doubt on what difference Playfordism played in producing this outcome. South Australia's rise from the bottom of the ladder of GDP per head at the end of the 1930s to the third rung occurred during the first half of the 1940s and can be attributed to the special effects of the War. South Australia then moved in step with the other states in the early part of the long post-war boom but, between the mid-1950s and the first half of the 1970s, it fell back to join Tasmania on the bottom (see Table 3). To a large extent, this can be explained in terms of the fact that the other two less populous states, Western Australia and Queensland, were entering on their long mineral boom while New South

Wales and Victoria benefited from economies of scale and agglomeration not available to South Australia and Tasmania. It would therefore be difficult to use the GDP estimates to support an argument either that Playfordism was responsible for the rise in incomes per head it presided over or for the comparative decline in the later years.

Table 3. Real GDP Per head (A$ equivalents)

	SA	NSW	Vic	Qld	WA	Tas
1938/39	125.8	143.8	150.6	132.0	140.6	125.4
1945/46	154.4	170.6	175.8	149.4	145.8	150.8
1955/56	200.0	219.6	234.0	188.1	187.6	106.4
1965/66	240.7	282.1	277.5	237.3	145.5	244.6
1973/74	301.8	360.4	366.2	306.7	340.4	297.0

Source: See text

A more complete counter-factual analysis would require an answer to the question of what would have happened if Playford had not taken his interventionist approach. Inter-state comparisons may be of little help here in that all states, with the possible exception of Western Australia, offered special inducements to manufacturers to locate within their borders. The resultant loss of allocative efficiency was thus felt across the board. For all that, Playfordism, was a more intrusive and wide-ranging package of government intervention in the economy than in other states and Playford was probably a particularly zealous proponent of forced industrialisation. The likelihood is therefore enhanced that the extent to which South Australia had moved down the road of industrialization had led to negative effects on incomes per head and had made it a hostage to the continuation of a benign external environment.

IV

As the small industrial state that it had become, South Australia was vulnerable to the effects of the sea change in the world economy dating from the mid-1970s and to the radical transformation of the Australian institutional structure of the 1980s. When the long post-war boom of the world economy came to an abrupt end, the Australian economy lost its buoyancy. The boom had also distracted attention from the effect of tariff protection of breeding an inward-looking manufacturing sector. The subsequent dismantling of the tariff therefore came as a major shock to the states which had larger manufacturing sectors. South Australia was particularly affected because, along with Tasmania, it lacked both the extensive mineral resources of the other less populous states and the population size which could ease the shift of resources into the services sector.

The transition to services as the dominant growth centre of the Australian economy had gathered pace after the mid-1950s. Services were always a major part of the economy, as high as 53 per cent of GDP in New South Wales and generally just over 40 per cent in South Australia in the second half of the nineteenth century. The sector, taken as a whole, tended to rise in importance over time although its composition changed significantly with a decline in the importance of domestic service and imputed house rents in favour of trade and transport and communications. The acceleration in the growth of services sector from the mid-1950s was particularly the result of the proliferation of financial and business services of many descriptions. In this development, New South Wales and Victoria, thanks to the economies of scale and agglomeration associated with the size of their metropolitan centres, led the way. By the late 1990s, financial and business services were claiming close to 25 per cent of GDP in these states compared with about 15 per cent in South Australia.

The differing opportunities for structural change between the states were reflected in a widening of the spread in their respective real GDP per head. Western Australia and Queensland, particularly the former, were better able to ride out the storm as a result of the strength of the mineral boom in those states. The growth of financial and business services enabled New South Wales and Victoria to avoid more than a short-term shock from the decline of the manufacturing sector. The result was that Western Australia broke from the pack to emerge as a clear leader in terms of real GDP per head followed by Queensland. South Australia and Tasmania, particularly the latter, fell back to the rear of the field.

Despite its laggard status, the South Australian economy was showing signs by the 1990s of adjustment to the new institutional framework established after the 1970s. The initial effect on the allocation of resources throughout Australia of the reversion to a market system had been to disadvantage South Australia. Even in the unbroken period of Australian economic growth from the

Table 4. South Australian Economic Growth (per cent per annum)

	Real GDP	Real GDP Per Head
1871–80	7.7	4.3
1955/56–1964/65	5.2	2.7
1990/91–1999/2000	2.1	1.7

Source: See text and ABS, *State Accounts*

early 1990s, South Australia brought up the rear. The state's economic performance at that time does not compare with the halcyon years of the 1870s or with the mid-twentieth century. Nevertheless, a new pattern of economic development was becoming apparent. In the earlier periods, rapid population increase had been a major element in economic expansion. By way of contrast, in the 1990s, the gap between the rates of increase of aggregate and per capita GDP had narrowed considerably (see Table 4). As in the other Australian states, the continuance of economic development was much more dependent than in previous growth periods on productivity increase with resultant gains for a slowly growing population.

South Australia is a region which made a propitious beginning as a new colony by drawing on its natural resources to trade with other parts of the Australian continent. It can, however, be seen as an extreme illustration of the difficulties encountered in Australia in switching from resource-driven growth to non-primary activities. This was a fundamental cause of the change of pace throughout Australia from the nineteenth to the twentieth century taken as a whole. The slenderness of the resource base as a generator of a large enough population to benefit from internationally competitive economies of scale is particularly noticeable in South Australia. Tariff protection of the domestic market for Australian manufactures provided the opportunity for a respite in the third quarter of the twentieth century. But when the state's economy was subsequently exposed to external shocks, the natural constraint re-asserted itself by impeding the transition to a services economy.

Notes

1 Butlin, *Australian Domestic Product.*
2 For a demonstration of the difference from the other large colony/state, see Sinclair.
3 For details of methods and sources used, see author. The estimates incorporate the earlier estimates for Western Australia in particular years by Snooks, *Depression and Recovery* and "Arithmetic of Regional Growth".
4 Butlin and Sinclair, "Australian Domestic Product".
5 ADP, *State Accounts.*
6 Cf. Pike, *Paradise of Dissent.*
7 See Butlin, "Long-Run Trends".
8 Haig.
9 This may be at variance with the analysis of colonial economic fluctuation in Boehm, *Prosperity and Depression*, pp. 23–62. Basing his findings on trade, fiscal and monetary indicators, Boehm does not make a clear distinction between South Australia and Queensland and Tasmania with respect to the severity of the depression.
10 As quoted in Stutchbury, "The Playford Legend", p. 1.
11 Stutchbury, "The Playford Legend". For a less negative assessment see Rich, "Industrialisation" and "Tom's Vision?"
12 This is consistent with the detailed account of early manufacturing development given by Richards, "Genesis of Secondary Industry".

References

Australian Bureau of Statistics, *Australian National Accounts: State Accounts* (Canberra, 1978–).

Boehm, E.A. *Prosperity and Depression in Australia 1887–1897* (Oxford, 1971).

Butlin, N.G. *Australian Domestic Product, Investment and Foreign Borrowing, 1861–1938/9* (Cambridge, 1962).

Butlin, N.G. "Long-Run Trends in Australian *Per Capita* Consumption" in Hancock, Keith (ed.) *The National Income and Social Welfare* (Melbourne, 1965).

Butlin, N.G. and Sinclair, W.A. "Australian Gross Domestic Product 1788–1860: Estimates, Sources and Methods", *Australian Economic History Review*, 26(2), 1986, 126–147.

Haig, B.D. "New Estimates of Australian GDP: 1861-1948/49", *Australian Economic History Review*, 41(1), 2001, 1–34.

Pike, D. *Paradise of Dissent: South Australia 1829–1857* (Melbourne, 1957).

Rich, D.C. "Tom's Vision? Playford and Industrialisation" in O'Neil, B., Raftery, J. and Round, K. (ed.) *Playford's South Australia* (Adelaide, 1997).

Rich, D.C. "Industrialisation" in Prest,W. (ed.) *The Wakefield Companion to South Australian History* (Adelaide, 2001).

Richards, E.S. "The Genesis of Secondary Industry in the South Australian Economy", Australian Economic History Review, 15(2), 1975, 107–135.

Sinclair, W.A. "Victoria's Economy in the Long Run", *Australian Economic History Review*, 36(2), 1996, 3–29.

Snooks, G.D. *Depression and Recovery in Western Australia 1928/29–1938/39* (Perth, 1974).

Snooks, G.D. "The Arithmetic of Regional Growth: Western Australia 1912/13 to 1957/58", *Australian Economic History Review*, 19(1), 1979, 63–74.

Stutchbury, M. "The Playford Legend and the Industrialisation of South Australia", *Australian Economic History Review* 24(1), 1984, 1–19.

Vitae

Born   4 January 1935, Murtoa, Victoria.

Education   B. A. (First Class Honours), Combined School of
                    Economics and History, The University of
                    Melbourne, 1955.

                    Ph. D., The University of London, 1959.

Present Appointments Professorial Fellow, National Institute of Labour
                    Studies, Flinders University; Honorary Visiting
                    Fellow, School of Economics, The University of
                    Adelaide. (Both appointments are honorary.)

                    Chairman, Energy Industry Ombudsman (South
                    Australia) Limited.

Employment Record Tutor in Economic History, The University of
                    Melbourne, 1956–57.

                    Lecturer in Economics, The University of Adelaide,
                    1959–63.

                    Professor of Economics, The University of Adelaide
                    at Bedford Park (1964–66) and Flinders University
                    (1966–79).

                    Vice-Chancellor, Flinders University, 1980–87

                    Deputy-President, Australian Conciliation and
                    Arbitration Commission (1987–89); Deputy
                    President, Australian Industrial Relations
                    Commission (1989–92) and Senior Deputy President
                    (1992–97).

Selected Distinctions Fellow of the Academy of the Social Sciences in
                    Australia since 1968, President 1981–84, Life
                    Member 1996– .

President, Industrial Relations Society of Australia, 1970–71.

Honorary Fellow of the London School of Economics and Political Science, 1982– .

Officer in the Order of Australia (1987).

Emeritus Professor, Flinders University (1987).

Honorary D. Litt., Flinders University, 1987.

Selected Publications (1960) "Wages Policy and Price Stability in Australia 1953–60", *Economic Journal*, vol. 70.
(1962) "The Reduction of Unemployment as a Problem of Public Policy, 1920–1929", *Economic History Review*, vol. 15; reprinted in Sidney Pollard (ed), *The Gold Standard and Employment Policies between the Wars*, Methuen.
(1970) *Economics, Australian Edition* (with Paul A. Samuelson and Robert Wallace), McGraw Hill; 2nd edn. 1975.
(1972) "The Occupational Wage Structure in Australia Since 1914" (with Kathryn Moore), *British Journal of Industrial Relations*, vol. 10; reprinted in J. R. Niland and J. E. Isaac (eds) (1975), *Australian Labour Economics: Readings*, Macmillan.
(1974–77) Three reports of the National Superannuation Committee of Enquiry (with K. Headley and R. G. McCrossin, AGPS. Vol. 1 (1974): *Interim Report*; vol. 2 (1976): *A National Superannuation Scheme for Australia*; vol. 3 (1977): *Occupational Superannuation in Australia*.
(1976) "The Relation Between Changes in Costs and Changes in Product Prices in Australian Manufacturing Industries 1949–50 to 1967–68", *Economic Record*, vol. 52.
(1979) "The First Half-Century of Australian Wage Policy" (in two parts), *Journal of Industrial Relations*, vol. 21.
(1985) *Australian Industrial Relations Law and Systems: Report of the Committee of Review* (with C. Fitzgibbon and G. E. Polites), 3 vols., AGPS.

(1985) "Discount Rates and the Distribution of Lifetime Earnings" (with Sue Richardson), *Journal of Human Resources*, vol. 20.
(1998) "The Needs of the Low Paid", *Journal of Industrial Relations*, vol. 40.
(1999) "The Deregulation of the Australian Labour Market", in Sue Richardson (ed.), *Reshaping the Labour Market*, CUP.
(2004) "The Economic and Social Effects" (with Sue Richardson), in Joe Isaac and Stuart McIntyre (eds), *The New Province for Law and Order: 100 Years Of Industrial Conciliation and Arbitration*, CUP.

METODEY POLASEK

Born   31 January 1932, Mistek, Czech Republic.

Education   B. Ec. (First Class Honours), The University of Adelaide, 1958.

                        Ph. D., Duke University, Durham N.C., U.S.A., 1961.

Present Appointment Honorary Visiting Fellow, School of Business Economics,
                        Flinders University, 1997– .

Teaching Record   Tutor in Economics, The University of Adelaide, 1958.

                        Lecturer in Economics, The University of Adelaide, 1962–64.

                        Assistant Professor of Economics, Queens University, Kingston, Ont., Canada, 1964–65.

                        Senior Lecturer in Economics, Flinders University, 1966–96.

Academic Awards	Fulbright Travel Grants, 1958 and 1961.
	Duke University Commonwealth Centre Fellowship 1958–60.
	Ford Foundation Dissertation Fellowship, 1960–61.
Selected Publications	(1962) "The Elasticity of Demand for Raw Apparel Wool in the United States" (with C.E. Ferguson), *Econometrica*, vol. 30.

(1962) "U.S. Wool Policy and its Effects on Apparel Wool Imports", *Australian Journal of Agricultural Economics*, vol. 6.

(1964) "Wool and Synthetics: A Statistical Analysis of Fibre Substitution in the United States" (with A.A. Powell), *Australian Journal of Agricultural Economics*, vol. 8.

(1965) "Synthetic Fibres and Australia's Economic Future", *Economic Record*, vol. 41.

(1970) *Applied Statistics for Economists*, 3rd edn. (with P.H. Karmel), Pitman; Portuguese edn. (1972), *Estatistica Geral Applicada para Economistas*, Editora Atlas; (1978), 4th Australian edn., Pitman.

(1971) "IMF Special Drawing Rights and the Currency Par Value System", *Economic Record*, vol. 47.

(1971) "The World Monetary System in Crisis", *Australia Quarterly*, vol. 43.

(1973) "IMF Special Drawing Rights and Economic Aid to Less Developed Countries", *Economic Record*, vol. 49, reprinted (1975) in *Kredit und Kapital¸*vol. 8. no. 1.

(1980) *State of Play: An Indecs Economics Special Report on the Australian Economy* (with B. Hughes, O. Covick, K.T. Davis, G.M. Scott), George Allen & Unwin; 2nd to 8th editions 1982–1995 (with B. Hughes, O. Covick, K.T. Davis).

(1985) "Foreign Exchange Markets and Capital Inflows" (with M.K. Lewis), in M.K. Lewis and R.H. Wallace (eds) *Australia's Financial Institutions and Markets*, Longman Cheshire.

(1985) "Australia's Transition from Crawling Peg to Floating Exchange Rate" (with M.K. Lewis), *Banca Nazionale de Lavoro*, June.

(1986) *Towards Active Voice: Report of the Committee of Review of the Adult Migrant Education Program* (with W.J. Campbell, chairman, J. Hoadley, W. Leslie and K. Young), Australian Government Publishing Service.
(1987) "Economic Expansion in South-East Asia", *Aussenwirtschaft/The Swiss Review of International Economic Relations*, vol. 42.
(1990) "Whither the Balance of Payments" (with M.K. Lewis), *Australian Economic Review*, 3rd quarter.
(1996) *Krise japonske bankovni soustavy (The Japanese Banking System in Crisis)*, (with J. Mervart), Research Monograph Series No. 62, Czech National Bank.
(2004) "Commodity Currencies: A Macroeconomic Interpretation", *Economic Analysis and Policy*, vol. 34, no. 1.
(2005) "The Commodity Currency View of the Australian Dollar" (with D. Hatzinikolaou), *Journal of Applied Economics*, vol. 8.

ROBERT HENRY WALLACE

Born	14 July 1930, Melbourne, Australia.
Education	B.Com. (First Class Honours), The University of Melbourne, 1952.
	B.Phil., Oxford University, 1956.
Present Appointment	Honorary Visiting Fellow, School of Business Economics, Flinders University.
Academic Awards	Wyselaskie Prize in Political Economy, 1952.
	Dafydd Lewis Scholarship for Graduate Studies, 1952.
Employment Record	Tutor then Senior Tutor in Economics, The University of Melbourne, 1952–54.

Lecturer then Senior Lecturer in Economics, The University of Adelaide, 1956–65.

Senior Lecturer then Reader in Economics, Flinders University, 1966–95.

Visiting Assistant Professor of Economics, Stanford University, California, 1964–65.

Visiting Associate Professor of Economics, University of Papua New Guinea, 1969.

Associate Commissioner, Industries Assistance Commission 1985–86.

Member, Commission of Inquiry into the Lemonthyme and Southern Forests, 1987–88.

Learned Societies Fellow of the Academy of the Social Sciences in Australia since 1978.

Selected Publications
Articles (1956) "Professor Arndt and the Labor Party" (with K.S. Inglis), *Quadrant*, December.
(1956) "Credit Creation in a Multi-Bank System" (with P.H. Karmel), *Australian Economic Papers*, September.
(1963) "Lessons of the 1960 Bank Credit Squeeze" (with R.W. Davis), *Australian Economic Papers*, June, reprinted in N. Runcie (ed) (1971), *Australian Monetary and Fiscal Policy*, University of London Press.
(1971) "Fiscal Policy in Post-war Australia" (with M.J. Artis) in N. Runcie (ed), *Australian Monetary and Fiscal Policy*, University of London Press.
(1973) "The Changing Rationale of Australian Monetary Policy" (with M.K. Lewis), *The Bankers Magazine*, September, reprinted in K. Davis and M.K. Lewis (eds) (1981), *Australian Monetary Economics*, Longman Cheshire.
(1975) "Taxation Reform: But What is the Agenda?", *Economic Record*, December.

(1977) "Medifinance: A Proposal for an Alternative Health Insurance System," *Community Health Studies*, October, reprinted in J.R.G. Butler and D.P. Doessel (eds) (1989) *Health Economics*, Australian Professional Publications.
(1983) "Health Economics" (with J.R. Richardson) in F. Gruen (ed) *Surveys of Australian Economics*, vol. 3, George Allen and Unwin, reprinted in Butler and Doessel (eds) (1989).

Books

(1964) *Studies in the Australian Capital Markets* (ed) (with R.R. Hirst), Cheshire.
(1967) *Economic Activity* (with G.C. Harcourt and P.H. Karmel), Cambridge University Press, Italian edn., *L'Activita Economica*.
(1970) *Economics: Australian Edition* (with P.A. Samuelson and Keith Hancock), McGraw Hill, 2nd edition 1975; 3rd edition 1992 (with P.A. Samuelson, W.D. Nordhaus, S. Richardson and G.M. Scott).
(1985) *Australia's Financial Institutions and Markets* (ed) (with M.K. Lewis), Longman.
(1993) *The Australian Financial System: Evaluation, Policy and Practice* (ed) (with M.K. Lewis), Longman.

Contributors

Michael Artis is Professor of Economics in the Institute for Political and Economic Governance at the University of Manchester where he directs the Manchester Centre for Regional Economics. He is also Professorial Fellow at the European University Institute, Florence.

Richard Blandy is Adjunct Professor of Economics at the University of South Australia. He is also Emeritus Professor of Economics at Flinders University.

Kevin Davis is Commonwealth Bank Chair of Finance at the University of Melbourne, and Director of the Melbourne Centre for Financial Studies.

Geoff Harcourt is Professor Emeritus of Economics at the University of Adelaide; Emeritus Fellow at Jesus College, University of Cambridge; and Emeritus Reader in the History of Economic Theory, University of Cambridge.

Joe Isaac is Professorial Fellow in the Department of Management, University of Melbourne. He has held chairs in Economics at the University of Melbourne and at Monash University, and was Deputy President of the Australian Conciliation and Arbitration Commission.

Philip Lawn is Senior Lecturer in Business Economics at Flinders University.

Daniel Leonard is Professor of Business Economics at Flinders University.

Mervyn K. Lewis is Professor of Banking and Finance in the School of Commerce at the University of South Australia.

The late **Richard Manning** was Professor of Economics at the State University of New York, Buffalo.

John McDonald is Professor of Business Economics at Flinders University.

The late **John McMillan** was Jonathan B. Lovelace Professor of Economics at Stanford University.

Eric Richards is Professor of History at Flinders University.

Jeff Richardson is a Professor in the Faculty of Business and Economics at Monash University, and Foundation Director of its Centre for Health Economics.

W.A. (Gus) Sinclair was Professor of Economic History at Flinders University from 1973 to 1982 and is now an Emeritus Professor of Monash University.